CHEQUERS

THE PRIME MINISTER'S
COUNTRY HOUSE AND
ITS HISTORY

THIS HOVSE OF PEACE
WAS GIVEN TO ENGLAND
FOR HER DELIVERANCE
AND AS A PLACE OF
FOR HER PRIME MINISTERS

AND ANCIENT MEMORIES
AS A THANK-OFFERING
IN THE GREAT WAR 1914-18
REST AND RECREATION
FOR EVER.

CHEQUERS

THE PRIME MINISTER'S COUNTRY HOUSE AND ITS HISTORY

Norma Major

Specially commissioned photographs
by Mark Fiennes

HarperCollins*Publishers*

First published in 1996 by HarperCollins*Publishers* London
Reprinted 1996

Text © Norma Major 1996
Specially commissioned photographs © Mark Fiennes 1996

A CIP catalogue record for this book is available from
the British Library

ISBN 0 00 470875 X

Colour origination by Radstock Reproductions Ltd
Printed and bound by Butler & Tanner Ltd, Frome, Somerset, UK

Dedication

To John, Elizabeth, James and Dee

Acknowledgements

My thanks first and foremost to Alan Samson and Andrew Lownie who persuaded me to write the book. It has been a fascinating voyage of discovery and I am indebted to all those who have helped and encouraged the project on its way and to all those who knowingly – or unknowingly – contributed to the story. In particular I should like to thank Clarissa Avon, Mary Wilson, Ted Heath, Jim and Audrey Callaghan, Margaret and Denis Thatcher, Mary Soames, Nicholas Soames MP, Winston Churchill MP, Caroline Douglas-Home, Eve MacLeod, Peter and Carly Thorneycroft, Willie Whitelaw, Alan Clark, Felicity Harwood, Joan Astley, Joy Crispin-Wilson, Jan Clutterbuck, Mary Henderson, Jack and Anne Page, Robert Armstrong, Robert Rhodes James, Oliver Everett, Ronnie Millar, David Renton, Patrick Telfer-Smollett, Robert Hakewill, James Alford, Ruth Ryder, Bill Johnson, Douglas and Jean Wilkins, Jeffrey Archer and Rod Lyne.

For their practical help and expertise I am most grateful to Sara Wheeler, Hubert Chesshyre, Robin Fletcher, Clifford Webster, Michael Reed and especially to Sir Martin Gilbert and Plantagenet and Fiona Somerset Fry for reading the text and making such helpful suggestions.

I am indebted to all those who made information available to me, in particular Christine Penney, Librarian of Birmingham University, Michael Doran, Librarian of the Courtauld Institute of Art, Guy Holborn, Librarian of Lincoln's Inn, Hugh Hanley, Archivist of Buckinghamshire County Records Office, John Green and Tina Sampson in the Downing Street Records Office, Sandra Green of English Heritage, Camilla Neil of Knight, Frank & Rutley, Camilla Costello and Sophia Gibb of *Country Life*, Sue Wiseman of Christie's, Anthony Camp at the Society of Genealogists, Angela Mace at the Royal Institute of British Architects, the British Library, the Victoria & Albert Museum and the House of Commons Library.

I am most grateful to Robert Cranborne and the Chequers Trustees for their encouragement and co-operation and also to Robin Catford, John Holroyd, Rodney Melville and Ken Stacey as well as to the curator Jane Uff and all the staff at Chequers.

For the photographs that form such an essential part of this book, my admiration and thanks go to Mark Fiennes. My thanks also to Caroline Evans for the flowers which greatly enhance the pictures.

A special thank you to all those involved with the publication at HarperCollins:
Polly Powell, Caroline Hill, Robin Wood, Sarah Riddell, Carole McGlynn, Sophie Gomm,
Becky Humphreys, Bridget Scanlon and especially to Eddie Bell for making it possible.

I could never have produced this book without the understanding of my family and the help and support of my secretary Lorne Roper-Caldbeck to whom I am especially grateful.

CONTENTS

INTRODUCTION

'*There are three classes which need sanctuary more than any others: birds, wildflowers and prime ministers.*'

STANLEY BALDWIN

OPPOSITE:

The Prime Minister and Norma Major
Norma Major is seated at her writing table in the Great Hall.

Chequers, Dorneywood and Chevening – today the official country residences of the Prime Minister, Chancellor of the Exchequer and Foreign Secretary respectively – are familiar names to politicians and public alike. For each of them the British Government owes a debt of gratitude to the philanthropy of men who recognized the need in public life for such retreats. Chequers was the first of these generous bequests.

Our first visit to Chequers was in February 1983 as guests at one of the many small lunches that Mrs Thatcher gave for her Ministers. At this time all we knew about the house was that it had been presented to the nation by Lord Lee of Fareham in 1921. The only visual image we had was the picture of Chequers in autumn that had featured on the Prime Minister's Christmas card the previous year. Even on a gloomy February day, it made a great impression on me.

My companions at lunch seemed no better informed. Did they know, for instance, that it was from the Hawtrey Room, where we had gathered for drinks before lunch, that Winston Churchill broadcast to the nation during the tense days of the Second World War? Or that in the Great Hall, Lloyd George entertained a Russian terrorist with a male-voice choir? Or that a potential claimant to the English throne had been kept prisoner for two years in a garret, now a guest bedroom? Were they aware that the elegant cabinet in the dining room was made from an elm tree believed to have been planted by King Stephen more than 800 years ago? Or how Queen Elizabeth I's ring, which Mrs Thatcher displayed for her guests, came to be in the jewel cabinet? Or what was the Chequers connection with Oliver Cromwell, whose death mask rested on a cushion in the Long Gallery?

We had no premonition in 1983, when John was a very junior minister, that we were to have the opportunity and privilege of knowing the house at first hand.

Nestling inconspicuously in a fold of the Chiltern Hills, Chequers is situated about forty miles from London's Downing Street, in a triangle between the Buckinghamshire towns of Great Missenden, Wendover and Princes Risborough. From Great

Missenden, Chequers is reached along a road which winds its way between neat Buckinghamshire hedgerows and stately beech woods.

Open parkland, dissected by the well-trodden Ridgeway Footpath, spreads before the house to the south. To the north it is protected by the rising ground of Beacon Hill and Coombe Hill, the highest points of the Chilterns. From here, on a clear day, seven counties can be seen, taking in the Berkshire Downs, Salisbury Plain and the Cotswolds.

All around, the countryside is steeped in history. Benjamin Disraeli's Hughenden Manor is close by, and John Milton took a cottage at Chalfont St Giles to escape the Great Plague in 1665. Jordans, the home of William Penn, is a place of pilgrimage for Quakers, and Edmund Burke, the political philosopher who regarded a country residence as a necessity for every statesman, lived at Beaconsfield. At Great Hampden is Hampden House, the ancestral home of Oliver Cromwell's cousin, John Hampden, the hero of the Civil War who died on Chalgrove field.

The park has even earlier associations. The northern boundary of the Chequers estate is formed by the Lower Icknield Way, the road of the ancient Britons linking the east of England with Salisbury Plain. To the north-west of the house, a maze cut in the turf, featured on a seventeenth-century map, has disappeared, but the park itself retains abundant evidence of early Romano-British occupation. Among these ancient remains is the stronghold of Cunobelinus known as Cymbeline's Mount where, as legend has it, his son Caractacus was born in AD1. The neighbouring villages of Great and Little Kimble derive their names from the Cymbeline connection. Amongst the treasures housed at Chequers are a gold stater of Cunobelinus, dug up in the park near Little Kimble, and a brass coin dating from the reign of the Roman Emperor Marcus Aurelius.

Below Cymbeline's Mount is Velvet Lawn, a picturesque area of mossy turf which was originally called Velvet Bottom until the Victorians – with the modesty that draped piano legs – gave it a more refined name. On the high ground around, box and beech grow in profusion.

Chequers is a sixteenth-century house of modest proportions, built of mellow russet brick with tall chimneys, gables and mullioned windows. The Elizabethan building is today something of an enigma, although we know the earlier dwelling was much restored and added to by William Hawtrey in 1565. The name Chequers is even older and probably derives from a twelfth-century owner, who was an official of the King's Exchequer.

Norma Major
*by the sundial in the
rose garden.*

Over the centuries, many of the occupants of Chequers have
had a role to play in their country's history. It fell, however, to
Lord Lee of Fareham, a Member of Parliament in the first quarter
of the twentieth century, to provide the link between the politics
of the past and the Prime Ministers of the future when, in 1917,
he bequeathed Chequers to the nation. It was his hope that future
Prime Ministers would thereby be enabled to maintain the dignity
of office without sacrificing their independence. The preamble to
the Trust Deed sets out the philosophy behind this noble – and, at
the time, controversial – gift:

> *It is not possible to foresee or foretell from what classes or conditions
> of life the future wielders of power in this country will be drawn.*

OPPOSITE:

The south front of Chequers

Rosa 'Norma Major'
This rose, which was launched at the Chelsea Flower Show in 1991, thrives luxuriantly against the south wall of the house.

Some may be, as in the past, men of wealth and famous descent; some may belong to the world of trade and business; others may spring from the ranks of the manual toilers. To none of these in the midst of their strenuous and responsible labours, could the spirit and anodyne of Chequers do anything but good. In the city-bred men especially, the periodic contact with the most typical rural life would create and preserve a just sense of proportion between the claims of town and country. To the revolutionary statesman the antiquity and calm tenacity of Chequers and its annals might suggest some saving virtues in the continuity of English history and exercise a check upon too hasty upheavals, whilst even the most revolutionary could scarcely be insensible to the spirit of human freedom which permeates the countryside of Hampden, Burke and Milton. And upon even the most hardened and least soulful politician the beauty of the place – within and without – would exercise, subconsciously, a humanising influence! Lastly, the better the health of our rulers the more sanely they will rule, and the inducement to spend two days a week in the high and pure air of the Chilterns and woods may, I hope, result in a real advantage to our nation as well as to its chosen leaders.

So quickly did Chequers become a part of political tradition that when Agatha Christie wrote *The Secret of Chimneys* a few years

BELOW:
The south front
at night.
FAR BELOW:
The swimming pool
*beside the rose garden
at night.*

later, she is supposed to have based her detective story on the Prime Minister's official residence. There is no evidence, however, that she ever visited the house, nor is there anything in the book to suggest it, yet the plot centres around an English stately home frequented by politicians and diplomats who go there to intrigue and, of course, to murder.

Lloyd George had the distinction of being the first official occupant of Chequers and thereafter all but one of Britain's Prime Ministers have made use of this house in the quiet Buckinghamshire countryside.

John Major became Prime Minister in November 1990. Since then Chequers has provided a respite from the demanding life of No. 10 and holds some happy memories for us, including many Christmas occasions and such family milestones as our daughter's twenty-first birthday and our silver wedding anniversary. We have staged operas and concerts in the Great Hall and have entertained large numbers of guests and foreign statesmen. We have also learned to appreciate the value of privacy. The burdens on Prime Ministers have greatly increased over the years and we, like our predecessors, can only be grateful to the far-sighted and magnanimous gesture that has allowed us to benefit from the peaceful Chequers environment. For, as Stanley Baldwin once

ABOVE:
The south front
*An autumn view of
Chequers.*

Norma Major
in the White Parlour at
Chequers.

said, 'There are three classes which need sanctuary more than any
others: birds, wildflowers and prime ministers.' And, he might
have added, Prime Ministers' wives.

CHEQUERS: THE HISTORY

> '...that dear delightful place, Chequers, where nothing but joy and tranquillity, health and pleasure can ever reign'
>
> COLONEL CHARLES RUSSELL TO HIS WIFE MARY
> *c.*1740

Although there is no architectural evidence of any dwelling on the site earlier than 1326, Maigno the Breton, the eleventh-century lord of Wolverton, is the earliest known owner of the land which now forms the nucleus of the Chequers estate in Buckinghamshire. The Domesday Book reveals that the lord of Wolverton held land in Ellesborough, in the Aylesbury Hundred, to the extent of fourteen-and-a-half hides. (In the twelfth century a 'hide', the equivalent of about 120 acres today, provided the basis for taxation and was considered enough to support a peasant family.) About a third of this holding was directly worked as the 'home farm', with labour supplied – as was the custom in feudal times – by Maigno's tenants on the other two-thirds.

In the century after the Domesday survey this land changed hands twice, from Maigno to his grandsons William and Richard and then to the Knights Hospitallers. A military religious order founded in the twelfth century to care for Christian pilgrims who fell ill on the way to Jerusalem, the Hospitallers were a prosperous organization; feudal barons often sold or mortgaged their estates in order to join the Crusades and perhaps Richard and William were among them. At the end of the twelfth century, this land was transferred by the Hospitallers to one Elias Ostiarius.

THE DE SCACCARIOS AND THE COURT OF THE EXCHEQUER

Elias was an official of the Court of the Exchequer, a branch of the medieval council which managed the financial affairs of the king. Not until the reign of Edward I (1272-1307) more than a century later was the Exchequer permanently settled at Westminster; up to that time it was itinerant, accompanying the king and his court on their progress around the country. Elias was the usher or *ostiarius*, the clerk responsible for guarding the privacy of the meetings, for arranging the attendance of the sheriffs who presided over the Exchequer Court, and for ensuring that

OPPOSITE:
The Russell and Revett (sic) families 'Syllabub straight from the Cow' (detail)
C. Philips 1708-1747.

Elias de Scaccario's
Coat of Arms

summonses were delivered. He was also responsible for setting up the *scaccarium* or chequer-board on which all the accounting was done and from which the term 'exchequer' is derived. In acknowledgement of this occupation Elias identified himself as Elias de Scaccario, sometimes written de Chekers or del Eschekere, a name which appears as a witness on the charters of several land transactions in Hampden and Ellesborough at the end of the twelfth century. It is not clear whether Elias took the name from his office and gave it also to the estate that he acquired, or whether Chequers itself, as the nineteenth-century county historian George Lipscomb suggests in *The History and Antiquities of the County of Buckinghamshire,* was 'the place of deposit of treasure belonging to the King's Court in which payments were anciently made ...'

Roger de Wallingford, the first recorded holder of this office, had held the post, by order of Henry II, from 1156 until his death ten years later. By virtue of his appointment Roger and his heirs had occupied the manor of Aston Rowant on the Oxfordshire side of the Chilterns. It is possible that Roger and Elias were related to each other, for on Roger's death Elias took up the post of usher and with it the small manor of Stokenchurch which was part of Aston Rowant. For twenty-six years Elias served as usher to the Exchequer until Roger's son succeeded him in 1192.

During this time Elias accrued land not only in Ellesborough but also beyond the parish of Stokenchurch and the county of Buckinghamshire. Among these new acquisitions was Tetchwick Farm in the parish of Ludgershall, about ten miles north-west of Chequers in the Vale of Aylesbury. Like Chequers, Tetchwick had been acquired from the Knights Hospitallers. Both of these transactions may have been straight sales, but though one of the more junior officials, Elias may have had influence at the Exchequer and the Hospitallers had amassed great fortunes. It is not unreasonable to suppose that they may have offered inducements to Elias to expedite their business through the Court of the Exchequer.

Elias's son Henry inherited a substantial estate and became a significant figure in mid-Buckinghamshire. He served two terms as sheriff for the neighbouring county of Berkshire and was knighted by Henry III. The King granted him hunting rights in Ellesborough and Tetchwick and gave him the responsibility of *custos* of the Royal Honour of Wallingford, which included Aston Rowant and now spread across seven counties. On the property deeds which were held at Missenden Abbey, the name that appears as a witness more frequently than any other is that of Henry de Scaccario.

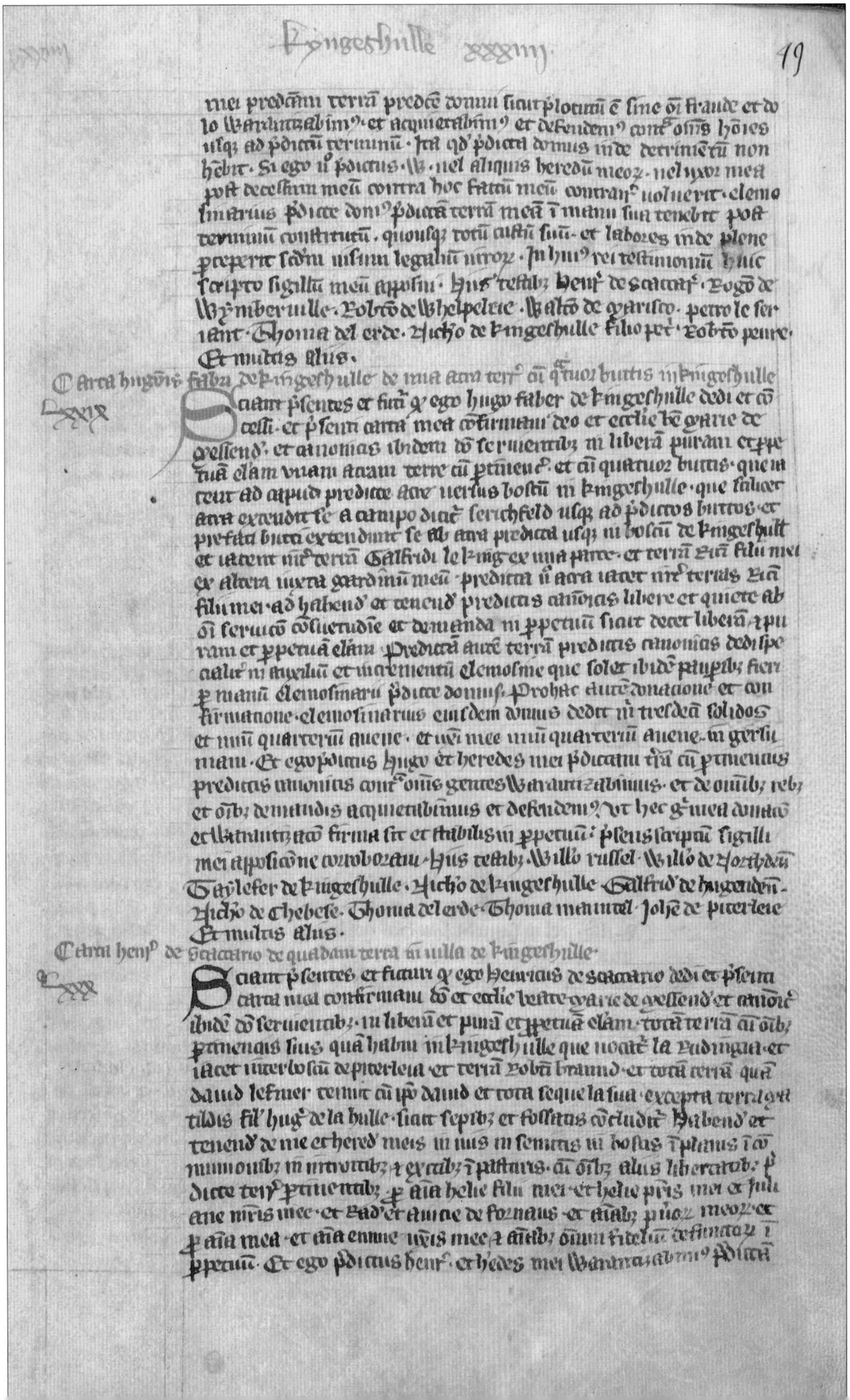

A page from the
Cartulary of
Missenden Abbey,
1330
*Henry de Scaccario's
name can be seen on
deed Lxxx. This
document is now held in
The British Library.*

Ringeshulle xxxiiij

Chequers Court,
View in Drawing
Room
Undated drawing by
nineteenth-century
architect, John Birch.
The costumes suggest his
impression of the
Hawtrey Room in late
seventeenth or early
eighteenth century.
J. Ackerman
photo-lithograph.

Henry's son Ralf, who succeeded him in 1243, acquired, probably through his marriage to Gundreda de Cheindut, still more land, some of which was in Cornwall. The Cheinduts, a prominent family, were amongst the early benefactors of Missenden Abbey. Ralf died ten years after the death of his father, leaving a widow and two young daughters, one of whom in later years seems to have had designs on the inheritance of the other. For when the elder daughter, Agnes, also married a de Cheindut, part of Agnes's inheritance was sold to Godstowe Nunnery on condition that they accommodate her sister Catherine as a nun. Whether or not Catherine was a willing party to this deal we do not know, but in the event she was spared the constraints of convent life by her marriage to William de Alta Ripa from Algarkirk, in Lincolnshire. In due course the name Alta Ripa evolved from its Norman French translation Haut Rive to the anglicized Dawtrey, and eventually became Hawtrey. Thus the ownership of Chequers was transferred from the de Scaccarios to the Hawtreys, in whose hands the estate was to remain for several centuries.

Chequers Court,
View in Organ Room
*Undated drawing by
nineteenth-century
architect, John Birch.
His impression of the
Hawtrey Room as seen
from the Reading Room
of today. The door to the
Prison Room staircase
can be seen to the right
of the fireplace.
J. Ackerman
photo-lithograph.*

THE HAWTREY FAMILY

William de Alta Ripa was of ancient descent and could trace his family to France before the Conquest. In her *History of the Hawtrey Family*, Florence Hawtrey, a nineteenth-century descendant, relates how an Alta Ripa ancestor came to England in the army of William the Conqueror. There is even a family legend which credits a knight of the same name with having fired the arrow which pierced King Harold through the eye at the Battle of Hastings, for which service he was rewarded with land in Lincolnshire. From Lincolnshire, generations of Alta Ripas spread themselves west, and in Plantagenet times, when the career of Henry de Scaccario was at its peak, Hawtreys were established in several English counties.

William de Alta
Ripa's Coat of Arms

    Catherine and William had no children, but in 1287 Catherine's inheritance was settled upon William's son by a previous marriage. This settlement included the Chequers land in Ellesborough as well as land in Tetchwick and Cornwall. In 1301 William's grandson Thomas married Joan Cheindut, Catherine's great-niece and the granddaughter of her sister Agnes, thus bringing about an amicable resettlement of the de Scaccario estates. The Cheinduts wound up with holdings in Berkshire and Cornwall, while the Buckinghamshire estates, including Chequers and Tetchwick, were settled upon Thomas and Joan Hawtrey.

Chequers was now the Hawtrey family seat and was to remain so for over three hundred years until the last of the Chequers' Hawtreys died in 1638. Generations of Hawtreys carried the name into the Tudor period, adding to the assets of Elias de Scaccario by speculation and marriage, and when his father died in 1522, the fifth Thomas Hawtrey inherited a sizeable fortune. A detailed inventory of the estate exists from this time which confirms that the land upon which the house stands was indeed that transferred by the Hospitallers to Elias, the usher of the Exchequer, at the end of the twelfth century. Although Chequers and Tetchwick were still the principal Hawtrey properties, to these had been added land and property in Great and Little Kimble, Stoke Mandeville, Wendover, Princes Risborough and Great Missenden. In his will Thomas Hawtrey specifically requested that he should be buried in the church of St Peter and St Paul at Ellesborough; he also made bequests to the church for the maintenance of the 'lights' and the repair of the bells.

His son, the sixth Thomas Hawtrey, added to his inherited wealth by his marriage to Sybil Hampden, the younger daughter of his near neighbour John Hampden – an ancestor of the Civil War hero – at Great Kimble; upon his death she inherited various properties in Hertfordshire. This Hawtrey, however, seems to have been something of a tearaway in his youth, for he was brought before the Court of Star Chamber for poaching from a hawk's nest belonging to the King. Sybil filled the house with children – a memorial brass in Ellesborough Church depicts eleven sons and seven daughters – and when her husband died in 1544 their son William became the owner of Chequers at the age of twenty-six.

WILLIAM HAWTREY AND THE REBUILDING OF CHEQUERS

William Hawtrey (1518-97) was the last of the male Hawtreys to occupy Chequers and was by far the most significant of the Chequers Hawtreys. As a founder member of the Muscovy Company of London, William Hawtrey was evidently a man of commerce. This company, of which his brother Thomas was also an employee, held a monopoly of Anglo-Russian trade for more than a century. In his contribution to local affairs Hawtrey was to

William Hawtrey's Coat of Arms

prove more responsible than his father, holding office on the right side of the law as commissioner for *oyer and terminer* ('hear and determine') and as a justice of the peace. He served two terms as sheriff of Bedfordshire and Buckinghamshire, and represented the latter in the parliament of 1562-3, earning himself a reputation as a man of honour and integrity. In due course he also came to be recognized as one of the wealthiest men in Buckinghamshire.

The inclusion of William Hawtrey of 'Chekkers and London' in the Pardon Roll of 1554 suggests he was absolved from any part he may have played in the political upheaval following the death of Edward VI, and Privy Council records show that under Mary Tudor he held office in a minor capacity at the Exchequer. In John William Burgon's *Life and Times of Sir Thomas Gresham* (published in 1839), he was described as a gentleman 'who represented an old and respectable family which had become enriched by several prudent alliances'.

The first of these 'prudent alliances' was his marriage to Mary Brocas, whose dowry included lands in the neighbouring parish of Edlesborough. But a memorial brass in Ellesborough Church states that Mary 'departed this lyfe in travell of her fyrst childe': since there is no record of a child by this marriage, presumably the child died too. Agnes, his second wife, was the wealthy widow of Hugh Losse, merchant and lord of the manor of Little Stanmore, Middlesex who had benefitted greatly from the dissolution of the monasteries.

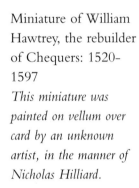

Miniature of William Hawtrey, the rebuilder of Chequers: 1520-1597

This miniature was painted on vellum over card by an unknown artist, in the manner of Nicholas Hilliard.

THE WALPOLE CONNECTION

William Hawtrey's second wife was a Walpole by birth and, in view of her connection with Chequers, the case that can be made for an ancestral relationship with the future Prime Minister, Sir Robert Walpole, is of particular interest.

Although records conflict with regard to the first name of Agnes's father, a shield in Little Stanmore Manor bore the arms of William Hawtrey incorporating a coat of arms for both Walpole and Holtofte. From this one might assume that Agnes was descended from a Walpole–Holtofte marriage and was likely to have been the daughter of Henry Walpole of Harpley in Norfolk and Whaplode in Lincolnshire, and Margaret Holtofte, also of Whaplode. If these antecedents are correct, Agnes and the Prime Minister, Robert Walpole, were first cousins five times removed.

Sir William Hawtrey
*A portrait by an
unknown artist of the
son of William Hawtrey,
the re-builder of
Chequers. He was
knighted by the Earl of
Essex on the battlefield
and was killed at the
siege of Rouen in 1591.
His daughter Mary
inherited Chequers when
her grandfather died in
1597.*

Combining his fortune with that of Agnes enabled William Hawtrey to undertake an extensive rebuilding project at Chequers. For it is her initial 'A' which can still be seen on the north front linked with his 'W' and the date 1565, commemorating its completion. The only documentary evidence we have of what the remodelled house looked like derives from a 1629 map showing the territorial possessions of his granddaughter, Mary Wolley. The map clearly shows a gatehouse to the south of two ranges of buildings running parallel to each other from east to west and facing north and south. Adjoining the east corner are stables and other outbuildings, but the east and west wings are missing, even though we know today that the east wing is one of the oldest parts of the house. The buildings almost certainly surrounded a central court which was typical of the Tudor period. Otherwise, Chequers does not conform to the more usual Tudor plan, which is presumably because Hawtrey was circumscribed by the foundations of an earlier house built by his de Scaccario predecessors. In 1911–12 the Historical Monuments Commission described Chequers as a 'fine example of sixteenth-century building'. It is clear that the exterior of the house we see today is, despite the vicissitudes of the intervening years, much as William Hawtrey planned it.

No sooner had Hawtrey completed his work in 1565 than he received, in August of that year, an unusual summons from the Privy Council, requiring him to 'repair to the Courte, and take into his charge and custody the Ladye Mary Greye'. Having offended the Queen by an ill-judged marriage, Lady Mary Grey's punishment was to be banished to Chequers, where she was to be confined in Hawtrey's protective custody.

William Hawtrey's initials
These initials are carved in the spandrels of the door which leads into the Hawtrey Room from the Stone Hall.

Lady Mary Grey

*A*s the great-granddaughter of Henry VII, Lady Mary Grey was, like her elder sisters Lady Jane and Lady Catherine, a potential claimant to the English throne. In the religious discord following Henry VIII's death, the Protector, the Duke of Northumberland, had attempted to secure the Protestant succession by persuading the dying Edward VI to name Lady Jane Grey as his successor in preference to his Catholic half-sister Mary, Henry VIII's daughter. Having hastily married Lady Jane to his own son Lord Guilford Dudley, Northumberland declared her Queen on the young king's death in 1553. This precarious position she held for nine days before Northumberland was deserted by his army and Mary was proclaimed the rightful sovereign. Northumberland went to the block at the Tower of London and six months later he was followed by Lady Jane, her husband, her father and her uncle. She was only sixteen years old at the time; her sisters Catherine and Mary were fourteen and eight respectively.

Although Mary I accorded the surviving sisters the respect due to princesses of the blood royal, when Elizabeth acceded in 1558 she refused to acknowledge Catherine as her heir and kept a close watch on her in the Palace of Whitehall. But she was not vigilant enough, for Catherine managed to marry the

Lady Mary Grey (1545–1578)
This small picture of Mary Grey by Hans Eworth, which hangs in the Prison Room, was acquired by Lord Lee. Ever on the look-out for artefacts with a Chequers connection, he presented it to the house in 1922.

Earl of Hertford secretly. Once evidence of her pregnancy could no longer be concealed, Catherine and her husband were confined in the Tower, their marriage declared void and their son denied legitimacy.

An Indiscreet Marriage

It almost defies belief that five years later Lady Mary Grey should commit the same indiscretion of marrying without the Queen's consent. Was Mary, hardly out of her teens, so consumed with passion that she was

blind to the dangers? Or could she have supposed that marriage to Thomas Keyes, a sergeant porter of the Royal Watergates at Westminster, should have posed no threat to the crown? Whatever the case, in August 1565 Thomas and Mary were married by candlelight in the sergeant porter's apartments. Lord William Howard, whose wife had witnessed the ceremony, wasted no time in writing to Elizabeth I's chief secretary of state, William Cecil, of 'a very fonde and lewde matter fallen owte betwixte my Lady Mary and the Serjeant-porter'.

It was not simply the clandestine nature of their marriage that offended the Queen: she was also unable to stomach a match the physical and social incongruities of which were bound to bring ridicule to the court. A widower with several children, Keyes was many years Mary's senior. Whereas he was a powerfully built man who stood seven feet tall in his stockings, the freckled-faced and red-haired Mary, every diminutive inch a Tudor, was described as being 'dwarfish' in stature. Elizabeth's retribution came fast: Mary was confined to Chequers and, to ensure that there were to be 'no little bastard Keyes', the sergeant porter was dispatched to the Fleet prison, where he was to suffer its notorious 'pestilent airs' along with his unfortunate children.

Hawtrey's instructions for Lady Mary's imprisonment called for a strict regime which did not allow her:

to have any talk or commerce with any stranger that shall come or send to hir otherwise than yourself or your wife shall be prive unto and shall be mete and convenient. Neither shall she go out of your house above, except it be necessarey for to take the ayre for .....hir helth...She shall have only with her a grome and a gentilwoman and you shall have reasonable allowance of hir Majesty for the charg of hir and the other two...she be not dieted otherwise than...for her sustentation and helth without respect to hir degree or place...

Mary accomplished the journey from London to Chequers mounted on a pillion behind William Hawtrey, followed by her groom and her maid. Mud-spattered, tired and weeping, she was guided up the narrow winding staircase into the attic room which was to be her prison. For the next two years Lady Mary saw little beyond the four stone walls of this 12-foot-square room, now called the Prison Room, on the north-east corner of the house. Accessible windows with a good aspect both north and east must have been some consolation, but if she did 'go abrode' it is doubtful that she would have been permitted to venture as far as Silver Spring or Velvet Bottom.

From this room Mary corresponded constantly with William Cecil, but apart from a reference to 'my great sorrowful estate', we learn nothing about the conditions of her confinement. This is perhaps an indication that Master Hawtrey, notwithstanding his instructions, was not a harsh gaoler. With fulsome apologies for bothering Cecil so often with her 'rude letters', Mary begs him to plead her cause with the Queen, assuring him that she repented of her 'haynusse cryme', and declaring that, rather than endure the Queen's disfavour, she would prefer to be dead. Hawtrey, who did not find the role of gaoler congenial and was anxious to see the back of her, heartily endorsed her pleadings.

MOVING ON

Although Elizabeth did not easily forgive, perhaps Cecil succeeded in persuading her that Mary sincerely repented her folly, for in August 1567 she was transferred to the custody of her maternal step-grandmother, the dowager Duchess of Suffolk. Totally unprepared and in straitened circumstances herself, the Duchess was none too happy to find Mary dumped on her doorstep one

The Prison Room
Lady Mary Grey was imprisoned in this room for two years, from 1565 to 1567. The glass panel on the right protects the original stone wall on which Lady Mary wrote an inscription. The door to the left leads to a secret staircase.

Lady Mary Grey's inscription
Nobody has ever been able to decipher this strange inscription etched on the stone wall of her prison by Lady Mary Grey.

fine summer evening. Arriving in London at the Minories, with her groom and her maid and little more than an old patched featherbed and a quilt of silk 'so torn as the cotton of it comes out', Mary was not welcomed with open arms. The Duchess was dismayed by the meagreness of her possessions and the first of the Duchess's many begging letters to Cecil was a sorry tale of woe: she was unable to provide for Mary as Hawtrey had apparently done, her son was ill and her maid had recently died. But not without heart, she expressed concern that Mary was pining away in her misery and remorse and could not be persuaded to eat so much as a chicken leg.

After two years relief came for the Duchess when Mary was on the move again, this time to cause distress and inconvenience to Sir Thomas Gresham, a rich city merchant, and his wife at Osterley. He too bombarded Cecil and Robert Dudley, Earl of Leicester, with letters urging 'the removing of my Lady Mary Grey', but to no avail.

When her sister Catherine died in 1568 after years of imprisonment and ill health, Mary, to protect herself from the same fate, renounced her right to the succession as set out in the wills of Henry VIII and Edward VI. Thomas Keyes also indulged in some fruitless plea-bargaining, offering to renounce his wife and allow his marriage to be annulled if he might be permitted to leave the Fleet prison and retire to Kent. In mitigation he referred to the services he had rendered to the Crown, but the only immediate concession was to allow him access to the garden of Fleet prison. His final days were spent at Sandgate Castle, in Kent, from where he pleaded with the Queen through the Archbishop of Canterbury that, 'according to the laws of God I may be permitted to live with my wife'. He died in 1571, his entreaty having fallen on deaf ears.

It fell to Sir Thomas Gresham to break the news to Lady Mary that her husband, his health and spirit broken by his incarceration, had died. Gresham saw it as his duty to ask the Queen if the grieving widow could wear mourning. Lady Mary Grey remained at Osterley for another two years before the Greshams were able to send her on her way, together with 'all her books and rubbish', to live with her step-father and his new wife. An exchange of gifts with the Queen suggests that, having been deprived of her freedom for almost eight years, she may have been restored to royal favour before she died in 1578.

In the meantime twice-widowed William Hawtrey had married the widow of Ambrose Dormer, thereby strengthening the links with a family with which he was already connected by the

Good master secrytary I muste craue humble
pardonn of you for thatt I haue nott befor this
tyme rendered my selfe thankfull to you for the
greatte goodnes and fryndshepe I haue founde in
you and also the greatte redynes you haue showed
in meuinge my moste petyfull and lamentable
sueth to the quenes maieste for her maiestes moste
gracyous fauor for me and also I truste you will
rather impuett it to the wantt of a conneyentt
messenger then to any forgettfullnes of my partte who
hathe hathe byne to muche bound to you to forgett
my selfe so farr most humbly desiringe you also
thatt as you haue begonn your goodnes towards
me in beinge so erneste a sueter to her maieste
for the obtayninge of her maiestes fauor for me
so you will contenewe untell you haue made me
so happy a cretur as thatt I maye be made in
thatt good estatt thatt I was in when I hade
her maiestes fauor the whiche unlesse by your
good meanes I gett agayne do lyue in suche
wofull casse as I had rather be outt of this
worlde then to wantt so greatt a iuell as thatt
sholde be to me and thus trustinge you will still
as occacyon dothe serue moue her maieste for
her moste gracyous fauor and remessyon I leue
to trubell you any mor for this tyme desiringe
god to sende you happy suksesse in all your affayrs
from chekers the xvij of aperell 1567

Your pore frynde
to comande Mary
Graye

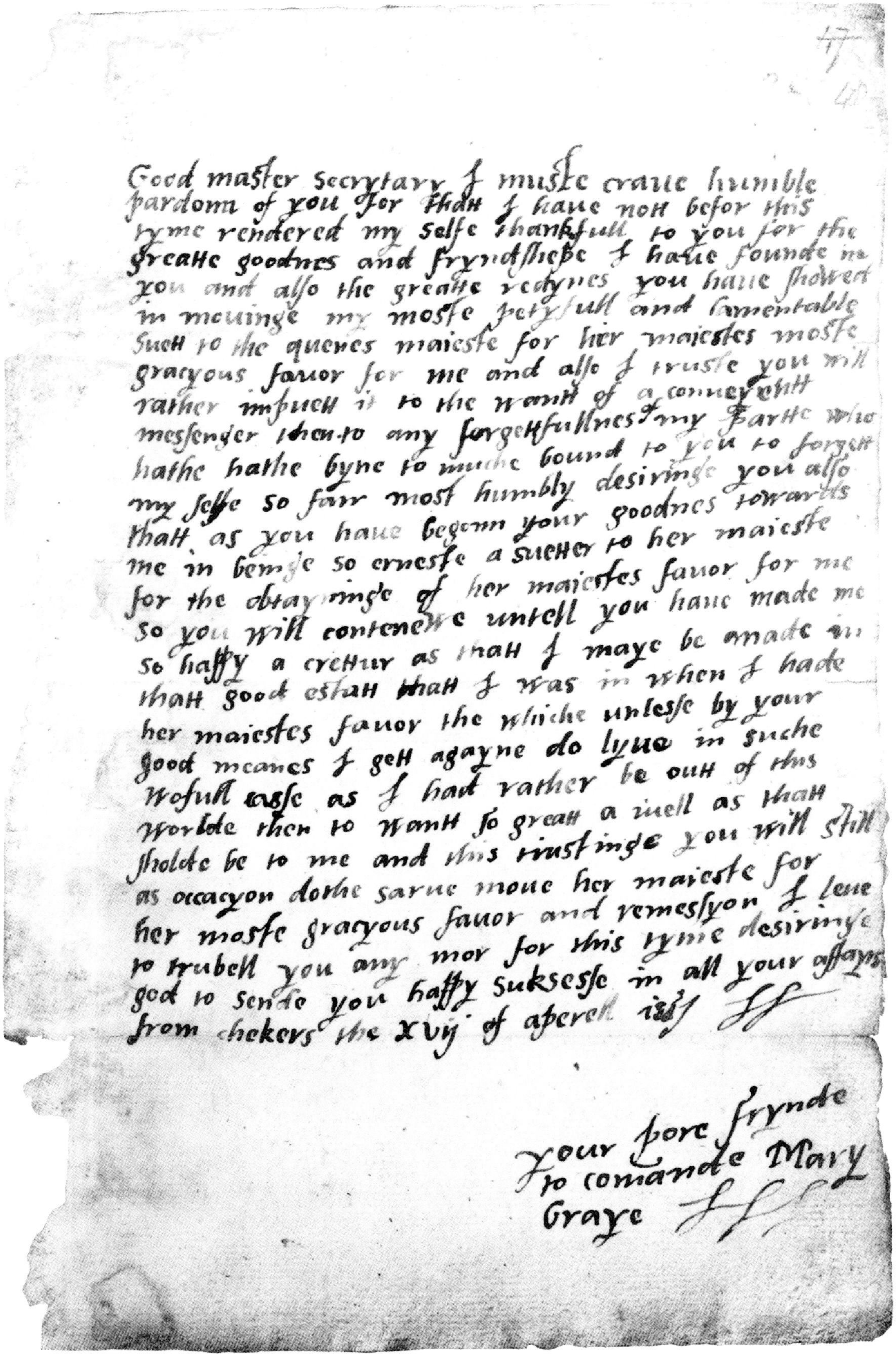

Letter from Lady Mary Grey to Cecil
This is one of the many letters which Lady Mary Grey wrote at Chequers to Cecil in which she pleads for the Queen's forgiveness and begs for her release. The originals are in The British Museum.

marriages of his Hawtrey cousins. Into this marriage Jane Dormer brought a son and a daughter as well as the Oxfordshire manors of Ascot and Hampton Poyle. The relationship between the two families was further cemented – not to say complicated – by the marriages of William and Agnes Hawtrey's second son William and daughter Dorothy with Jane's children Winifred and Michael.

When William Hawtrey's eldest son and heir Thomas died unmarried and without issue, the Hawtrey line seemed secure enough. Young William was the father of two daughters, and there was every possibility that sons would follow. Breaking with family tradition, however, William took to soldiering and in 1591, leaving a will and a pregnant wife, set off with the Earl of Essex's army to liberate Rouen from the Spaniards. He was among those knighted on the spot by Essex, but met his death a month or so later in the field. His widow gave birth posthumously to another daughter, Anne, and two years later Winifred married John Pigott of Edlesborough and produced three more daughters.

Thus deprived of a male heir, the old William Hawtrey made, to modern eyes, unseemly haste to secure a husband for his eldest granddaughter Mary. In his sights was Francis, son and heir of the scholarly Sir John Wolley, Elizabeth I's Latin secretary.

FRANCIS AND MARY WOLLEY

Francis Wolley, at ten years old, was two years younger than his bride when they were married in September 1594 by special licence of the Archbishop of Canterbury. At the time the Chequers estate was believed to have passed to Sir John Wolley for a sum of £400 and subsequently settled on Francis and Mary. As described in the legal document, the property now consisted of:

> thirty messuages [a dwelling house with outbuildings and land], forty tofts [homesteads], a windmill, a watermill, two dovecotes, thirty gardens, thirty orchards, fifteen hundred acres of land, sixty acres of meadows, sixty acres of pasture, five hundred acres of woodland, two hundred acres of heathland, and rents amounting to twenty shillings, situated in Chequers, Ellesborough, Wendover, Great Hampden, Little Hampden, Stoke Mandeville, Great Kimble, Monks Risborough and Bishopstone.

Within a few years of the marriage both William Hawtrey, who lived to the ripe old age of seventy-nine, and Sir John Wolley were dead, and Lady Wolley was appointed guardian to the child-

OPPOSITE:
Dame Mary Wolley (d.1637), English School
The granddaughter of William Hawtrey was married to Francis Wolley in 1594, at the age of 12, and widowed in 1609. Chequers was part of her marriage settlement. Painted in 1625, the portrait still shows evidence of mourning in the flimsy black threads tied to her ring and attached to her ruff, although the inscription, 'One thing is needfull [sic]', is thought to refer to her loveless marriage. The portrait hangs under the gallery in the Great Hall.

bride and her even younger bridegroom. Nothing suggests, however, that Mary and Francis Wolley lived at Chequers – or indeed lived together at all as man and wife. There were no children and Francis died in 1609 aged twenty-five, having enjoyed a more satisfying relationship with his mistress Jane Ferris, who produced a daughter for him. When Francis had come of age, he had been appointed Clerk of the Pipe, the official responsible for the Great Roll of the Exchequer upon which were entered debts and accounts due to the King. It was also one of the more important and remunerated offices of the Exchequer. Having inherited vast estates from his father, Francis died an exceedingly wealthy young man. In his will he bequeathed £400 to his widow, £200 and a life annuity of £100 to his mistress on condition that she remained unmarried, and the extravagant sum of £4,000 for the erection of a Wolley family memorial in the medieval cathedral of St Paul, which was destroyed by the Great Fire of 1666.

After her grandfather's death Mary may have trusted the Chequers estate to the care of the Plaistowe family of Little Hampden, for at the time of his marriage to her stepsister Katherine Pigott in the 1630s, William Plaistowe was said to have been Mary Wolley's steward for many years.

During this stewardship Chequers retained its parliamentary and court connections with the tenancy of William Hakewill, a distinguished Member of Parliament and constitutional lawyer. When he entered Lincoln's Inn in 1598 he gave his address as 'Chequers in the county of Buckinghamshire'. Called to the bar in 1606, Hakewill became 'a grave and judicious counsellor at law', who served as solicitor to Anne of Denmark, consort of James I. Well versed in the records of the Exchequer and other antiquities, he became a principal Bencher of Lincoln's Inn and was Master in Chancery from 1647 to 1652. Hakewill began his parliamentary career representing the Cornish borough of Bossiney. He was an active member of the House of Commons, and in 1603 attempted to revive a bill concerning soldiers, mariners and the maintenance of shipping with an argument that has an echo in our time: 'It was well said by one that ships were the walls of our kingdom, which if we suffer to decay, as I am certainly assured they are decaying, not only a quarter, or a third part, but even half, and as our strength diminisheth, so our enemies increase.'

Hakewill continued to represent West Country seats until, discovering that three Buckinghamshire boroughs with the right to return a member to parliament had allowed the privilege to lapse, he suggested they reclaim their rights and sought the nomination for Amersham. Having represented Amersham in the first two parliaments of Charles I, he retired from political life after

Coat of Arms of
Mary Hawtrey

The tombs of William Hakewill, d.1655, and of his wife Elizabeth, d.1652
The tombs are in St. Mary's Church, Wendover, in Buckinghamshire.

the historic dissolution in 1629, when the Speaker was forcibly held in his chair, while Parliament, in defiance of the King, passed resolutions against illegal taxation.

His appointment as Receiver for the Duchy of Lancaster in Buckinghamshire, Berkshire and adjoining counties gave him considerable influence in the area, where he also acquired substantial property. In due course he moved to Bucksbridge House, near Wendover, where he died in 1655.

The Hakewills appear not to have been the only tenants of Chequers during Mary Wolley's long widowhood. A memorial stone of 1632, in the Church of St Peter and St Paul at Stokenchurch, describes Bartholomew and Martha Tipping as 'of Checkers'.

Mary Wolley seems to have taken little active interest in Chequers and it was as 'Dame Wolley of Wandsworth, Surrey' that she sold most of the Hawtrey property in Little Kimble in 1612. The Chequers estate map of 1629 bears her name and the inscription 'widdow ladie and owner thereof', but her will describing her 'as of Bodicote in Oxfordshire', where she had Hawtrey cousins and died in 1637, carries instructions for her burial at Adderbury, about thirty miles away. (There is, however, nothing at Adderbury to commemorate or to confirm her death.)

On Mary Wolley's death the Chequers estates passed to her sister Bridget, but the only indication that she might have lived there is the impressive marble monument to her in the church at Ellesborough. In any event, her residence would have been brief, for she died a year after her sister. At that time Bridget had been married for thirty-one years to Sir Henry Croke, former Member of Parliament for Shaftesbury and Christchurch and Clerk of the Pipe. Thus once again, within the interval of a few years, Chequers renewed its ancient connection with the Exchequer.

Coat of Arms of Brigetta (sic) Hawtrey

THE CROKE FAMILY

A distinguished family of landowning lawyers who came from the neighbouring parish of Chilton, the Crokes had already earned themselves a place in the history books. Henry's father Sir John Croke had been Speaker of the House of Commons at the end of Elizabeth's reign, and was subsequently Recorder of London and Judge of the King's Bench. His uncle George, also a Judge of the King's Bench, was to secure a place in legal history by defying the majority and finding in favour of John Hampden's refusal to pay the iniquitous tax in the famous ship-money case (1637).

It was his uncle's distinguished patrimony that enabled Henry Croke to buy a half-share in a partnership in the Pipe Office in 1616. Croke was 'a man of letters, and of polite manners [who] by his prudence, and good conduct, raised a fair establishment of fame and fortune.' At least that was how he was described by a nineteenth-century family historian. While undoubtedly a man of some distinction, his conduct in office also earned him a fair degree of notoriety. Both he and his partner, Anthony Rouse, came under the scrutiny of a long-running inquiry by treasury

Lady Croke c.1620
*Companion portrait
by Marc Gheeraerts of
Bridget Croke,
granddaughter of
William Hawtrey, and* *the last of the Hawtreys
to own Chequers.*

commissioners into the levying of excessive fees by civil and church courts. Fees had last been regulated in 1598 so Croke and Rouse had devised new fees of their own as a way of staying ahead of inflation. This was profitable but not legal, and by this and other sharp practices they vastly increased the value of their office.

Fortunately for Croke and Rouse, the commission inquiry was grindingly slow, and the alleged abuses of his office did not come to a head until 1636, by which time Croke had been sole Clerk of the Pipe for six years. He had clearly learned how to cope with the Exchequer during this period because he succeeded in avoiding prosecution by voluntarily offering a schedule of his fees, and agreeing to come to terms with the Commissioners. The King's pardon cost him £4,300, but it absolved him 'from all charges pending against him in Star Chamber, as well as any other offences committed by him in office'.

In spite of all these attacks upon his integrity, he remained Clerk of the Pipe throughout the turbulent years of the Civil War, the Commonwealth and the Protectorate. But the Attorney General had been instructed to settle what Croke's fees should be and when he was assessed for parliamentary taxation in 1644, his fortunes seem to have waned and he swore that he did not have a hundred pounds to his name.

Henry Croke's difficulties, however, did not drive him to an early grave: born in the year of the Armada, he was seventy-one when he died 'of the stone' in 1659. Apart from a bequest of £5 to the poor of the parish, there is little evidence that he lived up to the epitaph on his monument in Ellesborough Church: 'He did not love the poor, and therefore that none might continue in poverty, was the constant object of his exertions and of the employment of his wealth.' Chequers and the Clerkship of the Pipe, however, reverted without interference to his and Bridget's only son Robert.

Born in 1611, Robert Croke was educated by his uncle, Dr Charles Croke, the Rector of Amersham, matriculated at Balliol and, following the legal tradition of the family, was called to the Bar in 1635. In 1636 he served in the same parliament as his father as the Member for Wendover, and he was awarded a knighthood in 1641.

During the Civil War, in a county which strongly supported the parliamentary cause, Sir Robert actively took up with the Royalists and joined the King's 'Rival Parliament' at Oxford. It was an allegiance which cost him dear, for he was obliged to contribute personal funds to the war effort and Chequers was confiscated by the parliamentary commissioners.

The Crokes, however, still owned a considerable amount of property, including Bridget's share in the manor at Hampton Poyle, one of William Hawtrey's Dormer acquisitions. This Oxfordshire manor had passed to Bridget in a complicated settlement involving her two sisters Mary and Anne and subsequently to her son Robert. By his marriage to an heiress he had acquired an interest in property in Essex and Berkshire, but the wealth he anticipated had not come with it. In 1648, ten years after Bridget's death, Hampton Poyle became another casualty of the Civil War when it was sold for £5,000 to settle Sir Robert's debts and pay for the restitution of the Chequers estate.

After the Civil War Sir Robert ceased to take an active interest in politics, and he and his large family of six sons and seven daughters returned to Chequers, where he took over the running of the estate from his father. Hampton Poyle apart, Sir Henry Croke had not added to the assets accrued to him on his marriage to Bridget Hawtrey, and at his death in 1659 the estate he left was somewhat smaller than that set out in the inventory following the death of the fifth Thomas Hawtrey in 1522.

When Sir Robert died, only three daughters survived him. With no male heir, Sir Robert bequeathed all his estates to his widow for her lifetime, and left her with the responsibility of apportioning that property to their three surviving daughters on her death as she saw fit. It was the middle daughter, Mary, who was ultimately the beneficiary of Chequers.

JOHN THURBARNE AND HIS DAUGHTER JOANNA

In 1683 Mary Croke married John Thurbarne. Like his father before him, Thurbarne was a Member of Gray's Inn and a practising barrister who represented Sandwich, in Kent, in several parliaments between 1679 and 1698. Although acknowledged as 'honest' on the Earl of Shaftesbury's list of supporters of his campaign to exclude the Roman Catholic Duke of York from the succession, Thurbarne was an inactive member of the first parliament, from which Catholics were excluded as a result of the Popish Plot fabricated by Titus Oates in 1677. Later, after the Duke of York succeeded to the throne as James II, a search of the Thurbarne house – Wingham Burton – had revealed a small supply of arms and ammunition indicating a sympathy, which his son shared, with Monmouth's rebellion. Thurbarne was recognized as a country Whig and at the Glorious Revolution he became a Sergeant-at-Law and was a supporter of the canopy at the coronation of William and Mary.

Sir Henry Croke, Clerk of the Pipe, c.1620 *Sir Henry Croke became the owner of Chequers on the death of his wife Bridget in 1638. The portrait, by the Flemish painter Marc Gheeraerts (1530-1590), hangs in the Great Hall.*

Coat of Arms of
Mary Croke

Well into middle age, with a young daughter and two wives behind him, John Thurbarne had fixed ideas of what he required in his third wife, and during their courtship he presented Mary with Milton's recently published *Paradise Lost*: in the margins he had indicated passages he particularly wanted to draw to her attention. We cannot know if Mary took to heart what she read, nor whether she lived up to his ideal image of a 'perfect, loving wife' as personified by Eve in the epic poem, but they were together until death parted them, within a year of each other, twenty-three years later.

Since Mary had inherited Chequers and the major part of her father's estate in 1685, Thurbarne was considered to have done quite well by his marriage. The marriage deed also provided that in the event of their demise without further issue the estate would pass to Joanna, his only daughter by his second marriage to Ann Cutts. There is nothing, however, like a perceived unfairness in the distribution of an inheritance for bringing out the worst in people. Mary's elder sister Susan made a fuss about the settlement of the estate under her mother's will and had to be bought off, and the house by this time was in need of considerable renovation and repair. Although Thurbarne had given up his legal practice to move from Kent to Buckinghamshire in order to share his life with Mary at Chequers, the family seat showed every sign of being a millstone round his neck.

The programme of repairs Thurbarne undertook at Chequers, which included a major renovation of the south front, appeared to have paid dividends when a great storm ravaged the south of England in 1703. According to his bailiff, the 'new building' had escaped substantial harm, while the old building sustained greater damage. Thurbarne was able to reassure an inquiring friend that, 'rotten as it is', Chequers had weathered the storm better than any other part of his Buckinghamshire or Kent estates. Further damage, however, became evident the following year when a Chequers workman reported evidence of subsidence and advised Thurbarne to 'retire to the other side' of the house.

John Thurbarne's troubles did not end there, for his daughter Joanna had married Colonel Edmund Rivett, whose relationship with his father-in-law was stormy. Thurbarne accused Rivett of squandering his daughter's income on a life of luxury and wantonness – and, worse, of ill-treating his wife because she was unable to coax money out of her father to sustain him. In return, Thurbarne's brother-in-law Lord Cutts reproached him for failing to pay Joanna the promised interest on her inheritance from her mother. In contemporary manuscripts, Edmund Rivett is consistently referred to as the 'gallant' Colonel Rivett, and he is never long from the front. His gallantry in Belgium at the siege of Namur earned him the rank of colonel, for which he had been given by William III a company of the Coldstream Guards, then under the command of Lord Cutts.

Joanna and her dashing Colonel clearly felt deeply for each other and from the camp at Cockleberg he wrote affectionate letters referring to her as 'his lovely child' and 'glorious heroine', and assuring her that her expressions of love and goodness have put his mind in 'a most heavenly state of tranquillity'. When he returned from this conflict unharmed, Lord Cutts received a grateful letter of thanks from Joanna.

In 1704 Rivett again covered himself in glory at the siege of Gibraltar, after which he was recommended to Queen Anne 'as one that during the whole siege and stay there since hath behaved himself with a distinguishable bravery and with a continual application to the service'. This commendation pleased his family and friends for the influence it might have in persuading Thurbarne to think well of his son-in-law. But soldiering was to be the death of him. In 1709 he commanded a battalion of Foot Guards in Marlborough's victorious battle over the French at Malplaquet, when heavy losses were sustained by the British army. Amongst them was the Colonel, who had returned to the field 'from which he had before been carried off as dead'. Dying so courageously in action may to some extent have redeemed him in the eyes of his father-in-law, but Joanna was nevertheless left a young widow with a legacy of debt which came as no great surprise to her father.

On the death of her parents three years later, Joanna Rivett inherited Chequers, and this was to be the first time in 500 years that the blood of the de Scaccario and Hawtrey families no longer flowed in the veins of the owners of Chequers. But Joanna's inheritance proved to be more of a burden than a blessing; having been dissipated over the years, all that remained of the Hawtrey estates were the manor houses of Chequers and Mordaunts. Having paid off her husband's substantial debts and with her family to provide for, she successfully petitioned the Queen for a pension on the strength of Colonel Rivett's twenty years of loyal service to two monarchs, and was able to buy a commission in the Foot Guards for her eldest son John. But before long she was married for the second time, to a widower with four children of his own. That widower was John Russell, the youngest and posthumous son of Sir John Russell, 3rd Baronet, and of Oliver Cromwell's youngest daughter, Frances.

Coat of Arms of Joanna Thurbarne

THE RUSSELLS AND THE CROMWELL CONNECTION

The Russells were a landowning family from Chippenham, in Cambridgeshire who had risen to prominence under Charles I. The 2nd Baronet, Sir Francis Russell, was a Colonel in the Parliamentary Army and two of his children married into the Cromwell family: his daughter Elizabeth marrying Cromwell's son Henry and his son John, later the 3rd Russell Baronet, married his daughter Frances.

Oliver Cromwell
Drawing or etching by Van Dyck.

Frances Cromwell

*F*rances Cromwell was the fourth daughter of Oliver Cromwell. Before her marriage to John Russell, she had been briefly married to the Earl of Warwick's grandson Robert Rich. Cromwell had considered Rich a dubious choice but Frances, a determined and strong-willed young lady, had set her heart on marrying him, and after her father's installation as Lord Protector, when he was no longer preoccupied with the question of kingship, Cromwell had given his grudging consent. In November 1657 she married this 'most noble gentleman' in Whitehall, amidst lavish celebrations the like of which, it was said, had never been seen before.

Their happiness, however, did not last long, for Rich died barely three months later, leaving her a widow at the age of twenty. Before the year was out Frances was also grieving for the death of her older sister Elizabeth (Bettie Claypole) and of her father, who died less than a month later.

A Second Marriage

Frances remained unattached for some time before marrying her brother-in-law John Russell; soon afterwards he inherited the title as 3rd Baronet and she became mistress of the Cambridgeshire family seat of Chippenham.

In 1670, Frances Russell was widowed for the second time, with

Frances Cromwell (1638-1721)
Portrait by H. Van der Myn of Oliver Cromwell's youngest daughter, Frances, which hangs in the Cromwell Passage. Her youngest son John married the owner of Chequers in 1715.

two sons and two daughters, and a fifth child on the way. Her eldest son William was still a minor when he inherited both Chippenham and the baronetcy. In due course, the 4th Baronet, with more patriotism than prudence, succeeded in dissipating his fortune in promoting the Glorious Revolution of 1689. His espousal of the cause brought distress and misery to his mother and reproach from family and friends, for the price of putting William of Orange on the throne of England proved a high one for the Russells.

Sir William sold Chippenham to the First Earl of Orford, Admiral of the Blue, a member of the Bedford Russells. This left his mother virtually homeless and in the humiliating position of having to draw her plight to the attention of the Duke of Devonshire, who had also supported William of Orange. Her hopes were to procure:

something if possible in this revolution that might have given me a small support; my necessities obliging me to accept any employment that might become a gentlewoman, many of which…will either be absolutely in your power as Lord Steward, or mediately so by your great and deserved interest with the King and Queen.

Ultimately, to save her son from ruin, Frances Russell was obliged to make inroads into her jointure and to take up residence at Sutton Court with her sister Mary. Lady Russell was well over eighty when she died in 1721, the year in which Sir Robert Walpole – to whom the title Prime Minister was first applied – became the First Lord of the Treasury. She had outlived her brothers, sisters and eldest son; she had also seen her youngest son John take Joanna Rivett as his second wife.

John Russell had spent the best part of his adult life in Bengal as an agent for the East India Company. Young Russell rose through the ranks ultimately to become Governor of Bengal, an office he held without distinction for a couple of years. In 1714 he returned to England a widower, in poor health, with four young children to look after. The following year he married Joanna Rivett and what little we know of Chequers at this time comes from letters written by her stepson Colonel Charles Russell and his wife Mary, Joanna's only daughter.

Mary Joanna Cutts Rivett
Portrait by T. Hudson (1701-1799).
The daughter of the owner of Chequers, Joanna Thurbarne and her first husband, Colonel Edmund Rivett. Mary married Colonel Charles Russell and their son, Sir John Russell, inherited Chequers in 1764. The portrait is one of two of Mary which hang in the Long Gallery.

THE RIVETTS AND RUSSELLS

Married life for Charles and Mary Russell was spasmodic, for as a Lieutenant-Colonel of the 1st Foot Guards, Charles was away from home, fighting for king and country in the War of the Austrian Succession. Although they had a home in nearby Great

Missenden, he was reassured by the knowledge that while he was abroad she and the children were at Chequers, from where she wrote copious letters to him. 'You can't imagine how often I peruse the accounts you give of my dear babies', he writes in response. 'Nobody but those that have 'em can know the joy they give.' His letters to Mary are also full of references to that 'dear delightful place, Chequers, where nothing but joy and tranquillity, health and pleasure can ever reign' – a far cry from the camp in which he had been laid up with a cold, because he had, 'indiscreetly dined without his wig'.

When peace came at last, Colonel Russell, having fought at the battle of Dettingen and distinguished himself at Fontenoy, cherished the hope of a home posting. Instead he went to Minorca, which the British had leased in 1709, to command the 34th Foot Regiment. It was to be his last posting, for he was invalided home in 1754. His hopes of finally enjoying the peace and tranquillity of family life were short-lived, and he died in the same year.

Coat of Arms of Mary Joanna Cutts Rivett

Meanwhile Mary's brother John Rivett, who had served in the same regiment as Colonel Russell, had retired as a captain in 1743 and come back to Chequers to manage the estate for his mother, now widowed for the second time. While looking after its maintenance, he undertook the major surgery of blocking up some forty windows to cut down the draughts and the window tax. He also cleaned out the farmyard, made alterations to the Great Parlour – mostly for the better according to his sister – and took in hand the restoration of many of the pictures. Two portraits by an unknown artist of the Russells' two children, which today hang in the Great Hall, date from this time.

John Rivett continued living at Chequers and married his stepsister Fanny Russell, Woman of the Bedchamber to George II's daughter Princess Amelia. Since their union came somewhat late in life, there were no children, but his will, made a year or so before his death, provides for one John Smith 'thought to be my son'. It is tempting to draw a particular conclusion from the generous provision he also made in his will for his servant, Mary Vere.

When Rivett died in 1763, his mother Joanna had been the mistress of Chequers for more than half a century. She died an octogenarian the following year, having outlived her three sons, all of whom had died childless.

It was therefore her only daughter Mary Russell who found herself in possession of the Chequers estate and the manor of Mordaunts. The will also mentioned land in Ellesborough: 'fifteen houses, two dovehouses, a mill, 200 acres of pasture, 370 acres of woodland, 100 acres of furze and heath', together with common pasture and free warren in Nashley, Kimblewick, and in the parishes of Ellesborough and Great Kimble. Mary did not, however, enjoy her inheritance for long: she died before the will was out of probate and the estate passed unhindered to her only son, John, who had inherited the Russell baronetcy from his cousin William, who died childless in 1757.

Only sixteen when he inherited the title, the 8th Baronet, Sir John Russell, left Christ Church, Oxford, with two degrees and when he was admitted to Lincoln's Inn in 1759 gave his address as 'Chequers Court'. An impecunious but amiable young man, with an ancient house and acres of land, he had been called to the Bar in 1763, but had shown no inclination to practise the law. Without ambition or obvious means of supporting a wife, it was not surprising that the parents of his intended bride should not wholeheartedly approve of the match.

His fiancée Kitty, the only daughter of General the Hon. George Cary and Isabella née Ingram, did not enjoy robust health. To add to the baronet's problems, Chequers had been occupied by tenants since the death of his mother, and was somewhat run down. Nevertheless, hoping that love would conquer all, Sir John Russell simultaneously announced his engagement and his intention to retire to Buckinghamshire; he was reconciled, he wrote to his friend John Baker Holroyd (later Lord Sheffield), to carrying his bride over the threshold and into a house 'full of dirt and rags', yet determined to manage as best they could. Since Holroyd, a Member of Parliament and leading authority of the time on agricultural matters, had commissioned the most successful architect of his day, James Wyatt (1747–1813), to carry out extensive alterations to his Sussex mansion, Sheffield Place, John Russell was keen to involve him in the work needed at Chequers. 'I am in such dirt,' he complained, 'I cannot even paper a room till I shall determine what is to be altered.' Wyatt visited Chequers on one occasion, when it was probably apparent that Russell's dreams exceeded his means. The architect did, however, submit sketches for new stables and a farmyard, but these came to nothing. Russell was therefore obliged to 'blunder on with [his] country bricklayer', though there is no record of how much of the work he accomplished in this way.

In the meantime John and Kitty dedicated themselves to cleaning and mending the furniture, pictures and china and adding a few contemporary pieces of their own. The 8th Baronet's one

Lady Catherine Russell (1748-1782) John Downman, A.R.A. (1750-1824). In 1775 Kitty Cary married Sir John Russell, 8th Baronet, who had inherited Chequers through his mother, Mary Joanna Rivett, in 1764. This watercolour portrait hangs in the White Parlour.

Coat of Arms of Sir John Russell, 8th Bart.

The Russell and Revett (sic) families
A conversation piece by C. Philips, 1708-1747: 'Syllabub straight from the Cow', which hangs in the Hawtrey Room.

great legacy to Chequers, however, was the fitting up of the Long Gallery as a library. In one letter to Holroyd he writes:

… tho' it is only whitewashed blue and has most of its books lettered upon little bits of paper gummed on the back by Kate and me … yet it has some good features let me tell you … it is 88 feet long and the book cases are very neat and it only wants two couches and 3 or 4 more tables.

The Russell and
Revett (sic) and
Greenhill families
*A companion picture by
C. Philips, 1708-1747,
which hangs in the
Hawtrey Room.*

Russell also sought Holroyd's advice on agricultural matters and
his friend sent him forty ewes from the Sussex Downs, which
produced some very satisfactory lambs. A herd of Alderneys
graced the dairy, which Russell described as 'the most beautiful in
the world'. To this day grazing sheep and cattle are a familiar sight
in the pastoral landscape of Chequers.

Russell devoted his life to Chequers, his farm and his wife;
when she died after only seven years of married bliss he was

plunged into inconsolable grief. Eight months later, in 1783, 'universally lamented by all who had the honour of his acquaintance', he too died – of inflammation of the bowels brought on, so it is said, by an over-indulgence of melons while dining at the home of a friend in Kent. He was buried at Ellesborough, alongside his wife Kate, and he left his estate in trust to his sons.

THE GREENHILL RUSSELLS

At the time of their parents' death John, the heir to the baronetcy, and his brother George were only six and four years old respectively. Under their father's will, their guardianship fell to their cousin the Reverend Dr John Greenhill Russell and his wife Elizabeth, who took them into the bosom of their family, nursing them through various childhood illnesses and bringing them up with the same affection as they had for their own son. As trustee of the Chequers estate, Greenhill appears to have managed affairs with competence and efficiency.

In due course young John inherited an ample fortune from the Ingrams, his mother's family, but in the meantime Chequers was mortgaged, in spite of generating income of £1,200 from a brisk trade in timber and rents from a succession of tenants, until Sir John came of age in 1798.

Although his father's plans for alterations had been frustrated, Chequers was evidently in a good state of repair. A few years earlier the *General Evening Post* had described it as 'a good comfortable old mansion house, part of which is fitted in the modern style and mostly new furnished within these few years... fit for the use of a moderate and genteel family'.

There was, however, to be no future for the Russell name down this line, for Sir John, the 9th Baronet, died a bachelor in 1802. His lengthy and complex will covered every eventuality, though the inclusion of any heirs 'male or female' of his aunt Mary Russell strikes an odd note: at this time she was unmarried, childless and well over sixty years old. In the first instance his brother George was the beneficiary, but he too died a bachelor a couple of years later and with him the baronetcy became extinct. He also considered Aunt Mary in his will, assuming that 'at her time of life she would not want to fatigue herself with the large establishment which would be necessary to keep Chequers in a proper state of repair'. Next in line to inherit the property was his guardian, John Greenhill Russell, but the Reverend Doctor was

Coat of Arms of Sir John Russell and Sir George Russell

47

well into his seventies by this time and, having managed the estate for a good few years, had no wish to resume the responsibility. In June 1805 Greenhill therefore joined Mary Russell in renouncing his interest in Chequers in favour of his own son Robert.

THE GOTHIC REVIVAL AT CHEQUERS

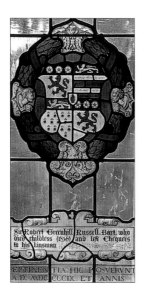

Coat of Arms of Sir Robert Greenhill Russell

It is evident that, although not in the vanguard of the trend, Chequers did not escape the Gothic revival that came to Buckinghamshire in the late eighteenth and nineteenth centuries. Whereas the hard-pressed 8th Baronet, Sir John Russell, had been unable to get beyond the drawing board with James Wyatt, his cousin Robert Greenhill Russell engaged William Atkinson, a pupil of Wyatt, to execute what a later generation described as the 'orgy of Victorian Gothic'. When Lipscomb visited Chequers in 1824 while researching his history of Buckinghamshire, the fabric of Chequers already conformed to the prevailing fashion of the time. Lipscomb approved of the modernization, while Sir Alexander Croke, the nineteenth-century family historian who believed the Crokes had been responsible for building the original house, was still more eulogistic, describing it as having been 'lately fitted up in the Gothic style with exquisite taste'.

This fit of Gothic enthusiasm, however, succeeded in almost totally obscuring William Hawtrey's house by covering everything with plaster inside and out. Panelling was ripped out and replaced with plaster, moth-eaten tapestries were torn down and burnt on the north lawn, and no aspect of the house remained untouched. A porch was added to the east wing, windows with curved transoms were fitted to the north front and the simple triangular gables were cut into battlements and decorated with pinnacles.

Thus 'transformed', the house became the fashionable and imposing residence of Sir Robert Greenhill Russell, a successful and prosperous lawyer who specialized in the drafting of pleadings in the Court of Chancery. He was also a Member of Parliament and represented Thirsk, in Yorkshire, for twenty-six years from 1806 until the seat, a rotten borough, disappeared with the Reform Act in 1832. Loyal to the Tories in and out of office, he witnessed the comings and goings of eight administrations from Lord Grenville to Lord Grey. He was a conscientious parliamentarian, voting among other things for an inquiry into allegations of ministerial corruption and into the Lord Chancellor's conduct during the illness of George III. In Parliament he was regarded by colleagues as 'a man of honour and kindness of heart', who

Chequers South and
East fronts about
1892, before the
removal of the
Greenhill Gothic

Chequers North and
West fronts about
1892, before the
removal of the
Greenhill Gothic

Chequers Court

refused to allow political disagreements to interfere with his friendships. But parliamentary duties were not very onerous, and Sir Robert had ample time to oversee the work being done at Chequers.

An inscription on the underside of a floorboard in the Hawtrey Room, signed and dated 'J. Hewitt 24 September 1813', discovered during restoration work in the twentieth century, suggests that at Chequers Sir Robert was a hard taskmaster. This same Hewitt tells us that he 'groined the breakfast room in May 1804', but is now 'under marching orders to smokey London'; he refers to the present 'Master Greenhill [as] a poor lousy vagabond', adding, 'God help all poor carpenters.' It is not entirely clear who might have been responsible for the decision to 'groin' the breakfast room. George Russell had died in April, and Mary Russell and the Reverend John Greenhill Russell had not officially renounced their right to Chequers by this date. Moreover, it seems unlikely that the latter would have bothered with such a major task, so perhaps Hewitt was finishing a phase of work begun by George Russell. No evidence remains today in any of the rooms likely to have been the breakfast room, although in a void above a small bedroom on the south-east corner of the house the remains of a groined ceiling can clearly be seen by anyone prepared to make the journey on hands and knees via a cupboard on the attic floor.

Sir Robert was also a beneficiary of the Enclosure Act of 1803, which enhanced the Chequers estate to the tune of several hundred acres of meadows, woodland and wasteland which

included Beacon Hill and twelve acres of Coombe Hill.
Unmarried, childless and without a natural heir, when he
contemplated the future disposition of his property, the story goes
that his attention turned to the Bedford Russells, the same family
to whom the 4th Baronet, Sir William Russell, had sold
Chippenham a century and a half earlier. In his high regard for Sir
John Russell, the 6th Duke of Bedford, he decided that Chequers
would pass, on his death, to a 'younger' son of the Duke. But
when he drove over to Woburn in his coach and four to acquaint
the Duke with his plans, he was received with such scant
hospitality that he returned to Chequers without having made his
offer. If the story were true, for the want of a glass of wine
Chequers failed to become a Prime Ministerial residence some
seventy years earlier than it actually did, for Lord John Russell,
one of the 6th Duke's younger sons, succeeded Sir Robert Peel as
Prime Minister in 1846.

Unfortunately, however, the facts get in the way of the story.
Since Chequers was entailed under the 9th Baronet's complex
will, the story must be dismissed as apocryphal. The rightful
successor was in fact his distant relation, Sir Robert Frankland of
Thirkleby, in Yorkshire. When Sir Robert died in 1836, his will
made generous financial bequests to a number of people, including
servants, and Chequers, now a pseudo-Gothic mansion standing in
1,700 acres of wooded parkland, was duly bequeathed to Sir
Robert Frankland on the sole condition that he adopt the name
Russell as part of his own name.

SIR ROBERT AND LADY FRANKLAND RUSSELL

Sir Robert Frankland Russell, as he became known, was directly
descended from Frances Cromwell and Sir John Russell; he had
inherited the baronetcy from his father in 1831. Although happy
to adopt the name of Russell as a condition of his inheritance, he
was less enthusiastic about taking up residence with his wife and
five daughters in the south of England. Chequers was therefore
put on the market, where it soon attracted the attention of
Benjamin Disraeli.

Disraeli, who had visited the house a couple of years earlier,
was then a successful novelist and flamboyant man-about-town,
struggling for recognition in a party which set great store upon
birth and wealth, neither of which qualifications he possessed. For
a Tory politician who aspired to high office, a country estate was
an almost essential prerequisite, and everything about Chequers

Coat of Arms of Sir
Robert Frankland
Russell

was perfect – except the price. 'Not under £40,000, perhaps £10,000 more, as there is timber', was Disraeli's estimate in a letter to a friend. But being deeply in debt, for the moment not only the country estate but also the Parliamentary seat eluded him.

Sir Robert soon abandoned plans to sell the estate, and, according to Lipscomb who visited Chequers again before his massive historical work was reprinted in 1847, continued to make improvements to the house. The architect Edward Buckton Lamb dedicated his book *Studies of Ancient Domestic Architecture* (published in 1842) to Sir Robert as a tribute to his patronage of

Sir Robert Frankland Russell Bart.
by himself.

Chequers Court
*by Sir Robert
Frankland Russell
line and wash.*

architecture and interest in the subject. Lamb's drawing of the
north front of Chequers, captioned 'Chequers Court, Restored',
is indistinguishable from how it appears today, suggesting that
there might have been plans to strip off the Gothic accretions and
restore the house to its former Tudor dignity. But Chequers was
to remain veiled in stucco for the best part of the nineteenth
century. In the meantime Lamb was responsible for some new
additions to Chequers in the form of several gatehouse lodges –
one of which, on the Butler's Cross road, was used until recently
as a sewing room – and a bailiff's cottage, together with the
village school in Ellesborough which was built at Sir Robert's
personal expense.

An artist in his own right, Sir Robert Frankland Russell was
referred to by Landseer as an 'artist spoilt' because he had not
taken up pencil and brush as a profession. There is evidence of his
talent at Chequers in two big albums of sketches and caricatures,
including one of himself and his bride on honeymoon walking
along a street in Brussels with the caption, '*Regardez les Anglais*'.
Charming portraits of his daughters still hang at Chequers. He is

Three of Sir Robert
Frankland Russell's
five daughters
by himself.
FROM THE TOP:
*Augusta, Caroline
Agnes and Julia
Roberta. The sketch is
of Caroline Agnes.*

also believed to have invented the pop-up picture books which amused his own children and have delighted countless generations of children since.

Sir Robert's wife, whom he married in 1815, was Louisa Anne Murray, the youngest and fifth daughter of the Bishop of St David's. If the Autissier miniature in the Long Gallery is anything to go by, Lady Frankland Russell was a strikingly beautiful woman. Her grandson later described how George IV, making play with her initials, dubbed her his 'pet lamb'. While she presided, Chequers was alive with glittering and intellectual house parties and there was plenty of time for drives to call on country neighbours, such as the Dashwoods at Wycombe Park. Amongst their political acquaintances in the county, Sir Robert and Lady Frankland Russell especially approved of Mr Disraeli, who 'thoroughly understood how to instruct the farmer, the Freeholder and the labourer' at Aylesbury political meetings.

Lady Frankland Russell particularly liked to watch the cricket matches played in front of the house. She extended generous hospitality to all, including her favourite charitable institutions, such as the annual show of the Velvet Lawn Cottage Garden Society, when tenants from Ellesborough and the Kimbles competed to produce the best vegetables and the best kept garden or allotment: for the winning garden there was a first prize of £10, a year's rent.

Picnics on Velvet Lawn were organized on a grand scale, and in 1860, 8,000 people were reported to have flocked to watch the Aylesbury Rifle Volunteers stage a sham fight as the highlight of their grand fete. According to the local newspaper, the occasion was graced by 'all the beauty and fashion of the neighbourhood, comprising a brilliant assemblage of ladies'. The band of the Ist Life Guards provided the music and the day ended with a dinner in a marquee attended by 400 people.

Lady Frankland Russell lived on at Chequers for more than twenty years after the death of her husband, the last of the Russell baronets, in 1849. To the end of her life she was a familiar figure driving in her landau and on Sundays in Ellesborough Church, sitting in the big square Chequers pew draped with blue cloth. She had been responsible for the church's restoration in the 1850s and presumably nobody complained when she decreed that the church bells should fall silent as she approached since she found their clamour disturbing.

Her grandson recalled his grandmother as a semi-invalid, 'a little old lady, garbed in black watered silk'. Every evening he was

Lady Frankland Russell
(Louisa Anne Murray)
Miniature by Louis
Autissier, 1772-1830.
Lady Frankland Russell
was the daughter of the
Bishop of St David's
and the granddaughter of
John Murray, the 3rd
Duke of Atholl.

ushered into her sitting room (the room which had the 'groined ceiling') to say goodnight and to receive an offering of a small flat chocolate covered in white 'tens and thousands' (sic). Once, when he wanted to stay up longer in order to read Lewis Carroll's recently published *Alice in Wonderland*, he remembered his grandmother growing impatient with him and packing him off to bed without more ado.

Lady Frankland Russell's sitting room *The room with the 'groined ceiling'*.

56

THE ASTLEYS AND THEIR CLUTTERBUCK TENANTS

It was the youngest of Lady Frankland Russell's five daughters who inherited Chequers on her mother's death in 1871. Rosalind Alicia Frankland Russell had married Colonel Francis L'Estrange Astley, the youngest son of the 15th Lord Hastings, but he had died after only eight years of marriage in 1862, leaving her a widow with three sons.

Rosalind Frankland Russell Astley was as devoted to Chequers as her mother had been. She took great pleasure in showing people around the house, explaining the Cromwell connection and pointing out its treasures. Equally, she loved to accompany her guests in the box woods or to drive them around the park in a trap pulled by a sure-footed pony. When she died at the turn of the century her son Bertram Astley inherited Chequers, but for a period of years it was let.

The Clutterbucks, an old brewery family from Yorkshire, had been attracted to Chequers by the shooting and stalking and had fallen in love with the house. Although the Astleys had retained the right to admit the public to the park (the footpath and the bridleways were not clearly defined), it is clear from some of the correspondence between the families that Mr Thomas Clutterbuck would not have agreed to the lease had he not been assured of protection for his coverts. 'Of course I do not object to neighbours to whom you have given leave to walk in the park', he wrote to Bertram Astley, 'but it would be very good of you if you could do something about the dogs.' Astley assured him that he would write

The Clutterbucks
A family group at Chequers in 1903.

The coat of arms on the west front *commemorates the marriage in 1815 of Robert Frankland and Louisa Anne Murray.*

A Game of Cricket
Chequers in 1903.

to the dog-walkers 'to stop them doing so in future', but Clutterbuck was in despair when he learned that both a fête in aid of the Ellesborough parish rooms and the annual Velvet Lawn flower show were to go ahead as usual. Perhaps the Astleys had never taken their shooting very seriously, but in any case after twelve years the flower show was no more.

Notwithstanding the problems of access the Clutterbucks liked Chequers so much that when they left in 1909 Thomas commissioned a house to be built in Bedfordshire, with a south front the almost exact replica of that of Chequers. The family had in fact hoped to extend their lease on Chequers, but in January 1909 Mr and Mrs Arthur Lee came to view the house and Chequers was set upon the course of a much higher destiny.

The Great Hall
Two photographs taken before the Lee restoration in 1909.

The Hawtrey Room
A photograph taken before the Lee restoration in 1909.

The Long Gallery
A photograph taken before the Lee restoration in 1909.

The Great Parlour
A photograph taken before the Lee restoration in 1909.

The Recess of the Great Parlour
A photograph taken in 1910 after the Lee restoration.

THE LEES' BEQUEST

OPPOSITE:
The stained glass bay window in the Long Gallery
Installed by Lord Lee, its 24 panels feature the coats of arms of the families that owned Chequers, from the de Scaccarios to the Astleys.

Arthur Lee was already a well-established Conservative Member of Parliament for Fareham, with a distinguished military career behind him, when he and his wife took over the lease of Chequers in 1909. The Lees had for some years been renting a house in their Hampshire constituency, but now wished, for the sake of Arthur's health, to move to the more bracing climate of the Buckinghamshire Chilterns. Theirs was a move that was to have profound consequences, for, after a twelve-year occupation and the expenditure of much love and money, Chequers was to become the subject of an extraordinary act of far-sighted generosity.

ARTHUR LEE'S EARLY LIFE

Born in Dorset in 1868, the year in which Benjamin Disraeli became Prime Minister for the first time, Arthur Hamilton Lee had begun his life in somewhat different financial circumstances. His father, an impoverished country rector, had died when he was only two years old, leaving his mother with little provision to bring up their three daughters and two sons. Arthur, the youngest son and a sickly child, was therefore from time to time farmed out to strangers.

At the age of four he was taken into the more or less permanent care of Miss Paterson, a formidable lady of independent means who had dedicated her life to looking after the children of poor gentlefolk. Her mixture of tyranny and generosity, however, left him not knowing whether to love her or loathe her.

A precocious child, he was sent to boarding school at the age of six, but unhappiness at school was not greatly relieved by the dreaded prospect of the holidays with Miss Paterson. At the age of eleven he won a classics scholarship to Cheltenham College. Here, inadequate food, bullying and regular doses of corporal punishment combined to ensure that his schooldays were a continuing misery.

Arthur Hamilton Lee,
1868–1947
*Later Lord Lee of
Fareham, who gave
Chequers to the nation
for the use of successive
Prime Ministers.*

With his sights firmly set upon an army career, in 1885 he passed into the Royal Military College at Woolwich. Three years later he left with a Queen's Commission as a second lieutenant in the Royal Artillery and applied to the War Office for a posting to Hong Kong, because he understood that there "it might be possible to live on one's pay".

In the colony, Lee soon earned himself a reputation as a loner. When not yet twenty, he engaged in a covert and totally unauthorized solo reconnaissance of a new Russian base at Vladivostock. This was not only the port and arsenal of the rapidly growing Russian fleet but also the supposedly impregnable terminus of the trans-Siberian railway. He succeeded in getting close enough to deposit a visiting card into the barrel of one gun emplacement. This remarkable feat of espionage brought his name to the attention of the military authorities but earned him a stern reprimand from the Foreign Office.

Lee was soon offered the post of adjutant of the Western Defences and staff officer at the Isle of Wight gunnery school. The headquarters of his new command at Freshwater were not far from Farringford Lodge, where Alfred Tennyson spent the winter months. Here, Arthur Lee became the elderly Poet Laureate's frequent companion on regular morning walks in the year before Tennyson died.

Lee's next post was as Professor of Strategy and Tactics at the Military College in Kingston, Ontario, where he remained until 1898. When war between America and Spain seemed imminent, Lee offered his services to the War Office, which appointed him a military attaché with the US army in the field.

A LASTING FRIENDSHIP

It was in Tampa, Florida, from where the American expeditionary force was to embark for Cuba, that Arthur Lee first met the American Vice-President Theodore Roosevelt, '... the most alive, the most compelling, and the most entertaining human being with whom I had ever come into contact'. Lee also noted that 'to my huge delight he seemed to take to me as instinctively as I did to him.' The two men formed a close friendship and when Roosevelt formed the first United States Volunteer Cavalry Regiment, known as the Rough Riders, Lee enlisted as an honorary member of the regiment.

At the end of the Cuban campaign Arthur Lee returned home to England, especially commended for his attention to the

Miniature of Ruth Moore, 1873–1967
This miniature by Amalia Kussner (1876–1933) in a pearl frame was painted at the time of her engagement to Arthur Lee in 1899. She was the daughter of John G. Moore of New York.

wounded while under fire at the battle of Santiago. The War Office had received bids from Washington that he be posted back to America as the British military attaché at the Embassy. As a mere second lieutenant, Lee was considered too junior for the post, so he persuaded his superiors to promote him to lieutenant-colonel and as such he was foisted upon the unsuspecting ambassador in Washington.

Once back in the United States, Lee made haste to New York. On an earlier visit he had met and fallen head over heels in love with Ruth Moore, daughter of the wealthy businessman-turned-banker, John G. Moore. After her father's death, Lee proposed marriage, and on their engagement in September 1899 Theodore Roosevelt, then Governor of New York State, wrote to Lee:

> *I congratulate you most heartily old fellow ... no possible success, military or political, is worth weighing in the balance for one moment against the happiness that comes to those fortunate enough to make a love-match – a match in which lover and sweetheart will never be lost in husband and wife ...*

Ruth and Arthur married quietly in New York just before Christmas 1899, when the Boer War was at its height. In Washington, Lee was able to review their future together. Since Ruth and her sister Faith had been handsomely provided for by their father, Lee had become, by marriage, a man of substantial means. Believing that further promotion in the army was unlikely, he was now in a position to be able to think seriously about a political career.

Silver inkstand
This silver inkstand on hoof feet was a wedding present from Arthur Lee's colleagues at the British Embassy in Washington in 1900.

MEMBER OF PARLIAMENT FOR FAREHAM

Having returned to England in May 1900, Lee was adopted unanimously as the prospective parliamentary candidate for Fareham in Hampshire. In the general election of 1900 he doubled the previous Conservative majority and joined the government benches at the same time as such future parliamentary luminaries as Andrew Bonar Law and Winston Churchill.

Lee soon proved himself to be a man of independent mind. He announced, 'I would not go to Westminster with my hands tied or committed to vote on this side or that before I had heard the matter debated.' The *Pall Mall Gazette* recorded his maiden speech in a debate on the new Army Scheme as one of the best such speeches the House had ever heard. By the end of his first session he was perceived to have vastly increased his reputation and was regarded as politically 'sound' by the Tory leadership. Early in 1901 he became a member of the War Office Committee of Military Education, for which he was eminently qualified.

In May 1903 Joseph Chamberlain's campaign for tariff reform, which was supported by Lee, divided the Government. Chamberlain resigned, and in the resulting shake-up Arthur Lee was surprised to be asked by the Prime Minister, Arthur Balfour, to join the Government as Civil Lord of the Admiralty. 'Would a duck take to water?' was Lee's response.

As the aftershocks rumbled on, Balfour vacillated in an attempt to keep the Free Traders happy. Ultimately, however, even his ingenuity could not keep the Unionist Party together and he resigned in 1905. Campbell-Bannerman formed a new Liberal administration and in January he went to the country on Free Trade; the Liberal Party was returned with an overwhelming majority and Balfour lost his seat.

1900 Election brooch
A brooch, showing Lee's majority, was given to Ruth Lee by his Fareham constituents after the general election of 1900.

Arthur Lee
Conservative and Unionist MP for Fareham from 1900 to 1918, when he was elevated to the peerage as Lord Lee of Fareham.

In the meantime, after the assassination of President McKinley in September 1901, Theodore Roosevelt had become the twenty-sixth President of the United States. When a change of ambassador seemed imminent in Washington in November 1906, Roosevelt wrote to the Foreign Office suggesting that Lee was ably qualified for the appointment. For his part Lee was ambivalent about the possibility of returning to Washington: he had no doubts that Ruth would adapt to the new role as ambassador's wife, but neither of them relished the prospect of exchanging their political life and constituency for the diplomatic treadmill. In his autobiography, *A Good Innings*, Lee wrote:

1910 Election brooch
A brooch, made of brilliants depiciting Lee's majority, was given to Ruth Lee by the constituents of Fareham.

> *Ruth, as always, took off my shoulders nearly all the burden of social and political calls and was in great demand for bazaars, fêtes and the like, at which she behaved as though she really enjoyed them. I, on the other hand, found them so intolerable that I could seldom conceal my aversion and eventually Ruth forbade any further attendance on my part lest worse things might befall.*

Miniature of Lady Lee
This miniature in a silver frame was signed by Lily Ogilvy and inscribed on the back, 'Ruth, later Viscountess Lee of Fareham:1913'.

The decision, however, was made for them by Edward Grey, the Foreign Secretary. He had no doubt that Lee would have been an excellent diplomat, but in the end other arrangements were made. So Fareham was spared a by-election and Lee remained in opposition, speaking when necessary in the House, mainly on

Painting for a *Vanity Fair* 'Spy' cartoon *Arthur Lee at the dispatch box in the House of Commons. Arthur Lee served in Lloyd George's last coalition Cabinet as Minister for Agriculture and First Lord of the Admiralty.*

naval and military matters and continuing to goad the Prime Minister. In April 1907 ill health obliged Campbell-Bannerman to resign and the way was clear for Asquith, the Chancellor of the Exchequer, to become Prime Minister. Before the end of the month Campbell-Bannerman was dead. Later, Lee was to record his remorse for all the annoyance he had caused him in his declining years.

HOUSE-HUNTING

It was at this point in his career that the Lees decided to look around for another country house. In addition to their Mayfair house, they had been renting Rookesbury Park, at Wickham in Lee's constituency, on which the lease was about to expire. On their short-list were two properties about thirteen miles apart – Chequers Court and a house at Watlington.

On their first visit to Chequers, they viewed the house through a storm of sleet in the fading light of a winter afternoon. What they found was a house larger than the one at Watlington, though not as big as Rookesbury. In the January 1909 edition of *Country Life*, it was described as a:

> *...beautiful old house with many historic associations and restored and partially rebuilt in 1566* [sic] *... situated in the centre of the Park of about 300 acres, and ... approached by two drives with entrance lodges. It is of Tudor character, in red brick with old stone mullioned windows, and presents a pleasing and dignified appearance. The House contains a lofty central hall 33ft square, with gallery, dining room 37ft × 21ft, drawing room 37ft × 21ft, fine library 83ft × 16ft, morning room, smoking room and boudoir and there are some 30 bed and dressing rooms ... extensive stabling, and shooting over 2,700 acres including some 600 acres of covert.*

The exterior lived up to all their expectations and, although the inside was described by Lee as 'an orgy of Victorian Gothic' in a very poor state of repair and perversely inconvenient, they both fell in love with it.

After a sleepless night at the George Inn at Aylesbury, Lee had come up with a scheme whereby it might be possible to lease the house for their joint lifetimes, at the same time as having a reasonably free hand with carrying out the essential restoration and improvements.

Mr and Mrs Arthur
Lee at the North
door of Chequers
in 1910
*The photograph was
first published in*
Country Life.

Ruth, on the other hand, had set her heart on owning rather than leasing and, although excited about the possibility of Chequers, dwelt upon the prospect of the work absorbing too much of Arthur's energy and their money. While they equivocated between Chequers and Watlington, Ruth wrote in her diary:

> *[Arthur] says Watlington is like being married to a nice comfortable little woman and Chequers Court like being carried off one's feet by Helen of Troy! One might be happier, though, with the nice little woman in the long run.*

A week later Ruth was writing that she thought the Chequers deal was 'off'. The lease was a non-starter and the asking price of around £130,000 for the house and estate put it beyond their reach. Nevertheless, they visited Chequers again, and continued to press their suit. Finally, with a sigh of relief, a life tenancy was signed and sealed on 28 April 1909. 'So far as anything could appear settled in mundane affairs', Lee later wrote, 'we are now provided with an ideal home for the rest of our natural lives.'

CHEQUERS RESTORED

The restoration work at Chequers began almost immediately. Arthur Lee engaged the services of Reginald Blomfield (1856–1942), the architect responsible for Lambeth Bridge, Swan & Edgar at Piccadilly Circus and Lady Margaret Hall, in Oxford. Blomfield, who had a reputation for restoring houses to their original form and was the author of *The Formal Garden in England*, was already familiar with Chequers. In 1892 Bertram Astley, the then owner of Chequers, had approached him with a view to improving the gardens, as a result of which he had designed a terrace to run along the south front.

At the same time Blomfield had called Astley's attention to a section of loose stucco beneath which could be seen the warm red brick that a century earlier had been decreed a blot on the landscape. Astley and his whole house-party had fallen with enthusiasm to picking off the stucco, and before long a large area of fine brickwork had been revealed, resembling the older parts of Hampton Court. In due course all the stucco was chipped away,

The east front at Chequers Court Restoration during two seasons in 1909, shown from the south-east corner.

the spurious battlements and finials were removed from the roof gables and the pseudo-Gothic windows were replaced with more harmonious stone mullions. Chequers was at last restored to something William Hawtrey would have recognized.

The external restoration was, therefore, virtually complete when the Lees took over the tenancy from the Clutterbucks in 1909. All that remained to be done before they could turn their

Mr Lee consulting
with Mr Blomfield
*The discovery of the
old door in the inner
courtyard during the
restoration work
in 1909.*

Mr. Bloomfield on the war Path!

The finding of the old Courtyard doors.

A Consultation!

attention to the 'orgy of Victorian Gothic' on the inside was to reinstate a couple of blocked-off windows, add a more substantial porch to the main entrance and create more space in what remained of the old inner courtyard.

Blomfield now turned his attention to the massive renovation of the interior: so dramatic were his changes that it is impossible to relate some of the photographs of Chequers taken at the end of the nineteenth century to the interior as we know it today.

Lee's guiding principle for the restoration was to preserve every aspect of the Elizabethan house, and to bring the rest of it as far as possible into harmony with William Hawtrey's imposing north

The Great Parlour, c.1870
China is displayed in the recess formed by the old staircase to the Prison Room. This staircase was restored by Arthur Lee in 1909.

ABOVE:

Chequers Court
The forecourt, after restoration.

RIGHT:

Chequers Court
The north and east front, with the new porch, after restoration.

Chequers Court
The north and west angle, after restoration (all photographs shown in Country Life, *31 December 1910).*

front. But not much of the original remained: there was no panelling and not a single old fireplace. The spiral staircase up which Lady Mary Grey had wearily climbed to her Prison Room had rotted away long ago, and the landing which gave on to the Great Parlour had been turned into a china closet. The only remaining feature of genuine antiquity appeared to be the balusters

The Great Hall
Three views of the Great Hall after the renovations. The painting of 'The Mathematician' is shown under the gallery (below).

Lady Lee in the
kitchen garden
*The gatehouse in the
background was designed
by Edward Buckton
Lamb for Sir Robert
Frankland Russell in
the 1840s.*

Lime Avenue (*above
left*), Velvet Lawn
(*above right*) and Silver
Springs (*bottom*)
*All these photographs
were taken in 1909.*

Entrance to the rose garden from the East forecourt
The entrance was designed by Arthur Lee. Above it the inscription reads: 'All Care Abandon Ye Who Enter Here'.

of the main staircase. For Lee the answer was to seek antiquity elsewhere and to import it to Chequers. Architect and client enjoyed a good relationship and, with the house 'restored to something of its former beauty and dignity', Blomfield was to acknowledge the 'fine taste and discernment' of the Lees.

A year later the Lees gave a dinner in the nearly completed Great Hall for more than 200 workmen. Little progress seemed to have been made, however, since before Christmas, when they had celebrated their tenth wedding anniversary with a picnic in the new dining room. Parts of the house still resembled, in Ruth's words, 'scenes from the San Francisco earthquake', but they felt the only way to speed the workmen up was to move in. They slept in the Astley Room and Arthur used the Prison Room as a dressing room.

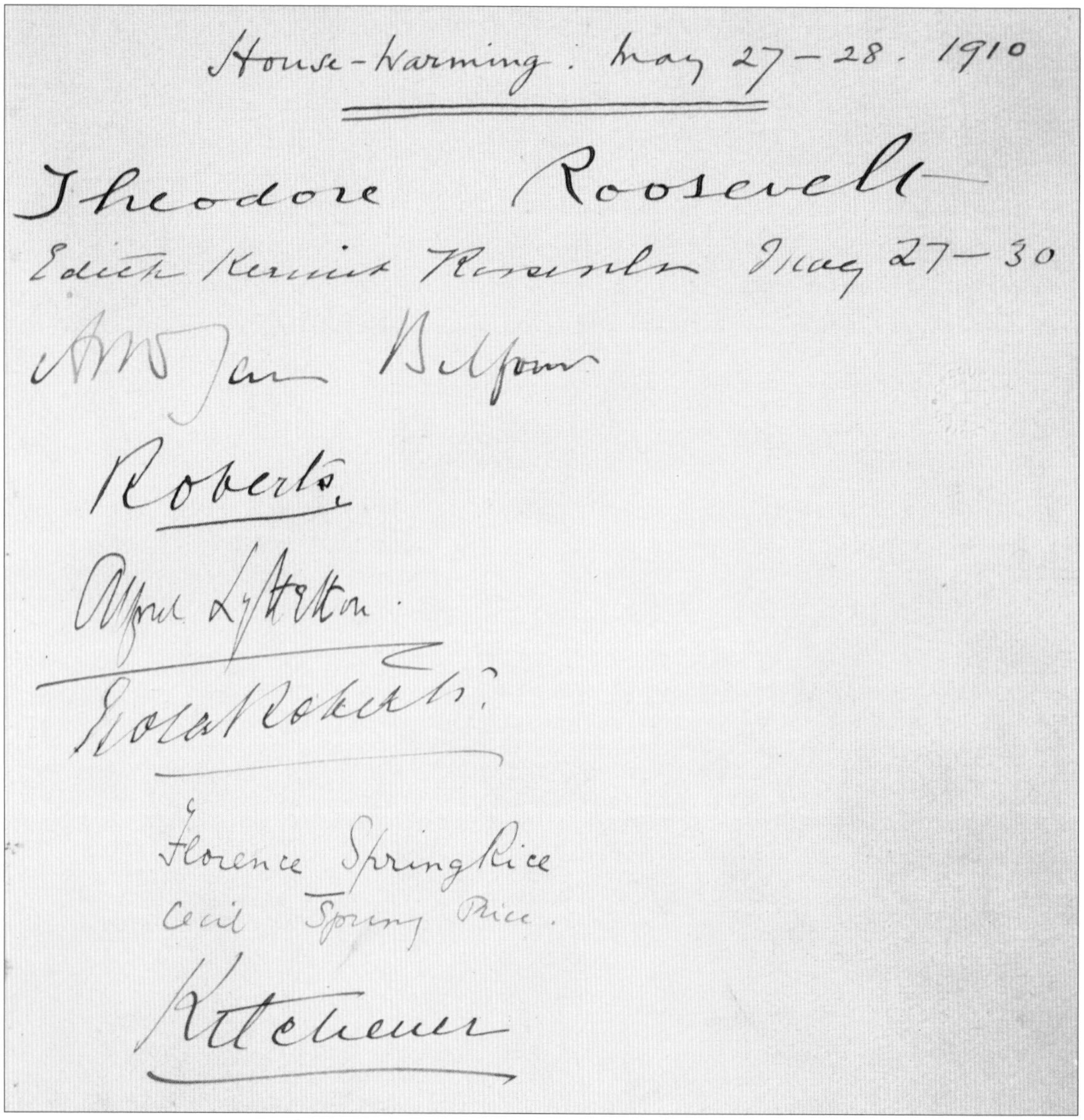

House-Warming: May 27–28. 1910

Theodore Roosevelt

Edith Kermit Roosevelt May 27–30

Arthur James Balfour

Roberts.

Alfred Lyttelton.

Florence Spring Rice

Cecil Spring Rice.

Kitchener

The Chequers Visitors' Book
The first page, with the signatures of the guests at the house-warming party which included the Roosevelts, Arthur Balfour and Lord Kitchener.

A HOUSE-WARMING PARTY

With the coming of spring, house and staff were gradually brought under control and then the Lees were presented with the opportunity to throw a rather grander house-warming party. Edward VII had died in May 1910 and the Roosevelts, who were attending his funeral, were invited to Chequers. The invitation particularly irked Lord Curzon, who had tried to lure them to Hackwood with the promise of congenial and interesting guests. The Lees' own house-party, however, was far from dull. Gathered together for the occasion was a former Prime Minister, a former Secretary of State for the Colonies, two distinguished Field Marshals and a future American Ambassador – Arthur Balfour,

Alfred Lyttelton, Lord Roberts, Lord Kitchener and Cecil Spring Rice respectively. Only Lord Kitchener, who joined them later, proved less than congenial to the ex-President, who complained in a letter of his 'bumptious and posing' manner. The only regret the Lees had was that it was not as President that Roosevelt planted the first of the commemorative trees at Chequers on 28 May 1910.

DELAVAL ASTLEY

It was the untimely death of Delaval Astley, in 1912, that at last gave the Lees the opportunity to buy Chequers. He was the son of Bertram Astley and his wife Florence, the youngest daughter of the 3rd Marquess Conyngham, who had spent their honeymoon at Chequers. Baptized in Ellesborough Church, he grew up with names that were a tribute to several branches of the family – Henry Jacob Delaval Frankland Russell Astley – and was still a minor when he inherited Chequers on the death of his father. Having completed his education at Eton and Sandhurst, he was too much on the move to be interested in a country estate; in any case the house had been occupied by tenants since the turn of the century.

Delaval lived life on the edge – enjoying pursuits such as shooting, hunting and motor racing. He earned a pilot's certificate

Henry Delaval Astley
The courageous young flyer who inherited Chequers from his father, Bertram Astley, in 1904.

Delaval Astley
Photographed shortly before his last fateful flight in September 1912.

at Brooklands in the pioneering days of aviation, joining a band of those 'magnificent men in their flying machines'. In September 1912, while taking part in a flying display near Belfast, his Bleriot monoplane was caught by a freak gust of wind and crashed to the ground. At the inquest the coroner commended Astley's determination to keep the plane aloft long enough to bring it down away from the crowd. Thousands of sympathizers watched as his body was embarked on the steamer for England and for burial in Ellesborough Church.

Three years earlier Astley had married, to his family's disapproval, the beautiful musical comedy actress May Kinder. She now became the absolute owner of Chequers, subject to the Lees' life interest in the lease. With no personal attachment to the house, she was prepared to negotiate with the Lees. But it was another five years before the Chequers estate, which had changed hands only by will or by marriage for over 800 years, finally became theirs.

THE WAR YEARS

When war broke out in August 1914 Chequers was turned into a military hospital. Lee rejoined the army, serving as a colonel with the British expeditionary force in France, where he was twice mentioned in dispatches. A year later he was appointed personal military secretary to Lloyd George in the newly created Ministry of Munitions in Asquith's Coalition Government. Although on opposite sides of the tariff reform question, Arthur Lee had fallen under the spell of the charismatic Welshman. Lloyd George, for his part, had seen Lee in action in the House, had been impressed by his efficiency and intelligence and respected his military courage and a judgement 'not paralysed by an opinion expressed by a senior rank'. When Lloyd George was called upon to form a second Coalition Government in 1916 Lee, who had served Lloyd George well, was hurt and disappointed when no offer of a job was made. But Bonar Law had reached an agreement with Lloyd

Convalescent officers on the North terrace *Chequers was used as a voluntary hospital for wounded soldiers for two years of the First World War, from 1914-1916.*

*Sister Williams, Mr Dillon, Miss MacKenzie, Sister Oswald, Mr Beagley,
Sister Turney & Mr Lawton,
Mr Williams, Mr Thorne, Mrs Lee, Col. Lee, & Mr Greenwood.*

George that Unionist appointments should rest with him and, with other more able men waiting in the wings, Arthur Lee's name was vetoed by the Conservative leader.

A few months into the new administration, however, Lloyd George, in his capacity as Chairman of the War Council, appointed him Director General of Food Production with direct responsibility to the Board of Agriculture. With characteristic resourcefulness and efficiency, Lee set about trying to bring an additional three million acres of grassland into food production. He set an example at Chequers by ploughing up more land and, to compensate for the national shortage of skilled labour, he ordered 10,000 new tractors from Henry Ford in America, on behalf of the Board of Agriculture, and set up a tractor training school at Chequers.

Convalescent officers
at Chequers
*Taken on the steps of the
rose garden with Arthur
and Ruth Lee during
the First World War.*

THE CHEQUERS SCHEME

In April 1917 the final documents for the sale of Chequers were signed. With them came some IOUs from a Jermyn Street money-lender to whom Delaval Astley had pawned some Cromwell memorabilia and other family relics which were due for redemption. Lee dispatched his lawyer to retrieve them, Astley's debt was paid off and the Cromwelliana were safely restored to Chequers, where they now form part of a remarkable permanent collection.

It was this transaction that focused Lee's mind on the future of Chequers, this 'house of peace and ancient memories' as he reverently described it. The Lees had no children of their own to inherit, and were desperately anxious to preserve what they had created with such painstaking care. Now that Delaval Astley's widow had parted with the freehold, they could proceed with their ultimate plan to bequeath Chequers to the nation as the official country residence for successive Prime Ministers.

Since Ruth and her sister Faith Moore together had put up the money, they became the effective owners of Chequers, but the ink was hardly dry on the deed of sale when they handed it over to Lee, 'in deepest gratitude and appreciation for the rare and

The Great Parlour
These photographs show the plaster frieze designed by Arthur Lee which features in relief the initials of William and Agnes Hawtrey, romantically joined by a lover's knot and interspersed with 'haw trees'.

Lady Lee
This portrait by Philip de Lazslo hangs in the Stone Hall.

The Ante Room to
the Great Parlour
*As it was in 1921, with
the portrait of John
Rivett. The eighteenth-
century inlaid Chinese
chest was brought from
the East by his step-
father, Governor Russell.*

remarkable qualities he has shown in his life from the two people who know him best and most intimately in the whole world'. Arthur was deeply touched by the unconditional generosity of their gift: even though a year earlier he had been honoured with a KCB for public service, he was inclined to believe that his achievements went unappreciated and unrecognized.

Now, as the absolute owner of an English country estate, he turned his attention to the detail of his Chequers scheme. Over lunch at Downing Street in July 1917 he outlined it to Lloyd George and asked if he thought that the Government would accept it. On the face of it Lloyd George could see no objections, but he took the documents away for more careful consideration. As the conditions of the gift clearly stated that the Lees reserved the right to remain at Chequers as tenants of the Trust for the rest of their lives, there was no reason for Lloyd George to believe that he might become a beneficiary of the scheme himself. It was a further frustrating six weeks before the Lees heard from the Prime Minister that, in principle, the scheme had been fully approved and accepted:

> *My dear Lee*
>
> *Your offer in regard to the Chequers Estate is most generous and beneficent, and one for which PMs of England in the future will have much to thank you. The gift which you are now bequeathing in advance to the nation is in its very essence an indication of the practical thoughtfulness which is characteristic of you; and the public spirit which the scheme displays is worthy of that which its originator has shown in all my dealings with him. Future generations of PMs will think with gratitude of the impulse which has thus prompted you so generously to place this beautiful mansion at their disposal. I have no doubt that such a retreat will do much to alleviate the cares of state which they will inherit along with it, and you will earn the grateful thanks of those whose privilege it is to enjoy it.*
>
> *You have my full authority to go ahead with the scheme, to approach the other Trustees, and to take whatever steps may be necessary to bring the Trust into effective existence.*
>
> *As soon as these preliminaries are completed, I shall be glad to attend and preside over the first meeting of the Trustees.*
>
> *Yours sincerely*
> *D. Lloyd George*

Within days, several copies of the scheme had been prepared, and placed in large sealed envelopes which the Lees delivered personally to several prestigious London addresses. The Prime

Minister received one at Downing Street; another went to the Speaker's house, copies were delivered to Bonar Law and to several government ministers as well as a copy to Buckingham Palace.

THE GIFT

The Chequers scheme became public early in October 1917 to become the subject of much comment. The sale of the house had been accomplished with evident pain to the Astleys, for whom perished all hope of buying the family home back again. Reginald Astley, Delaval's uncle, wrote to Lee to express his appreciation of the care that had been taken in drawing up the Trust, but added:

I am sure you will enter into my feelings when I say that it is a little difficult for one to look on it with absolute satisfaction as, when one has been brought up in a place like Chequers with all its beauty and family traditions, one cannot but worship it, and it makes one feel sad to think it is gone forever. There was not the smallest reason why you should do so, but after the conversation that we had at the House [Chequers] a few years ago I was always in hope that you might at a future date give the family an opportunity to buy the old place back, if they could find the money. However, that is past and gone now, and I can only say that the Scheme is a very big and noble idea and worthy of you and your great generosity.

Reginald B. Astley

There were those, of course, who refused to believe that Lee's gift was of a purely altruistic nature. The founder of *John Bull* addressed an open letter in his magazine to 'Lord Lee', with a thinly veiled suggestion that Lee was in pursuit of a peerage. In his view the scheme was ill-conceived and unpatriotic: if the Lees had really wanted to demonstrate their generosity they would have given up Chequers to provide accommodation for several VCs and their wives instead of handing it over to Prime Ministers who were already adequately housed. (It had evidently escaped *John Bull's* notice that until recently Chequers had been used as a hospital for wounded soldiers.) Such hurtful comments, however, were more than outweighed by messages of appreciation and understanding. Edward Wood, later 1st Earl Halifax, described the scheme as 'the most inspiring and exalted thing' that had been done in his time.

As luck would have it, when the second reading of the Chequers Estate Bill came before the House of Commons it fell

ABOVE: White Parlour
After the restoration of 1909 this room became Lady Lee's 'boudoir'.

BELOW: Stone Hall
The entrance hall, one of the oldest parts of Chequers.

Both photographs were taken in 1921.

to Bonar Law, Chancellor of the Exchequer and Leader of the Conservative Party, to make the opening speech. Believing Bonar Law to be as much out of sympathy with the scheme as he was with him, Lee found his sponsorship particularly distasteful, and asked him to move the reading of the Bill without any comment.

On 10 December 1917 Bonar Law made a gracious speech to the House, recognizing the spirit and generosity of Lee's gift to the nation, but said he had 'been asked especially by the Honourable Gentleman ... to use no words of praise in connection with it. I am sure the House will all sympathize with his having that objection. I am going to obey those instructions.' Nevertheless, Bonar Law recalled the occasion five years earlier when his honourable and gallant friend had first mentioned his intention of handing Chequers over to the nation. He acknowledged the great advantage to a Prime Minister of having a country house at his disposal without incurring added personal expenditure, and the value of it as a place of rest, which was impossible 'as everyone connected with it knows, so long as he is stationed in Downing Street'.

In his response Walter Runciman, the Liberal Member for Hartlepool, took up the theme:

> *All of us who, in office, have seen Prime Ministers at work realize that the severe and continuous strain is not even relaxed during Saturdays and Sundays so long as they reside in Downing Street. Although the weekend habit is a somewhat recent creation, the necessity for relief for our Prime Ministers is greater than it ever was.*

There were no dissenting voices and the Chequers Estate Bill was carried and passed on the third reading.

UNITY OF COMMAND

Once the Chequers scheme had been accepted, Lee was eager to impress upon Lloyd George that Chequers was available at any time either for him to entertain foreign visitors, or for the Cabinet to have a quiet weekend conference. Thus in October 1917, when the British front line was still a mile or so from Passchendaele, Chequers was the venue of a meeting between Lloyd George and the French Prime Minister, Paul Painlevé, who was accompanied by Franklin Bouillon, the French Minister for Propaganda, and General Ferdinand Foch, who was then Chief of Staff to General Philippe Pétain. General Jan Smuts, South Africa's representative at

OPPOSITE: 'The Last Days at Chequers' *This portrait of Arthur and Ruth Lee was painted by Philip de Lazslo to mark their departure from Chequers in 1921. It features the Hawtrey Room, where Ruth is shown working on a piece of needlepoint while her husband, with his ministerial box at his side, works on his papers.*

the Imperial War Cabinet, Sir Maurice Hankey, also a member of the War Cabinet, and Arthur Balfour made up the rest of the party.

Arthur Lee was well aware of Lloyd George's concern that the failure of the Allies to make substantial inroads on German military power lay in the fact that military strategy was in the hands of four separate governments and General Staffs. What was required was a co-ordinated effort to provide the one great push that would halt the German advance. It was at this so-called first Chequers conference that the principle of unity of command was agreed.

Lee had turned out of his own bedroom for Lloyd George, and while the Prime Minister rested before dinner, Painlevé received news from Paris which appeared to agitate him. The French Prime Minister had been in office only a few weeks and Lee assumed that he was finding it a heavy burden. Dinner was

The State Bedroom in 1921
The Elizabethan oak four-poster is carved with lions' heads, shells and foliage and inlaid with animals and flowers. Carved figures stand sentinel in niches at the base. The Lees refurbished the bed with hangings made of stamped blue and gold velvet which had originally been used to deck Westminster Abbey for the Coronation of George V.

The Long Gallery
This photograph was taken in 1921.

reported to be a light-hearted affair despite Painlevé's preoccupation, but he was noted to be not greatly amused when Lloyd George related a story of how Sir William Robertson, Chief of the Imperial General Staff, had said of one recent French Prime Minister, 'Well, 'e won't last long.' That evening talks continued late into the night, while Painlevé left to catch a destroyer called up by the Admiralty to take him back to France. Within a month his government was defeated in the French Chamber and he was succeeded by Georges Clemenceau.

The following day at Chequers, when talks resumed around the fireplace in the Long Gallery, unity of command was at the top of the agenda. Anxious to demonstrate his sincerity about the Chequers scheme, Lee had relinquished the role of host to Lloyd George and effaced himself as an unobtrusive guest. For Lee, a former professor of strategy who had seen service in the field, it must have been galling to have been excluded from this meeting. As he paced up and down the lawn, Lloyd George appeared at a window. 'It's all settled,' he called down, 'and we would like to have something to eat.'

Lord Hankey's later account of these unofficial talks confirmed that they formed an important stage in the creation of the Supreme War Council and several years later Lloyd George went out of his way to remind Lee of the momentous decision taken at Chequers. (It fell to a different group, however, gathered together at Doullens in France the following year, finally to settle the unity of command issue. With Foch as Commander-in-Chief of the Allied Forces, the tide turned in the summer of 1918 and the Germans were driven back across France.) Before leaving Chequers, Foch, who was aware of the Lees' plan for its future, had signed in the Visitors' Book with these words: '*Les Affaires de l'Angleterre iront encore mieux quand son Premier Ministre pourra se reposer à Chequers*' (England's affairs will run even more smoothly when her Prime Minister is housed at Chequers). Lloyd George, who had visited the hospital at Chequers the previous year, had taken great delight in the tour of the house and its contents. After lunch he insisted on walking up Beacon Hill through Velvet Lawn, the box trees and Silver Spring, and planted an oak tree in the park.

One year after the Armistice, inspired by the success of the first Chequers conference, the Lees took the momentous decision to hand Chequers over to the nation without delay, and to dedicate the scheme to the nation's achievements during the war. Arthur Lee believed that there was unlikely to be a time when the surrender of Chequers would be more appreciated, or when a Prime Minister would be more in need of it. Above all, the Lees wanted to see their cherished scheme up and running during their lifetime and, once the decision had been made, Lee was eager to complete the formalities as soon as possible.

At this time, apart from the house and its contents, the estate consisted of around 1200 acres of gardens, wooded park and farmland in Ellesborough and Great and Little Kimble, together with rents from estate cottages. (This acreage excluded Coombe Hill, which Lee had already given to the National Trust.) All profits from the rents, woodlands and farms were to be credited to the Chequers Trust Fund, set up in 1917 with an endowment which Lee doubled in 1921. The Prime Minister was to receive a

OPPOSITE: Lord and Lady Lee of Fareham *This photograph was taken in Washington, at the time of the Naval Conference of 1921, where Arthur Lee played a significant role.*

Double window in
the Ante Room
*The stained glass
window in the Ante
Room to the Great
Parlour features the coats
of arms of Lord and
Lady Lee of Fareham,
with the interlaced
monogram AR and RA
and the inscription of
dedication.*

THIS HOVSE OF PEACE
WAS GIVEN TO ENGLAND
FOR HER DELIVERANCE
AND AS A PLACE OF
FOR HER PRIME MINISTERS

AND ANCIENT MEMORIES
AS A THANK-OFFERING
IN THE GREAT WAR 1914-18
REST AND RECREATION
FOR EVER.

Napoleon
Bonaparte's effects
*His army records, letters
and his scarlet and gold
dispatch case are displayed
on a fine Regency oak
pedestal table, inlaid
with ebony, made by
George Bullock. The
brass plaque is inscribed:
'This table belonged to
Napoleon Bonaparte and
was constantly used by
him at St Helena to the
day of his death, 1822'
(sic). They were all
acquired by Arthur Lee.*

housekeeping allowance of £15 for every weekend he was in residence, so that he could live at Chequers and entertain on a moderate scale without any additional calls upon the public purse.

The Lees had taken an immense pride in restoring Chequers and adding to it furniture and *objets* with a relevance to its past, and this was reflected in the Trust Deed. By seeking to preserve for as long as possible 'the furnishings and works of art which represent, so far as they survive, the tastes, collecting enthusiasms, historic relics and ancient belongings of its long line of owners from the sixteenth century up to the present day', it ensured that never again would Chequers become a victim of architectural fashion. The name also was to be preserved in perpetuity: known for generations as Chequers Court, the house would henceforth be called simply Chequers.

Elizabeth I's ring
*Bought by Lee in 1919
and now in the Long
Gallery.*

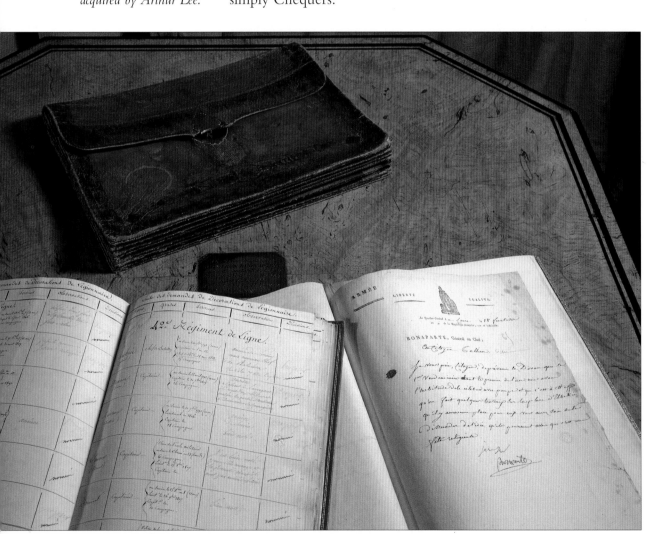

The Admiralty Chest
Covered with leather and studded with brass, this chest, acquired by Arthur Lee, was used by James II when, as Duke of York, he was Lord High Admiral It is decorated with the anchor and cross keys of the Admiralty badge. The George II stand has carved cabriole legs and lion's paw feet. The portraits after Van Dyck are of Charles I and Queen Henrietta Maria.

In October 1920 Lee wrote to Lloyd George saying that to see the scheme inaugurated during his term of office would be a huge source of personal satisfaction and 'the bitterest disappointment if you should deny us this great privilege and pleasure'. On the same day Lee wrote also to the Chief Whip, for he did not want any misunderstanding about his motives for giving up Chequers.

The struggle to get his Agriculture Bill through parliament, which led to his resignation as Director General of Food Production, had compounded Lee's growing disenchantment with politics. He still felt he had a role to play in the service of his country and, perversely, never gave up hope of a seat in the Cabinet. But he had begun to look beyond politics and to the possibility of going to India as viceroy or to Washington as ambassador – both ideas for his future which had been the subject of press speculation. Washington no longer had any appeal but India, where the movement for Home Rule was gathering momentum, presented the kind of challenge Lee relished. It would have been a logical step to leave the country once they had handed Chequers over although, given Lee's loathing of heat, insects and pomp and ceremony, together with recurring bouts of renal colic, the job could have been the death of him. Now, fearing that the gift of Chequers might be seen as a *quid pro quo* for the viceroyalty, he decided that he would not wish to accept the job if it were offered. In the letter to the Chief Whip, in which he withdrew his Indian candidature, he added, 'and there is nothing else I want (that you could give me), of any sort or description.'

When the Prime Minister did not respond by return of post to his letter, Lee was plunged into despondency. Ruth was distressed by the realization that Arthur would regard the scheme as a failure if Lloyd George did not wish to live at Chequers. The scheme after all was not originally intended for the benefit of this generation but, as Ruth wrote in her diary, 'to exercise a slow and subtle influence through the centuries ahead'. A week later they received a wholehearted and enthusiastic acceptance from Lloyd George. He was apparently impatient to move in as soon as possible and his Private Secretary said he had seldom seen the Prime Minister so excited about anything. The first meeting of the Trustees, with the Prime Minister as Chairman, took place at 10 Downing Street on 13 October 1920, when a formal resolution was passed accepting the gift of Chequers.

Meanwhile the Lees continued to live at Chequers and, in recognition of his achievements in managing the nation's wartime production of both food and munitions, Lee was created a baron and took the title Lord Lee of Fareham. Although the continuing opposition to his food production programme had obliged him to resign from the government in 1918, he was soon back in office. The 'khaki' election of December 1918 had been a resounding success for the coalition and, brushing Bonar Law's objections aside, Lloyd George brought Lee into the Cabinet as Minister for Agriculture.

Chequers Court
*The South front in
1920, with the lavender
terrace designed by
Avray Tipping in 1912.*

Seeking, however, to give permanent effect to the lessons of war with regard to home-grown corn, his path was no smoother in Lloyd George's 'Peace Cabinet' than it had been in the War Council. His Agriculture Bill had a long and stormy passage through Cabinet and an even more difficult one through the House of Lords. The Bill succeeded at the eleventh hour but only, according to Ruth, 'by super-human endeavours on A's part', as the Peers' Amendments passed back and forth between the Lords and the Commons, and Lee had to fight for every dot and comma.

Success brought Lee no feeling of triumph, only a deep sense of bitterness at what he considered to be the treachery of some of his colleagues and the lack of support from Lloyd George. Not for the first time Ruth relegated Lloyd George's picture to the box room and swept his Toby jug from the mantelpiece. 'And to think,' she wrote in her diary, 'that in two weeks' time we are handing over to them our dear Chequers, with more than half of our whole fortune, and all the things that we love most in the world.'

FINAL ARRANGEMENTS

In the event, the handing over of the house, as planned, on Armistice Day 1920 had proved a practical impossibility. There were a thousand and one things still to be done – inventories to be prepared, book-plates to be pasted in, prints and pictures to be hung, many of which had been gathering dust in the box room, drawers to go through and ornaments to find their rightful place. Lee was busy writing a little guide to Chequers, copies of which he was to leave for the use of future occupants and guests. While the furniture was being carefully arranged, the Lees had moved once more to the second floor and were using the rooms where they had spent their first nights at Chequers just over eleven years earlier. 'We ended as we began,' Ruth recorded in her diary, 'in the Astley Rooms.'

At the beginning of 1921, as they picked snowdrops for the last time under the big chestnut tree in the park, great waves of homesickness swept over them. 'Sometimes,' wrote Ruth, 'I feel as though the old house itself does not quite like our giving it away to strangers.' By way of cheering themselves up they walked up Beacon Hill to inspect the spot they had chosen for their burial-place, which had already been lined with bricks. To anyone who

was curious, it was explained that the excavation had been done in connection with a wireless station for the Prime Minister.

The Lees did, however, achieve a rapprochement with Lloyd George, and persuaded him to visit Chequers once again before the official hand-over. Ruth had had a rather unsatisfactory meeting with Margaret Lloyd George, at which housekeeping arrangements had been discussed but no word given of thanks or appreciation. But Megan, who accompanied her father, was captivated by the peace and tranquillity of the place and Lloyd George, at his most agreeable, more than made up for his wife's lack of effusion. He left the Lees feeling more warmth towards him than had been possible for some months and, with harmony restored, they were able to face the final sacrifice with greater equanimity.

THE LEES' FAREWELL TO CHEQUERS

Fourteen guests were expected for dinner on the evening of the final renunciation, 8 January 1921. Among them were the President of the Board of Trade Sir Robert Horne, the Secretary for Ireland Sir Hamar Greenwood, Lord Milner, the just retired

Two aerial views of Chequers
These photographs, taken in 1921, show Chequers with its gardens and tennis court, within its setting of the lovely Buckinghamshire countryside.

Secretary for the Colonies, the King's physician Lord Dawson of Penn, Lord Riddell, the Chairman of the *News of the World*, and John Davis, the American Ambassador. Megan Lloyd George accompanied her father and, when word was received that Dame Margaret Lloyd George would not be arriving until the next day, the widow of the former Rector of Ellesborough was hastily invited to avoid an unlucky thirteen at dinner.

For the guests it was evidently a cheerful occasion. For the Lees the evening was one of mixed emotions and we can only imagine their thoughts as they sat down for the last time as host and hostess in the panelled dining room. Although they were agonized by leaving, neither had any doubts about the sacrifice they were making. Arthur Lee had written a note to the Prime Minister earlier in the day:

> *I feel that you and Dame Margaret will forgive us if we slip away tonight after dinner. My wife especially has been under a terrific strain for the past three months … I know that she could not bear the emotional strain beyond this evening and our only chance of*

The Dining Room
Two aspects of the dining room in 1921, showing the William and Mary cabinet made from King Stephen's elm, and the sixteenth-century Ouchak carpet.

departing creditably is to do so whilst it is dark … We have perhaps completed our work here and leave everything as ready and ordered as we can. We only hope you will be happy and comfortable. I think perhaps at the end of dinner, I must say a few words of welcome, and then if you will reply we will leave you with your guests.

At the end of dinner Arthur Lee rose to make a speech which Ruth noted was perfect for the occasion. The Prime Minister responded with typical eloquence. 'It seemed to come from his heart,' wrote Ruth in her diary, 'and it was satisfying to us both because he showed in it how thoroughly he understood our idea. He not only made us feel that he had need of Chequers and that his successors were likely to have ever-increasing need of it and what it represented, but that our great sacrifice, as he realised it was, would in his opinion bear great fruit and have a deep and subtle and far-reaching effect on the destinies of the country. The most striking feature of his speech was a real *cri de coeur* about what a PM of these days has to suffer and how much he has needed – what Chequers would give him – inside and out.'

January 8. 1921

Tonight we leave this dear place, with a sense of loss which cannot be measured, but content and happy in our faith that Chequers has a great part to play in the moulding of the future and that in freeing it for this high task we are doing the best service to our Country that it is in our power to render.

We are also sustained by the confident belief that our successors here will honour and guard our Trust, and that Chequers, in return, will give to them — above all in times of stress — those blessings of peace, health and happiness which, for so long, it has given to us.

Lee of Fareham :

Ruth Lee of Fareham —

OPPOSITE:

The Chequers
Visitors' Book
*Lord Lee's last
inscription,
8th January 1921.*

The Hawtrey Room
*This photograph was
taken in 1921.*

Later, beneath portraits of Hawtreys and Crokes in the Hawtrey Room, the Lees signed the Deed of Settlement and inscribed in the Visitors' Book the words opposite. Then, as quickly as they could, they climbed into their car and drove off into the night.

The next morning the papers were full of comments. Many applauded the altruistic gesture of a patriotic man who wanted not only to preserve what he had created but also to leave a permanent contribution to public life; inevitably there were others less generous in their praise. On the whole, however, Lee was cheered by the response he received both in the press and from personal letters written to them both.

Three days later the house-warming party was still in full swing and word reached Ruth Lee that the staff were becoming mutinous. Lloyd George had indeed shown such reluctance to return to London that there was a distinct possibility that the Prince of Wales, who had an appointment with the Prime Minister, would have to see him at Chequers. Encouraged however by the Prime Minister's evident satisfaction with Chequers, the Lees sent temporary reinforcements in the form of three of their own under-parlour-maids. 'The relief of Lucknow would have been as nothing to it,' wrote Ruth in her diary.

POSTSCRIPT

Once they had irrevocably parted with their country estate, the Lees first stayed with Faith Moore at Downshire house, Richmond. In 1927, after several years in central London, they took a lease on White Lodge in Richmond Park. This Georgian house, a former royal hunting lodge, was where Queen Elizabeth the Queen Mother began her married life as the Duchess of York. It had also been home to George II's youngest daughter, Princess Amelia, to whom Fanny and Mary Russell were Women of the Bedchamber.

White Lodge, like Chequers, needed extensive renovation, but this time the Lees found the challenge somewhat depressing. 'There is dirt and dust everywhere,' wrote Ruth in her diary, 'scaffolding, as well as piles of furniture, packing cases, rolls of carpet; the perpetual noise of hammers, and the all-pervading smell of perspiring and unwashed workmen.'

On leaving Parliament in 1922, Arthur Lee continued to play an active role in public life. He was number two to Balfour at the Washington Conference on Disarmament in 1922 and chaired several royal commissions and public committees. He became a Trustee of the Wallace Collection, and Chairman of both the National Gallery and the Royal Fine Art Commission; in 1932, with Samuel Courtauld's financial backing, he established the Courtauld Institute of Fine Art, in the University of London.

Although affected by the Wall Street Crash, Lord and Lady Lee continued as generous benefactors of numerous institutions. To Westminster Abbey, for example, they made several anonymous donations, including the presentation of a bronze candelabrum by Benno Elkan, who had come from Germany as a refugee in 1933. Having left his entire art collection at Chequers, Lord Lee assiduously acquired another, which embraced almost every phase of European painting up to the end of the eighteenth century.

The Lees' last country house was High Quarries in Avening, Gloucestershire, to which Arthur added a private art gallery. This enabled him, during the Second World War, to perform one more service for his country by providing a safe haven for some of the contents of the National Gallery – fortuitously, as the Gallery was bombed in the blitz of October 1940. Lord Lee died in July 1947 and was buried, not in the plot he and his wife had so carefully marked out at Chequers, but in the Avening Parish Churchyard. He left his art collection to the Courtauld Institute, but it was his noble gift of Chequers that will always be best remembered.

Arthur Lee lived long enough to see six Prime Ministers benefit from the 'spirit and anodyne' of Chequers; Lady Lee, who died in

Lord and Lady Lee's stained glass window in the Long Gallery

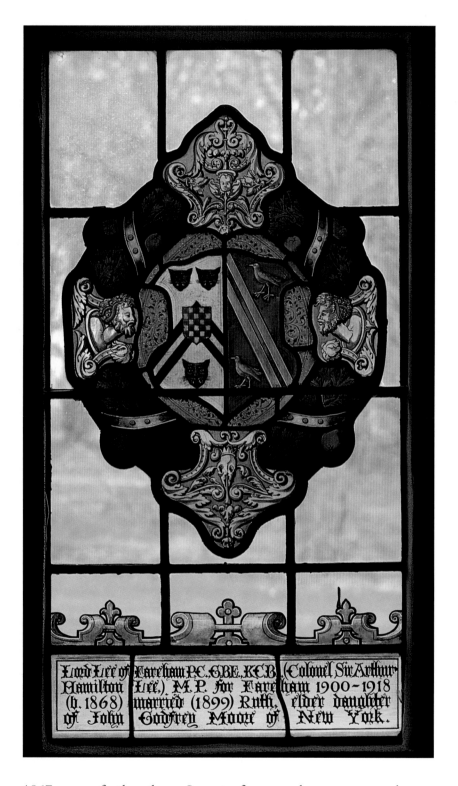

Lord Lee of Fareham P.C., G.B.E., K.C.B. (Colonel Sir Arthur Hamilton Lee,) M.P. for Fareham 1900–1918 (b. 1868) married (1899) Ruth, elder daughter of John Godfrey Moore of New York.

1967, saw a further three. Seventy-five years have now passed since Chequers became the official country residence of the Prime Minister. It has served the nation well and I see no reason why Chequers should not continue to provide, as Lord Lee intended, 'A place of rest and recreation for her Prime Ministers for ever.'

CHEQUERS: THE HOUSE

Only the Prime Minister and visiting heads of government approach Chequers from the south, through the imposing lodge gates and along Victory Drive. Everyone else arrives at the inconspicuous eastern entrance a mile or so short of Butler's Cross. Nobody arrives unexpectedly and everyone is required to present proof of identity at the Bothy gate. But both entrances take you through the park, past the memorial trees planted by Presidents and Prime Ministers and into the walled forecourt, in the centre of which the statue of the Greek goddess Hygeia stands gracefully upon her plinth.

This 'house of ancient memories' is not a museum but a surrogate home for Prime Ministers who have little respite from the cares of state. Carved above the arched doorway into the rose garden is the inscription 'All care abandon ye who enter here', and as the front door swings open in welcome and one steps across the threshold into the panelled stone-flagged hall, it is soon evident that there is every encouragement to do so. The mellow oak panelling, the smell of wood smoke from the huge fireplace in the Great Hall, and the presence of so many beautiful things that have grown old together combine to create an atmosphere of peace and tranquillity which is everything that Lord Lee intended when he bequeathed his house to the nation. For the sanctuary of Chequers, Prime Ministers have good reason to be thankful to Arthur Lee for his vision and generosity.

Chequers can never be open to the public and I like to think that Arthur Lee would have no objection to this book, which takes the reader behind the scenes of an intriguing part of our national heritage.

OPPOSITE:
The Great Hall
created in the nineteenth century from an inner courtyard. Beyond the window is all that remains of the old inner courtyard.

THE EXTERIOR

The approach to Chequers is from a driveway leading to the east front and it was here that Reginald Blomfield made the most significant changes to the exterior of the house. By the time the

The north front of
Chequers

BELOW:
The Tudor door on
the north front
leading into the north
Garden Hall
*Typical of the period, the
door has two moulded
orders with Tudor roses
in the spandrels.*

OPPOSITE:
The east front of
Chequers
*and the forecourt, with
the quatrefoil lawn and
the statue of Hygeia.*

Lees arrived in 1909, the external brickwork had been stripped of
the stucco applied in the nineteenth century, but a porch in the
east front, which Lee described as a 'spurious Gothic and
battlemented atrocity', remained. Blomfield demolished this in
favour of a two-storeyed porch in well-proportioned Tudor style
with a room above it. At the same time, the architect reinstated a
previously bricked-up window to the left of the entrance.

A walled forecourt was added to create a more imposing
approach and the gravel drive sweeps round a quatrefoil lawn, in
the centre of which stands a lead statue of Hygeia, the goddess of
health. In the forecourt, one of the finest tulip trees in England
used to cast its shadow over the Greek goddess, the clear yellow of
its autumn colours giving the illusion that the sun was always
shining. When Neville Chamberlain measured the tree in 1939 it
had a girth of over 15 feet (4.5m). Alas, in 1979, despite all
attempts to save it, the tree was discovered to be rotten to the core
and, to Mrs Thatcher's distress, it had to be felled.

The gates giving access to the forecourt are supported by piers
inspired by those at Canons Ashby, in Northamptonshire. The
two doors in the wall on either side of the forecourt, leading to
the north lawn and the south garden, were designed by Lord Lee
and it is above the latter that he inscribed the exhortation to
'Abandon care'.

OPPOSITE:

The south front of Chequers

1629 The Chequers Estate map
showing the territories of Dame Mary Wolley. The representation of the house here is the only idea of how Chequers might have looked after the rebuilding in 1565.

There is a theory that the original Elizabethan house consisted of a central building with an east and west wing projecting south from it. These wings were thought to have been linked by a wall through which an entrance gave access to an inner courtyard. At some point, the wall must have been removed because by 1629 – the date of an early estate map showing the outlines of the house – a range of rooms had been built between the main gables at either end to form the south front. With its grey stone gable copings and two rows of stone-mullioned windows separated by grey stone string courses, the south front is in perfect harmony with the north side of the house, though it presents a more friendly aspect. One pair of windows forms the central bay, above which is the crest of the Frankland Russell Astleys, and on either side in large stone

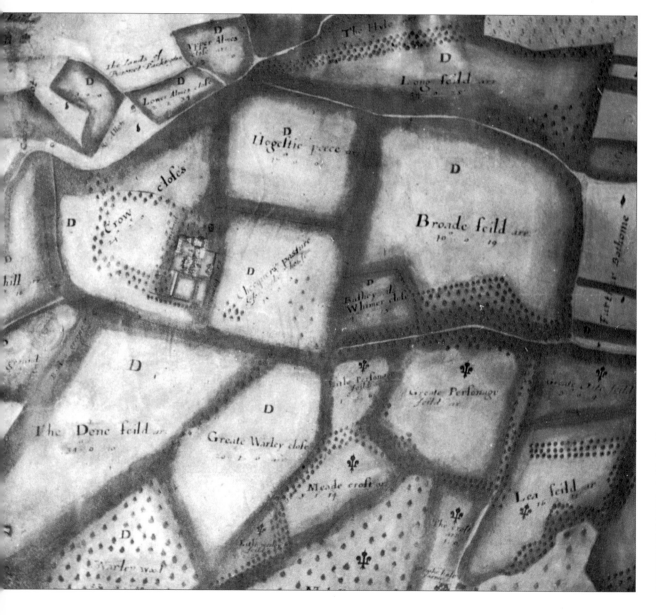

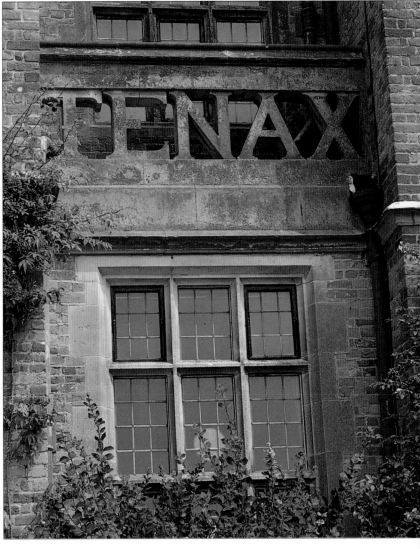

letters is the family motto *JUSTITIAE TENAX*.

The north front of Chequers, with its imposing red-brick façade of almost perfect symmetry, remains largely the work of William Hawtrey. It rises to two storeys and an attic, with each of the five attic windows topped by a plain gable. Double-transomed stone-mullioned windows in two rows of eight are separated from each other and from the attic by grey stone string courses. Two pairs of windows project in bays with battlemented parapets. Carved into the stone battlements of the west bay are the arms of Sir Henry Croke. The other battlements feature the chequered shield of the de Scaccarios and the crest of William Hawtrey, together with his initials, those of his wife Agnes and the date 1565, when his restoration was completed. Following the example of Hawtrey and the Astleys, Arthur Lee mounted his coat of arms on the new porch above the main entrance.

The south front of Chequers
The motto JUSTITIAE TENAX (literally, 'tenacious of justice') in large stone letters on either side of the central bay commemorates the restoration of the south front by the Astleys.

THE STONE HALL

The Stone Hall, so-called because of its flagged stone floor, leads directly from the front entrance porch. This small but welcoming hall is believed to be one of the oldest parts of the house. Certainly, when Reginald Blomfield began his restoration work in 1909, he considered the staircase which rises from it to be the only item of 'genuine antiquity' in the house.

The Jacobean panelling of the Stone Hall, like that of the rest of the house, came from elsewhere. Here, it is interrupted by a hand-carved balustrade which allows natural light from the hall into the staircase behind. On the panelling hangs a portrait of Ruth Lee by the Hungarian artist Philip de Lazslo (1869-1937), in an oval frame.

OPPOSITE:

The Stone Hall
*This moulded stone
doorway leading from the
Stone Hall into the
Hawtrey Room was
discovered when the
Victorian Gothic plaster
was stripped away
during the 1909
restoration.*

It was Arthur Lee's wish that her portrait should one day hang in the Stone Hall and, when she died in 1966, Lady Lee bequeathed this picture to Chequers, together with the de Lazslo portrait of her husband which also hangs here. It remains a mystery as to why the oval head and shoulders was cut out of de Lazslo's full-length portrait of Lady Lee.

A small Bokhara rug softens the stone floor, and two Hawtrey coats of arms are mounted in the windows beside the entrance. The Stone Hall is simply furnished with a seventeenth-century porter's chair and a couple of oak open armchairs. Opposite the entrance stands an ebonized oak coffer, banded with wrought iron, believed to have been used for storing ecclesiastical vestments in the sixteenth century. It is here that departing guests are invited to sign the Chequers Visitors' Book.

The Stone Hall
*as it was when the Lees
left Chequers in 1921.
Only the pictures have
been rearranged. The
main staircase is behind
the balustrade.*

THE HAWTREY ROOM

Leading off the Stone Hall is the Hawtrey Room, originally the Great Chamber of the Elizabethan house. For several hundred years it remained the principal room of the house and when the Lees arrived it was known as the Cromwell Room. It was renamed the Hawtrey Room when Blomfield's restoration uncovered, over the door, the moulded stone archway which had been hidden for more than a century under Victorian Gothic plaster: in the spandrels above the door were found the initials, in the original black wax, of William Hawtrey. Arthur Lee believed that this doorway dated from the much earlier fifteenth-century house of the de Scaccarios. But the discovery of the Hawtrey initials, together with the age of the beams, the doors and the brickwork, seemed to confirm Bertram Astley's theory that the east wing was contemporaneous with William Hawtrey.

The elegant proportions of this panelled room are similar to those of the Great Parlour above it on the first floor. Although we know that the room was panelled in the eighteenth century, it probably fell victim to nineteenth-century Gothicism and the fine panelling we see today was put in by Arthur Lee. The striking feature of the room is the north-facing bay window with its heraldic panels of stained glass depicting the Hawtrey marriages.

Portraits of the Hawtreys have long since been re-hung in the Great Hall and the wall space on either side of the fireplace is now occupied by a charming pair of conversation pieces of the Russell, Rivett and Greenhill families by Charles Philips (1708-47). Over the fireplace hangs a large landscape by N.T. Dall (active 1760-77)

and there is a full-length portrait of James Murray by Sir Joshua Reynolds (1723-92) and a head and shoulders portrait of Sir Robert Frankland Russell by Sir Thomas Lawrence (1767-1830). The other two pictures are *Dedham Vale*, a questionable John Constable (1776-1837), and an authentic landscape by John Crome (1768-1821).

Shortly before the Lees left, a visitor described the room as being 'panelled from floor to ceiling and hung with Hawtrey

OPPOSITE:
The Hawtrey Room
*It was Edward Heath
who transformed the
Hawtrey Room into a
comfortable drawing
room. The heraldic
glass in the north
window features the
coats of arms of the
early Hawtreys.*

tapestries'. A long table occupied the centre of the room and around it was grouped a set of seventeenth-century 'Seven Crown' chairs, made to commemorate the Restoration of Charles II; these now stand in the Cromwell Corridor. Today the Hawtrey Room is furnished as a drawing room, with side tables and comfortable sofas and armchairs covered in a faded rose and cream linen print. The principal piece of furniture in the room is a seventeenth-century scarlet and cream japanned cabinet, but, despite its undeniable merit, I confess it is not among my favourite pieces of furniture at Chequers.

The Hawtrey Room
*in 1909, before the
Lees' restoration.*

A seventeenth-century japanned cabinet
One of the most important pieces in the house, this is decorated with oriental figures in red lacquer and gold. The doors open to reveal eight drawers inside. The ornate giltwood stand, with elaborately carved cupids' heads and floral swags, is Dutch.

THE GREAT HALL

The Great Hall *in 1909, before the Lees' restoration.*

This lofty room which rises through two storeys, with a gallery along the south side, is the central focus of the house today. It was created out of the old inner courtyard of the Tudor mansion which was roofed in by Sir Robert Frankland Russell in the nineteenth century. It is dominated by a massive stone-mullioned window which separates the Great Hall from all that remains of the old courtyard. When Blomfield undertook the remodelling of the Hall, to allow more light into the interior, he removed from this window the rather undistinguished stained glass which featured coats of arms installed by the Frankland Russells.

The quasi-baronial interior was stripped of its plaster and a gallery, which gave access to the Library along the east side, was removed, thereby exposing an old mullioned and transomed window. Originally opening on to William Hawtrey's open courtyard, today this window overlooks the Great Hall from the staircase landing. Blomfield redesigned the elaborate gallery of the bedroom corridor to incorporate the classical oak columns of a Palladian arcade inlaid with coromandel and snake-wood. He adorned it with the arms of de Scaccario, Hawtrey, Croke, Russell, Frankland Russell Astley and Lee.

The walls are clad in Jacobean wainscotting, surmounted by a dentil moulding. The ceiling, a copy of a seventeenth-century example preserved in the Victoria & Albert Museum, is embellished with the chequerboard of the de Scaccarios. A brass chandelier with eighteen candle-lamps hangs from an octagonal cupola which sheds natural light on to the space below. The hearth, with its wooden overmantel, around which the Russells and Astleys might have sat, was replaced by an impressive chimneypiece of alabaster which is now the principal feature of the room. In the centre of the headpiece the arms of William Hawtrey, supported by a pair of Rubenesque cherubs, is flanked by those of de Scaccario and Lee.

Thus remodelled, and the floor covered with Persian Feraghan and Khorassan carpets, the Great Hall provided an appropriate setting for some military memorabilia and items from Lord Lee's collection of Chinese and Japanese porcelain. Above the fireplace he hung the flags of local volunteer units formed at the beginning of the nineteenth century to meet Napoleon's threatened invasion. A Union Jack, flown at Chequers for a month from the Armistice of the First World War, was hung on the east wall. In the grate stood a machine-gun captured from the Germans in one of the final battles of 1918 and a place was found for a German rifle and a Saxon helmet – two souvenirs from the first battle of Ypres in 1914.

OPPOSITE:

The Great Hall *The alabaster fireplace features the arms of de Scaccario, Hawtrey and Lee; on the mantelpiece are two pairs of seventeenth-century Imari dishes. Above it hangs a portrait of the children of Charles I by John Stone after Van Dyck; the original is at Windsor Castle and there is another copy at Burghley House. To the right of the fireplace is James II's Admiralty Chest.*

OPPOSITE:
The Great Hall
*The arcaded screen,
which was part of the
1909 restoration, is
inlaid with coromandel
and snake-wood, and
adorned with the arms,
from left to right, of de
Scaccario, Hawtrey,
Croke, Russell,
Frankland Russell
Astley and Lee; in
carved relief above the
frieze is the Tudor
rose, the portcullis
and the device of the
Hawtreys.*

Arthur Lee was a prodigious collector who regarded auctions at Christies as one of the best events in town. Lining the walls of the Great Hall are many of the fine pictures which he acquired, including, for example, two large Peter Lely canvases: one of the Perryer family, signed and dated 1655, and another of Edward Hyde, 1st Earl of Clarendon. Both the latter painting and a full-length portrait after Van Dyck of Queen Henrietta Maria, with the infant Charles II on her lap, were bought at the auction in 1919 to raise death duties on the estate of the 12th Earl of Home.

Another of Arthur Lee's acquisitions was an unfinished self-portrait by Sir Joshua Reynolds. Reynolds left his estate to his niece, Mary Palmer, who later married the 1st Marquis of Thomond, in whose collection the painting was found. It is interesting to speculate whether Lord Lee was aware that the second wife of the 7th Earl of Thomond was the sister of Sir John Russell, 3rd Baronet, and was therefore the sister-in-law of Frances Cromwell.

The Great Hall
*before the Lee restoration
in 1909, showing the
east gallery which was
removed.*

Unfinished self-portrait of Sir Joshua Reynolds
(1723–1792)
*This is believed to be the
last portrait found on the
artist's easel at the time
of his death. There are
several copies extant.*

Amongst the family portraits connected with the history of Chequers are those of William Hawtrey's granddaughters, Mary Wolley and Bridget Croke, the last of the Hawtrey owners. The portrait of Mary, painted in 1625 by an unknown artist, shows her in a richly embroidered farthingale and bodice and bears the inscription 'One thing is needfull' (sic) which is assumed to refer to her loveless marriage. But sixteen years after the death of her husband, there is still evidence of mourning in her costume, so perhaps she cared for her errant husband more than was supposed. The companion portraits of Bridget and Henry Croke have been attributed to Marc Gheeraerts the Elder (c.1530-90), the Flemish painter responsible for the famous Ditchley portrait of Queen Elizabeth I. There may be some doubt about this attribution, since Gheeraerts died some time before the Crokes were married in 1608. Nevertheless, the Croke portraits make a handsome pair.

OPPOSITE:
The White Parlour
The portrait of the Lees' 'Last Days at Chequers' was painted by Philip de Lazslo to commemorate their departure from Chequers in 1921. The late seventeenth-century walnut long-case clock, decorated with marquetry flowers and birds in a variety of woods, was made by John Hill of Princes Risborough. The nineteenth-century semi-circular china cabinet contains a collection of blue and white Chinese porcelain.

REGINA · FILLIA

Queen Mary I
This small portrait of Queen Mary I, the daughter of Henry VIII and Catherine of Aragon, hangs under the gallery between the Great Hall and the White Parlour. It is attributed to the school of the Dutch painter, Antonio Mor. Mor was a favourite of Philip of Spain who sent him to England to paint Mary Tudor before their marriage.

THE WHITE PARLOUR

Tucked away under the gallery of the Great Hall is the White Parlour. This delightful room has changed little since 1921, when Lady Lee made a specific request that the room – her boudoir – should be preserved as she had left it, including the knitting and her glasses lying on the table.

Throughout the nineteenth century, this room had been arched and beamed and stuffed with heavy furniture. Blomfield stripped out the Gothic beams and groins and replaced them with a plain ceiling and panelling which he painted white, thus giving the room a delicacy not found elsewhere in the house.

The suite of eighteenth-century furniture was a wedding gift to Kitty Cary, the wife of Sir John Russell, from her father. In the

1950s it was rescued from the ravages of wood-beetle and reupholstered. In one corner stands a walnut English long-case clock, made in Princes Risborough during the seventeenth century and decorated in marquetry with carnations, tulips and other flowers. A late eighteenth-century china cupboard with a semi-circular front displayed, until recently, some of the large collection of blue and white china brought from the East by the Russells. At present, it houses a riotous miscellany of china and porcelain, including a pair of Gwendolen Parnell figurines of Ruth Lee and her sister Faith in eighteenth-century costume.

The painter Philip de Lazslo carried out several commissions for the Lees, three of which hang in the White Parlour. He had painted their former home, Rookesbury Park, in Hampshire, and commemorated their departure from Chequers with a joint portrait, set in the Hawtrey Room, depicting Ruth working a piece of needlepoint while her husband, with his ministerial box at his side, works on his papers. Another, painted in the White Parlour, shows Faith, with her face turned towards the window, at ease on the sofa. Among other paintings in this room are two small ovals – a watercolour of Kitty Cary by John Downman (1750-1824), and a pastel companion by John Vaslet (d. 1721) of her husband Sir John Russell. Two small Constables, *A Study of Sky* and *The Beach at Harwich*, F.W. Watts' *Strand on the Green* and *A Windmill*, and *A Street in Dordrecht* by J.H. Prins, complete the collection in the White Parlour.

The two sixteenth-century oval medallions suspended in the windows are of Flemish origin. Inspired by a series of drawings on the life of Joseph at the Liège Musée de l'Art Wallon in Belgium, and painted *en grisaille* in sepia paint and yellow stain,

LEFT:
Two stained-glass medallions
These sixteenth century Flemish medallions are two of a series of twenty-one, depicting scenes from the Biblical story of Joseph.

Faith Moore

Philip de Lazslo's fine portrait of Faith Moore, Lady Lee's sister, who contributed so generously to the house. Painted in the White Parlour, it shows Faith on the sofa above which the painting once hung. When Lady Lee died in 1966, this portrait was among her last bequests to Chequers.

they depict in intricate detail scenes from the Biblical story of Joseph. Although the Liège collection has seventeen of these designs, it is thought that there were originally twenty-one in the series. One of the White Parlour medallions, showing Joseph being lowered into the pit, is believed to be inspired by one of the missing four designs, and is therefore of unique interest.

The White Parlour is one of the few really 'feminine' rooms

The Mathematician
*G. van den Eeckhout
(1621–1674)
Arthur Lee bought this
painting as a Rembrandt
from the Earl of
Ashburnham's collection
and hung it in the Great
Hall. It was later re-
attributed to the Dutch
artist, G. van den
Eeckhout – a pupil of
Rembrandt. It now
hangs in the South
Garden Hall with its
companion mezzotint
engraving by Charles
McArdle.*

OPPOSITE:
Wrought-iron
firebacks
*Dining Room (top left)
showing an oak tree,
royal crown and
cypher CR.
Recess of Great Parlour
(top right) showing an
equestrian figure and
cypher CR.
Long Gallery (bottom
left) featuring an anchor
with fleur-de-lys and
Tudor roses, the date
1588 and the
initials IFC.
Bedroom 3 (bottom right)
showing the crowned
anchor and the
monogram CR.*

in the house and has long been a favourite retreat for the occupants.
On her first visit, seeing the room with the morning sun streaming
through the windows, Neville Chamberlain's wife Annie decided to
make it her 'den'. The Douglas-Homes were charmed by its
intimacy and Mary Wilson wrote to tell me how much she had liked
the room. Both John and I, like Denis and Margaret Thatcher before
us, very much enjoy the informality of a 'television' meal on a tray
here, when the contents of the red boxes can be set aside for an
hour or two.

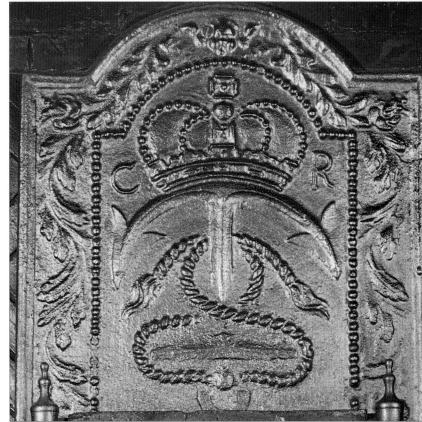

THE DINING ROOM

At the request of their tenants, the Clutterbucks, the Astleys had undertaken several minor alterations to Chequers, which included a hot-water supply to the kitchen and the improvement to a staircase which provided the servants' access to the dining room. In fact this was one of the first problems that Blomfield had to tackle when he turned his attention to the interior of the house, for in 1909 the dining room (now the Hawtrey Room), situated on the other side of the Great Hall, was about as far as possible from the kitchen. A journey between the two, invariably laden with dishes, involved a descent to the cellar, a scurry under the Great Hall and a hazardous climb up the steep and narrow staircase that emerged on to a landing between what was then the

The Dining Room
The Georgian mahogany dining table is laid with the George III silver-gilt dessert service presented by Lord Lee to Neville Chamberlain in 1938 as a token of admiration.

smoking room and the dining room. In consequence, the food was often cold and the butler and parlour-maid took their lives in their hands each time a meal was served.

Blomfield created the present dining room out of the old south-facing kitchen and the butler's pantry. By the end of 1910 Chequers had also been fitted with a completely new kitchen wing, which today includes the staff canteen. The only external evidence of this new wing, which occupies space in the yard to the west, is the tiled hipped roof surmounted by a cupola.

The early seventeenth-century panelling in this room may have come from the Ipswich house which was the source of so much of the material for Blomfield's restoration work. The panelling stops a little too short of the ceiling to give complete visual satisfaction, but nothing detracts from the fine geometric carving of the flat pilasters and the intricate detail of the frieze. Above it, Blomfield covered the remaining area of wall with an exact reproduction in sheepskin of an original fragment of Elizabethan leather. This frieze, with the same grape motif featured on the panels of a wardrobe in the State Bedroom, remained in place until it fell apart in the 1980s; it is now plain and painted white.

The Georgian mahogany pedestal dining table was given an extension during Margaret Thatcher's term of office and now comfortably accommodates twenty people. For more intimate occasions, a smaller Victorian round table, made of burr-elm and rosewood, stands in the recess of the bay window overlooking the rose garden. The dining-room chairs, veneered with figured walnut and partly gilded, have seats covered in now faded *petit point*, embroidered by the Russell ladies in the eighteenth century.

The Dining Room in 1921

Dining-room chairs
The Georgian dining chairs have seats covered in petit point *worked by the ladies of the house in the eighteenth century.*

The William and
Mary cabinet on stand
*Concealed behind a pair
of hinged doors, is a
series of drawers
surrounding a central
compartment. A long
drawer with a convex
front forms the cornice;
the stand has another
five drawers supported on
elaborately turned
baluster legs joined by
intersecting serpentine
stretchers. The drop-
handles and escutcheons
are of gilt metal.*

This room has one of the most interesting pieces of furniture in the house: a William and Mary cabinet made towards the end of the seventeenth century from part of an elm tree believed to have been planted on the Chequers estate by King Stephen in the twelfth century. When this tree was blown down by a storm in the nineteenth century, it was said to have a circumference of almost 33 feet (16m): by tradition, it also shed a branch every time an owner of Chequers died. In one of the drawers is a piece of old veneer, a reminder of the cabinet's condition when it was retrieved, in 1838, from an old woodshed where it had been used to store seeds. The cabinet-maker in Aylesbury to whom it was sent for repair reported that the wood was so hard that it turned the edges of all the tools used to work on it. The cabinet's exterior was restored using new wood grown at Chequers.

Hanging on the panelling here are two of the most important paintings in the house: *A Dutch Port* by L. Backhuysen (1631-1708), the celebrated painter of seascapes; and *A View of Arnhem* by Jan van Goyen (1596-1656), one of the earliest Dutch landscape painters. There is also a pair of especially fine portraits by Nicolas Elias (c.1590-c.1655) of Mr and Mrs Symon van Swieten. Two pictures dating from the Civil War are the portrait of Cromwell's General, John Lambert, by Ferdinand Bol (1616-80) and *A Cavalry Skirmish* by Esaias van de Velde (c.1591-1630).

Unfortunately, the famous Ouchak rug left behind by the Lees, described as one of the most valuable items in the house, became too expensive to maintain. It has since been replaced by a fitted Wilton carpet with a Persian pattern designed especially for the room. The curtains are of a golden floral silk damask.

A two-handled soup-tureen and cover
This is by Frankenthal about 1760.

THE GREAT PARLOUR

The Great Parlour on the first floor, through which access can be gained to the Long Gallery, is L-shaped, but it is possible that the recessed portion might at one time have been shut off to form a separate room. Of all the rooms at Chequers, the Great Parlour bears the least resemblance to its turn-of-the-century counterpart, although photographs taken before the Lee restoration show – among the parlour palms and typical Edwardian clutter – many pieces of furniture found in the house today.

Margaret Thatcher always felt that the Great Parlour was the only room at Chequers which did not feel like part of a private house. It was in the 1960s that Harold Macmillan decided to add the table which transformed the Lees' former living room into the

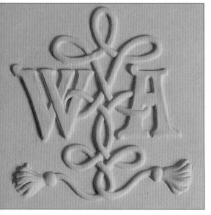

conference room he felt the house needed. He had suggested a table such as the one that the Ministry of Works had supplied for him at Admiralty House, where he and Lady Dorothy were living while No. 10 Downing Street was undergoing major reconstruction. This was the famous 'boat-shaped' table, covered in brown baize, which is now in the Cabinet Room at No. 10; it was designed so that everyone sitting around it can see and hear everyone else. Finding it difficult to justify the expense of a new table, the Trustees instead explored the possibility of a second-hand one and in due course a William IV dining table of immense proportions was found, with seven extra leaves and fourteen matching chairs.

OPPOSITE:

The Great Parlour
*The William IV dining
table, installed by
Harold Macmillan,
enables the room to be
used for conferences and
seminars. The plaster
frieze (detail) displays
Lee's design for William
and Agnes Hawtrey's
initials, romantically
joined by lovers' knots
and interspersed with
'haw trees' – a play on
words which appealed to
Lee. To the right of the
fireplace hangs a portrait
of William Pitt by
Joseph Highmore
(1692-1780).*

It set the Trust back around £400 but it has increased dramatically
in value and more than earned its keep. Another piece of furniture
worthy of special note is a large coromandel chest, brought from
the East by John Russell, Governor of Bengal. It is beautifully
decorated with incised and coloured oriental figures in a landscape
setting, and has carrying handles at each end. The engraved brass
of the lockplates and angle-plates has been lovingly burnished.

The panelling in this room is by far the most elaborate of all the
panelling brought into the house by Arthur Lee. Complex
geometric patterns and floral motifs adorn the door panels and
mantelpiece, and the strap-work ornamentation of the pilasters is
typically Elizabethan. During Margaret Thatcher's tenure, centuries
of varnish were removed, revealing the intricate fretwork and inlay
of holly and bog oak believed by Lord Lee to have been the work
of Dutch refugees who had fled from the Low Countries during
the Spanish occupation at the end of the sixteenth century. The
restoration work was given added impetus by the promise of a visit
from President Gorbachev in 1988. Tragically, the Armenian

The Great Parlour
in 1921

A detail of the
panelling in the
Great Parlour
*This shows the intricate
holly and bog oak
inlay revealed during
restoration work
in 1987.*

Detail from the plaster
ceiling of the ante-
room to the Great
Parlour
*Blomfield copied this
from a ceiling at Burton
Agnes, the Yorkshire
home of Captain
Thomas Wykeham
Boynton.*

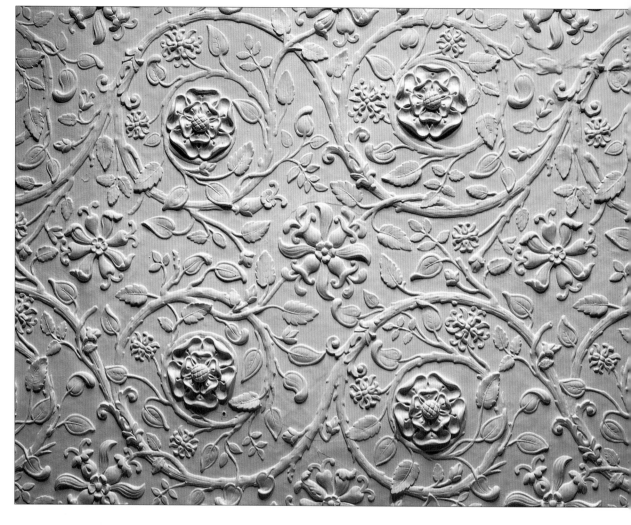

BELOW:

A pedestal table in the
Chippendale style
*This has plate-sized
indentations on its tip-
up top, and stands in
the ante-room of the
Great Parlour.*

earthquake gave him problems to attend to at home. The
proposed visit to Chequers never took place, although Gorbachev
did come to London the following year.

Mounted on the panelling are lights carried on silver wall-
sconces of Charles II design. Above the panelling Lee added a
plaster frieze featuring in relief the initials of William and Agnes
Hawtrey. Blomfield was also responsible for the elaborate ceiling
here; he based the design on one at Broughton Castle, in
Oxfordshire, the home of Lord Saye and Sele. A large Feraghan
carpet covers the polished wood floor.

On either side of the fireplace hang portraits of William Pitt, 1st
Earl of Chatham, by Joseph Highmore (1692–1780) and of Sir
Robert Walpole by J. B. van Loo (1684-1745). Arthur Lee bought
the portrait of Walpole at the same time as a smaller version,
which today hangs in the Cabinet Room at No. 10. Portraits of a
Dutch Officer and the heiress Susan Vanlore, wife of Sir Robert
Croke, both by B. van der Helst (1612-70), keep them company.

An eighteenth-century Dutch bureau
Decorated inside and out with ivory, mother-of-pearl and intricate marquetry of various woods, it stands in the recess of the Great Parlour.

BELOW:
'Isle of Man' tip-up tripod table
These human legs, with buckled shoes, support the oval table top.

The ante-room ceiling is decorated with especially fine relief. In the recess of the Great Parlour stands an eighteenth-century Dutch marquetry *bombé* bureau, inlaid with ivory and mother-of-pearl. Also here is one of my favourite pieces of furniture: a three-legged, 'Isle of Man' mahogany table, which has an oval tip-up top, supported by 'human' legs with buckled shoes on the feet.

Above the fireplace, in the panelled recess of the room, hang black and white photographs of all the thirteen Prime Ministers, from Lloyd George to Margaret Thatcher, who have occupied Chequers. John Major will join them when his term of office ends. This collection has had a somewhat peripatetic existence, having been at one time on the main staircase. Here, in Mrs Thatcher's view, they were less effective than a similar collection on the stairs at No. 10. When it was suggested to her, however, that the photographs could be replaced with pictures, she replied that perhaps it was best to leave them where they were, for her guests loved them and she no longer noticed them.

THE LONG GALLERY

The Long Gallery on the first floor houses the Chequers library. Running almost the entire length of the north front, this impressive room, redolent of book-restorer and wood smoke, was long enough for indoor exercise in the sixteenth century and has been used for indoor cricket in the twentieth. The walls are lined with the bookshelves put in by Sir John Russell at the end of the eighteenth century. Today they hold some 5,000 books, reflecting the tastes of Chequers' previous owners. Many of the leather-bound volumes were acquired by the Rivetts and the Russells, and in recent years they have been carefully restored and catalogued.

Amongst a number of rare books are two items of incunabula that Lord Peter Wimsey would have died for. The most treasured is an exquisitely illuminated fifteenth-century manuscript Missal from Bressanone in the Tyrol, immaculately preserved in its original velevet binding with gilt bosses and clasps. The other is a first edition of Albertus Magnus' *Paradise Animae*, printed in Cologne in 1483, seven years before Caxton first brought printing to England. There is a first printed edition (1503) of all but four of Euripides' tragedies, added to the library by Sir George Russell, as well as sixteenth-century first editions of Aristophanes' *Lysistrata* and *Thermophoriazusae* and a translation by Erasmus of Lucian of Samosata's *Saturnalia* (published in Cologne), with the arms of Louis XIII on the binding. In a first illustrated edition of Milton's *Paradise Lost* (1688) are Sergeant Thurbarne's annotations; and a sixteenth-century volume of Foxe's *Book of Martyrs* has Sir Robert Croke's name inscribed on the fly-leaf.

John Rivett added a 1545 leather-bound edition of Chaucer, an early edition (1609) of Spenser's *The Faerie Queene* together with a first edition of Dryden's tragedy of the Spartan hero *Cleomenes* (1692). Rivett's nephew, Sir John Russell, added a fourth folio edition of Shakespeare in the original binding (printed in 1685), a second edition of Richardson's *Clarissa* (1769), Sterne's *Tristram Shandy* (1760) and a new edition of *The Works of Francis Bacon* (1753).

The library also houses a 'Breeches' Bible and Archbishop Laud's Book of Common Prayer (1633). There is a second folio edition of Graevius and Gronovius' *Classical Antiquities* (1722-37), a massive work in twelve volumes, and a first edition of William Painter's *The Pleasure Palaces* (1566), dedicated to the Earl of Warwick. The latter work is interesting since its short stories, translated from the Latin, Greek and French versions, provided the plots for Shakespeare's *Romeo and Juliet* and Webster's *The Duchess of Malfi*. Of the seven copies believed to have survived, the only

The Long Gallery
in 1909

OPPOSITE:
The Long Gallery
*Looking west towards
the stained glass
windows which feature
the coats-of-arms of the
owners of Chequers,
from de Scaccario to
Astley. The bookshelves
were put in by Sir John
Russell at the end of the
eighteenth century.*

A secret door in the Long Gallery *lined with 'dummy' books. The globe is one of a pair of celestial and territorial globes by Cary.*

other one in England is in The British Library, in London. Arthur Lee collected several rare first editions of nineteenth-century works, including those of Tennyson and Dickens. Faith Moore, who generously endowed Chequers with so many pictures, pieces of furniture and other works of art, also presented a collection of the works of Thackeray.

Departing Prime Ministers are all expected to donate their Memoirs and there is a growing collection of Prime Ministerial biographies in the Prime Minister's Study.

Two false doors faced with dummy books, at opposite ends of the Long Gallery, conceal a fire hose and the 'secret' door which leads to the Cromwell Passage; keen readers need not be frustrated, however, since many of these 'books' can be found on real bookshelves elsewhere in the library.

Blue and white Chinese porcelain is displayed on top of the bookshelves and blue and white Delft and seventeenth-century Japanese Imari-ware are also represented here. On the wall space above hang family portraits of many of the early owners of Chequers. Amongst those of the Russells and Rivetts is the only existing portrait of Joanna Thurbarne. Her second husband John

An illuminated fifteenth-century manuscript Missal
This is from Bressanone, in the Tyrol. The velvet binding with gilt bosses and clasps is original.

Russell – Cromwell's grandson – her second son James Rivett, her only daughter Mary Rivett and Mary's husband Colonel Charles Russell are also here. These canvasses, attributed to Thomas Murray (1666-1724), are all the same size, suggesting that they were painted as companion portraits. The 8th Baronet, Sir John Russell, and his son and heir, also Sir John, are featured in two portraits by Nathaniel Dance (1735-1811). An unattributed portrait of the English School depicts Sir John's younger brother George, the 10th and last Russell Baronet. There are eighteenth-century English School companion portraits of the Reverend John Greenhill Russell and his wife Elizabeth, and a fine painting by Sir William Beechey of their only son Sir Robert Greenhill Russell.

The couches and occasional tables which Sir John Russell thought the room needed have been added over the years, and Feraghan and Kazak rugs relieve the wall-to-wall beige carpet which replaced the straw matting of the 'twenties. The room is lit by numerous table lamps and a pair of seventeenth-century silvered brass chandeliers. The bookshelves have once again been 'white-washed blue', as they were in the seventeenth century, and the blue is echoed in the furniture and curtains. Efficient central heating has long since replaced the single-bar electric fire which could have done little more than take the chill off a few square feet of this long room. When a log fire burns in the grate, afternoon tea – still poured from a silver pot bearing the initials of Faith Moore – has a cosy timelessness about it.

There are few pieces of furniture of note in the Long Gallery. One exception is the Regency oak pedestal table, standing at the west end, which belonged to Napoleon Bonaparte and was used by him during his exile in St Helena until his death in 1821. In a box nearby is a pair of Napoleon's flintlock pistols, which Arthur Lee believed had been presented by the Emperor's brother Lucien to Arthur Lee's grandfather, Sir Theophilus Lee, soon after the Battle of Waterloo. The connection is unclear but Sir Theophilus Lee served as a midshipman with Nelson at the Battle of the Nile in 1798. At the other end of the Long Gallery is the eighteenth-century bureau which houses his Nile medals, Nelson's watch, Arthur Lee's collection of miniatures and other memorabilia and the gruesome mask of Oliver Cromwell.

Pride of place in the jewelcase, however, goes to a fine collection of miniatures of the Cromwell family by Samuel Cooper (1609-72), one of the greatest English miniaturists. These may well have been among those described as being kept 'under lock and key' during the ownership of the 8th Baronet, Sir John

Joanna Thurbarne
Rivett *(1684-1764)*
Joanna was the only
daughter of John
Thurbarne and his first
wife, Ann Cutts. After
the death of her first
husband Colonel
Edmund Rivett, at the
Battle of Malplaquet in
1709, she married
Oliver Cromwell's
grandson, John Russell.
Joanna inherited
Chequers through her
stepmother in 1712.

Russell. One, of the Protector's favourite daughter Elizabeth
(Bettie) Claypole, has traces of an inscription on the back, and a
rare signature by the artist. Another, signed with a gold 'SC', is of
John Pym, the Parliamentary statesman whose attempted arrest by
Charles I in 1642 triggered the Civil War. William Hawtrey, the
rebuilder of Chequers, is depicted, by an unknown artist, seated at

his writing desk, wearing a figured black doublet and high ruff; in the background is a town landscape. There is also an exquisite pearl-edged miniature of Ruth Moore painted by Amalia Kussner at the time of her engagement to Arthur Lee.

The jewelcase also houses Queen Elizabeth's ring, which Arthur Lee bought from a Bond Street jeweller in 1919. The ring is mounted in a special perspex box, with an illuminated magnifying glass with which to inspect the intricate detail. On the oval bezel of another ring is a likeness of Oliver Cromwell; although the present setting is eighteenth-century, there is a tradition that Cromwell gave this gold ring to his youngest daughter, Frances, on his deathbed.

Occupying the whole of the west end of the Gallery is a bay window with twenty-four panels of heraldic glass, installed by Arthur Lee. The panels relate the genealogical history of the house from the de Scaccarios to the Astleys, a theme which is taken up in the double-transomed windows overlooking the north lawn towards the wooded copse known as Crow Close. Here, beginning with the arms of Lord and Lady Lee, heraldic stained glass commemorates the official occupancies of thirteen Prime Ministers, from Lloyd George to Margaret Thatcher. For many years there was a space reserved for Edward Heath, but it was not until he became a Knight of the Garter in 1992 that he approached the College of Arms to design his coat-of-arms. Sir Edward Heath's window was finally installed in 1994, twenty years after he left office.

Cromwell's mask
Once thought to have been taken from life, this is now believed to have been cast from a wax funeral effigy some years after Cromwell's death. Arthur Lee made another cast from this for his friend Theodore Roosevelt, who had written a biography of Cromwell.

Oliver Cromwell miniatures
The miniature of Oliver Cromwell (above), which he gave to his daughter Frances, set in the bezel of a gold ring, is after Samuel Cooper; the miniature (left) is by an unknown artist.

THE CROMWELL CORRIDOR

A secret door faced with dummy books at the western end of the Long Gallery links the Long Gallery with the Cromwell Corridor. Behind it is concealed another door of linenfold panelling, which was retrieved from a woodshed and is believed to be one of the few surviving fragments of the earlier Tudor building predating William Hawtrey's house. The Cromwell Corridor derives its name from the unique collection of portraits of the Cromwell family. Two of the fine paintings displayed here are by Robert Walker (d. 1658) who might almost be described as the court painter to Oliver Cromwell. One is of the Protector

Oliver Cromwell
by Robert Walker
(d. 1658)
Oliver Cromwell with
his page Peter Temple
tying on his sash.

in armour, with his page Peter Temple tying on his sash; the other
portrays Cromwell's son Richard, who succeeded him in 1658.
There is a small portrait of Cromwell's mother, and a large one of
his daughter Bettie Claypole, depicting her seated with one hand
resting upon a celestial globe and the other holding a pair of
dividers. A book lies open upon her knee with a scroll inscribed
Altiora Sequor (I pursue higher things). Both of these portraits have
been attributed to Huysmans (1656-96), but if this is correct they
must be posthumous since their subjects had been dead more than
a year before Huysmans arrived in this country from Antwerp in
1660. Lord Lee added to the collection with a copper engraving
of Cromwell in armour on horseback, by the French engraver
Pierre Lombart (c.1620-81), and a picture of the battle of Marston
Moor, by the English artist Abraham Cooper (1787-1868),
featuring the Earl of Manchester and General Lambert with
Cromwell on a horse in the centre. In the latter picture,

Cromwell, nursing one arm in a sling, brandishes in the other a sword which Lord Lee believed to be the same as that which today rests upon the mantelpiece in the Long Gallery. Alas, the facts do not support this theory, for the sword belongs to the mid-eighteenth century.

The fine portrait of Frances Russell by the Dutch painter H. Van der Myn (1684-1741) completes the Cromwell collection. It was taken for granted by her descendants that these portraits and

Oliver Cromwell aged 2 years
A portrait of the English school.

Frances Cromwell (1638-1721) by H. Van der Myn. Oliver Cromwell's youngest daughter was married to Sir John Russell, 3rd Bart. Their youngest son John married Joanna Thurbarne Rivett, the owner of Chequers, in 1715. It was through this marriage that many of the Cromwell portraits and relics came to be in the house.

the Cromwell relics were contemporaneous with his youngest daughter. They assumed that since Lady Russell had made her home at Chequers, Oliver Cromwell would have been a visitor. But, in fact, the Protector had been dead for many years before his daughter had any connection with the house, and she was

Detail from a 'Seven Crown' chair

certainly never mistress of it. She did, however, live well into her eighties and was therefore still alive when her grandson John married the owner of Chequers. When Lady Russell's eldest son, the 4th Baronet, sold the roof over his widowed mother's head, she went to live with her sister Mary and her husband Lord Fauconberg at Newburgh Priory, in Yorkshire. Legend has it that Cromwell's remains, disinterred after the Restoration in 1660, were secretly taken to Newburgh, where they were bricked up. Many family portraits and possessions subsequently moved with the Fauconbergs from Newburgh to Sutton Court, in Chiswick, in 1676. Sutton Court eventually passed to Fauconberg's nephew, the 2nd Baronet, Sir Thomas Frankland, who, in 1683, married Frances Russell's only daughter Elizabeth, with whom the old lady spent the last years of her life.

On the evidence of an early nineteenth-century visitor, who compiled a work entitled *Families Allied to the Cromwells* (published in 1804), many Cromwell portraits and memorabilia were present at Chequers during the ownership of the 8th Baronet Sir John Russell in the late 1770s. These must have followed a circuitous route to Chequers from Frances Russell, via her son John Russell and thence to her Rivett grandchildren and finally to her great-grandson Sir John Russell.

In the bay of the Cromwell Corridor a sixteenth-century window put in by Blomfield looks out across what remains of the old inner courtyard towards the huge mullioned window of the Great Hall. Suspended in the window are medallions of stained glass, some of which were thought to have come originally from York Minster and to have been brought to Chequers by the Frankland Russells. There is also a fragment of stained glass salvaged from the Houses of Parliament after a German air-raid in May 1941. In the bay window stands an early eighteenth-century chestnut wood coffer of Spanish origin. This corridor leads to another, which gives access to all the first floor bedrooms on the south side of the house.

One of a set of 'Seven Crown' chairs
These chairs stand in the Cromwell Corridor. They were made to commemorate Charles II's Restoration. The crown was a popular symbol with royalists.

A sturdy little seventeenth-century Dutch strong-box
Made of walnut and lined with lignum vitae, it is mounted with brass bands. The drop front conceals a pair of drawers.

The Greenhill Room
The coats-of-arms of the Greenhill family are featured in the stone spandrels of the fireplace and to the left is a William and Mary bureau inlaid with marquetry. Above the fireplace is H. Huyssing's portrait of George II's daughter Princess Amelia, to whom both Frances and Mary Russell were Women of the Bedchamber.

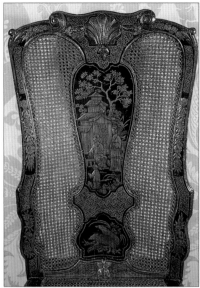

Detail from one of a set of six Queen Anne lacquered beechwood chairs
They stand in the bedroom corridor and each one is different.

A small seventeenth-century Indo-Portuguese cabinet
This was brought from the East by Governor Russell. Veneered with horn and tortoiseshell, it is intricately painted with equestrian figures. The ornate Charles II oak stand with putti legs, is decorated with foliage and flowers.

A late seventeenth-century oak wardrobe
This stands in the former State Bedroom. The doors are made from twelve panels carved in the Tudor period with interlaced strap-work and vines. Curiously, one of the panels is different from the others.

THE GREENHILL ROOM

This bedroom derives its name from the coats-of-arms of the Greenhill Russell family featured in the stone spandrels of the fireplace. The portrait above the fireplace is of George II's daughter, Princess Amelia.

In 1920 the Lees invited the Maharajah of Alwar to stay at Chequers. He slept in this bedroom and in the mornings the maids found bowls of water all over the floor. Ruth Lee could only explain such eccentric behaviour by imagining that he had used the bowls as stepping stones to avoid contact with the polluted carpets.

BEDROOM TWO

This was Winston Churchill's bedroom during the Second World War. Seldom up before lunchtime, Churchill would sit propped up in bed, puffing on a cigar, while he worked on his boxes, dictated to his secretary and received colleagues and officials. It was here also that his first grandson was born in 1940.

The wallpaper and matching hangings on the mahogany four-poster bed were replaced during Margaret Thatcher's premiership. In the spandrels of the fireplace are the Hawtrey coat-of-arms and above it hangs Churchill's painting of Lake Geneva, a gift from Lady Churchill to Chequers in 1971. Just visible in the photograph is Robert Frankland Russell's portrait of one of his daughters. In the window stands a George III rosewood sofa-table; the footstool beneath it contains a tin-plated hot-water bottle.

Bedroom Two
This bedroom, with its view across the park, is one of the prettiest rooms in the house.

Bedroom doorhandle
An irresistible moustachioed 'merman'.

The Lee Room
This is a room of dignified proportions, enhanced by the imposing George III four-poster bed which is carved with wheatears.

THE LEE ROOM

This room, with its imposing carved George III four-poster bed, is allocated to visiting Heads of State or other distinguished guests. During the war, Molotov, the Soviet Foreign Secretary, slept here with a loaded revolver under his pillow. This room was refurbished during Margaret Thatcher's premiership and the bed is hung with floral chintz. It is furnished with seventeenth-century and Regency pieces, and there are several classical landscapes on the wall, as well as an eighteenth-century Dutch townscape.

Lady Mary Grey
*This small picture by
Hans Eworth
(1520–1573), which
hangs in the Prison
Room, was acquired
by Lord Lee. He was
always on the lookout for
artefacts with a Chequers
connection, and presented
it to the house in 1922.*

THE PRISON ROOM

The Prison Room, on the second floor directly above the recess
of the Great Parlour, is reached either by a spiral staircase leading
from the Hawtrey Room or from an upper corridor. Today, this
pretty guest bedroom, its once-forbidding stone walls plastered
and painted white, bears little resemblance to how it must have
been when William Hawtrey was asked to take Lady Mary Grey
into his custody. Perhaps a fire burned then in the huge fireplace.

Protected under a glass panel is a section of the original stone
on which can be seen the indecipherable writing of the prisoner.
Framed on the wall are facsimiles of several of her numerous
letters to William Cecil (the originals are in the British Museum).

The Gollywogg Book *together with the original Gollywogg (sic) and his friends, Peggy, Sarah Jane, Meg Weg and Midget, came to Chequers during the First World War. Created by an American called Florence Upton to illustrate the books her mother wrote, the dolls were bought by Faith Moore in an auction to raise money for the Western Front. The presence of the dolls at Chequers aroused great public interest, and the Trustees decided that, as they had no historic significance to the house, they could be more appropriately displayed in the Bethnal Green Toy Museum, where they have been since 1983. The book remains in the second floor corridor, where Golliwogg lived, which is still known as the Golliwogg Corridor.*

But even wooden limbs get tired
And want a change of play.
So "Golliwogg"
A "jolly dog"
Suggests they run away.

The big shop door
But through th
Peggy ha
One ope
Which she w

A nineteenth-century elm exercise horse *The seat formed of springs is upholstered in leather. There are only a few other examples in existence today. It is on the second floor.*

THE GARDENS AND PARK

Once Blomfield's work on the interior of the house had been completed, Lee turned his attention to the gardens. It was clear to him that the flower beds, shrubbery and shapeless areas of lawn which formed what Lipscomb had described as a 'small but very elegant parterre' now appeared to have been dropped in front of the south elevation, with little attention to its relationship with the newly renovated house. In 1911 Arthur Lee commissioned H. Avray Tipping, a former Member of Parliament and distinguished contributor to *Country Life,* to create a more appropriate architectural setting. Tipping was the creator of many large and admired gardens, among them Brinsop Court in Herefordshire, the house of Bertram Astley.

The south garden of Chequers occupies what would have been the outer court of William Hawtrey's house and a black line carved into the paving still marks the outline of a fifteenth-century gatehouse, the foundations of which were unearthed during the 1911 excavations. Access from the South Garden Hall gives on to a broad paved terrace, running the whole length of the south front, which Blomfield laid for Bertram Astley. A low brick wall and a lavender hedge separate the terrace from a rectangular grass walkway on a lower level. From here steps lead to the sunken garden, laid out with box hedges in the formal pattern of an Elizabethan knot garden. In the centre, on a sandstone plinth, is an octagonal copper sundial, designed by Lord Lee, who composed the inscription: 'Ye houres do flie/ For soone we die/ In age secure/ Ye house and hills/ Alone endure.' It amused him to see these lines often credited with an antiquity it did not have.

At the southernmost corners of the grass walk stand two summerhouses, joined by a buttressed wall which screens the garden from Victory Drive and the broad expanse of the south park. A lower wall borders it to the east and it is here, close to the garden wall, that the remains of the ancient elm known as King Stephen's tree can be seen. Towering above it is the oak planted by Stanley Baldwin and a gigantic chestnut, beneath which the ground is carpeted with snowdrops and crocuses in early spring.

Tipping's new brickwork was mostly Dutch, with a sprinkling from Surrey, to give the garden the variety of materials which prevailed in William Hawtrey's time; the stone dressings came from Northamptonshire. On completion of his work, Tipping was conscious of the 'bare and staring walls' that only time would mellow and soften with roses and perennials. But the Lees had nothing but praise for Tipping, who had created what Chequers

OPPOSITE:
Sculpture by Henry Moore *(top left) on the north lawn, on loan to Chequers from the Henry Moore Foundation.*

A garden house *(top right) in the south garden.*

The lavender hedge *(bottom left) on the terrace of the rose garden.*

Sundial *(bottom right) on the south wall above the terrace.*

most lacked: 'an adequate frame for an old and beautiful picture'. Like the house itself, the gardens at Chequers remain virtually as he conceived them more than eighty years ago. The topiary birds, planted in pots, which Tipping stood at the four corners of the parterre, have given way to sculptured topiary of a more abstract kind, growing proudly in the ground. The lavender hedge

A view across the rose garden from the north-west to the south-east
The topiary remains faithful to Avray Tipping's original plan. The oak tree in the background was planted by Stanley Baldwin in 1928.

continues to provide the house with bowls of lavender and the box hedges, with their paved borders, are now mature. The eight beds they enclose are planted with roses, as Tipping intended, although the old-fashioned varieties have given way to hybrid teas. Elsewhere, however, the tradition of old-fashioned roses prevails and many of those planted by Lady Eden in the 'fifties, flower luxuriantly. 'Albertine' and 'Cécile Brunner' climb freely over the walls and jasmine cascades down the walls of the house. On a summer's day there is no more beautiful or fragrant place at Chequers than the lavender terrace of the rose garden.

To the north side of the house, the garden has changed little since the nineteenth century and is simplicity itself. A broad paved path, at each end of which stand two pairs of stately yews, separates the house from the north lawn. This expanse of grass has served in its time as a tennis court and croquet lawn and is an ideal site for a marquee when the occasion demands. A steep bank with a wide flight of stone steps leads up to a longer grassway and to the wooded copse known as Crow Close. To the west, a thick beech hedge screens the lawn from the track that winds its way through the woodlands of The Junipers and Ellesborough Plantation to the church at Ellesborough. On the east side, a wall which returns to meet the house allows for greater privacy and forms one side of the main forecourt; in the angle of the wall stands a summerhouse. Beyond the bank, to the north and east, iron railings stop cows and sheep in the park from straying on to the north lawn.

Prime Ministers and visiting heads of state have continued the tradition of planting memorial trees at Chequers. Between the beech hedge and Crow Close many have been added to the cedars planted by the Lees and Theodore Roosevelt. Ramsay MacDonald planted a cedar in 1924, and President Eisenhower commemorated his visit in 1959 with a dawn redwood – a rare Metasequoia. Harold Macmillan chose a copper beech, Jim Callaghan a South American beech and we keep an eye on the English oak John planted in 1992. Margaret Thatcher and Edward Heath planted their trees – a lime and a beech respectively – in the south park, on opposite sides of the drive. There are beeches planted by three French Presidents – Giscard d'Estaing, Georges Pompidou and Jacques Chirac. The German Chancellor, Helmut Schmidt, planted a horse chestnut and President Yeltsin a black poplar.

In the east park are the oldest of the prime ministerial trees, with the tulip tree dedicated to Neville Chamberlain and the mature oaks of Stanley Baldwin and David Lloyd George, the first Prime Minister to occupy Chequers who planted the first of them in 1917.

OPPOSITE:
A fine group of memorial trees on the east lawn Winston Churchill's Valonia oak (left), Clement Attlee's hornbeam (centre) and Harold Wilson's evergreen holm oak (right). Anthony Eden's plane tree and Alec Douglas-Home's walnut are on the other side of the drive.

POLITICAL LIFE AT CHEQUERS

OPPOSITE:

The only absentee from this gallery of 'official occupants' of Chequers is Bonar Law. John Major's photograph will be added when he leaves office.

A month after relinquishing Chequers in January 1921, Arthur Lee moved from Agriculture and, without hindrance from Bonar Law, became First Lord of the Admiralty. Accommodation went with the job and as the Lees settled into the First Lord's Whitehall residence at Admiralty House, the Prime Minister, Lloyd George, was spending more time at Chequers, holding political conferences and meeting international statesmen.

Amongst them was Marshal Foch, making a return visit with the French Prime Minister Aristide Briand, ostensibly to discuss the pressing question of war reparations and armaments. According to Sir Henry Wilson, Chief of the Imperial General Staff, Foch described the occasion with wry amusement. After '*le lunch*', and the inevitable photographic session on the terrace, Lloyd George took them up Beacon Hill. From there, looking down on Cymbeline's Mount, the Prime Minister delivered a lecture on Roman encampments. In Foch's view, the conference had been fairly 'futile', but he was impressed, once again, by the dignity of Chequers, especially in comparison with the nearby Rothschild mansion of Halton (now an RAF station), considered to be merely a caricature of a Louis XIV château. Briand's verdict on Chequers was '*trop authentique*'.

More productive was a meeting in May 1921 of miners' leaders, convened to try to avert the coal strike threatening to paralyse the country. One newspaper expressed the view that since Chequers now belonged to the nation it would be a most suitable place for a settlement. After eight hours of uninterrupted talks, the coal strike was called off. Chequers had made such a deep impression upon the miners' leaders that they told Lloyd George of their intention to occupy it themselves as soon as possible.

The Lees were gratified that Chequers already appeared to be fulfilling its intended role, but although Lloyd George told them what they most wanted to hear – that he loved the place and that it meant everything to him – his enchantment was in reality far from complete.

DAVID LLOYD GEORGE

Chequers was certainly proving to be an indispensable amenity to the premiership, but Lloyd George's secretary, Frances Stevenson, who was later his mistress, recorded in her book, *The Years That are Past,* that he was never really happy there. Lloyd George felt confined by its history, resenting 'the atmosphere of preceding generations which seemed to swamp and encroach upon the essential independence of his nature which refused to be contained.' But if Lloyd George cared little for an old house haunted by the spirits of the past, his dog, a black chou called Chong, liked it even less. Chong was particularly restless in the Long Gallery, where his master liked to rest in the afternoon. With his eyes fixed on one spot in the room, the dog used to set up a persistent barking. Although he himself never found any evidence of a supernatural presence, Lloyd George felt sure that Chong could see a ghost.

David Lloyd George's window at Chequers

For Lloyd George, however, there was another overwhelming disadvantage for, situated in a valley, Chequers lacked a view. To him, this was a fatal flaw, and he was deeply envious of a colleague who had built a small house, near Wendover, with an expansive view of the Vale of Aylesbury. To Lloyd George, a small house with a view was infinitely preferable to a large house without one.

In the early nineteenth century, Lipscombe had also lamented the fact that from the North Front the view across the Vale was blocked by an 'inconveniently interposed' range of hills, some of which he suggested should be either lowered or removed. In the eighteenth century, landscape gardeners thought nothing of diverting a river or moving a hill, but fortunately Beacon Hill and Coombe Hill still protect Chequers from the North and give it a welcome seclusion. Perhaps if Lipscombe had had his way, Lloyd George might have taken more wholeheartedly to Chequers.

David Lloyd George's
housewarming
Chequers
January 1921.

Although both their children and their grandchildren came to
Chequers regularly, Margaret Lloyd George was a rare visitor
there, for house-parties at Chequers were emphatically political
and she disapproved of the company her husband kept. Lloyd
George hated the sanctimonious humbug of the majority of
Liberals, and his friends were mostly in the Tory Party; even
Philip Sassoon, his Parliamentary Private Secretary, was a Tory.
'He always says,' wrote Frances Stevenson in her diary, 'that there
are no Liberals who would make a jolly dinner party such as we
used to have in the days of the old coalition.' Even Lloyd George's
youngest daughter Megan, who took over the role of hostess in
her mother's absence, was often accompanied by her friend
Thelma Cazalet, who later became a Conservative MP.

For Megan, untroubled by the supernatural or the lack of a
view, the only thing that marred Chequers was the presence of
Frances Stevenson, who had originally come to Downing Street as
her tutor. When it became evident that Miss Stevenson had come
to mean more to her father, Megan was deeply hurt and went out
of her way to make life difficult for her. She was quite capable of
putting on a fine show of rudeness if she arrived at Chequers to

David Lloyd George with Marshal Foch (left) and M.Briand (right) on the terrace at Chequers in February 1921.

find Frances in the role of hostess. Since wife and mistress never met, Megan knew that Frances Stevenson would stay away if her mother was at Chequers. So when Lloyd George entertained the Japanese Crown Prince Hirohito in May 1921, she told her mother that her father wanted her there as well, although he had said no such thing. Lloyd George had taken immense pains over the visit, which was a prelude to the Imperial Conference in June. Dame Margaret, who hated formal occasions, especially when royalty were involved, appeared in a glowering mood. 'It is the fortunes of war, and cannot be helped,' wrote Frances philosophically in her diary. The Crown Prince perhaps noticed nothing amiss, for he extended his visit well into the evening.

In December of that year, a most unusual guest was received at Chequers in the person of Boris Savinkov, an ex-Russian revolutionary turned anti-Bolshevik. Having fought tirelessly with bomb and bullet to promote the revolution, he discovered that he had merely traded one kind of tyranny for another. Since the Russians needed help in the fight against Bolshevism and Winston Churchill was an ardent champion of Savinkov's cause, Lloyd George invited them both to Chequers to discuss the possibilities of overthrowing the four-year-old communist régime. It was a

Sunday when they arrived at Chequers and Lloyd George greeted his visitors in the Great Hall with a Welsh choir lustily singing Welsh hymns. Although Lloyd George was greatly moved by Savinkov's appeal on behalf of the Russian people, he took the view that revolutions, like diseases, must run their course. According to Churchill's account of this meeting in *Great Contemporaries*, the Prime Minister expounded his theory that Bolshevism would inevitably fail and ' … others weaker or more moderate would succeed them, and by successive convulsions a more tolerable régime would be established.' An unconvinced Savinkov reminded the Prime Minister that 'after the fall of the Roman Empire there ensued the Dark Ages.' What must this terrorist patriot have made of his visit to an English country house, where he was served afternoon tea before a log fire and serenaded by a male voice choir?

A few days later Louis Loucheur, the French Minister for Reconstruction, came to Chequers with his proposal for the economic re-integration of Russia into Europe, and for its recognition in return for the agreement to the right of private ownership. As we know, little progress was made on either front for nearly seventy years, but the real purpose of the visit was to discuss German war reparations. Lloyd George was seeking to distance Britain from the sabre-rattling of the French in favour of a payments moratorium. He argued for the opening-up of eastern and central European markets to Germany and the creation of an all-European organization to supervise the economic reconstruction of the war-torn continent, thus facilitating Germany's long-term capacity to pay reparations. A little over a year later these negotiations broke down and the French occupied the Ruhr.

When Lloyd George took up residence at Chequers, security became a problem for the first time, for the lengthy negotiations leading to the Irish treaty had put him and other members of the Cabinet at risk from Sinn Fein. The treaty of peace with England, signed in December 1920, retained Ulster as part of the United Kingdom and gave the Irish Free State the status of a dominion with allegiance to the Crown. Since this did not satisfy the rabid republicans in the south, the Irish problem continued to fester. When Irish Republican Army slogans were discovered on the walls of some outbuildings close to Chequers, the police arrested a group of young Irishmen in the grounds, who professed to be medical students on holiday from Dublin wishing to see the house. They were released after a night in the cells, although neither Lloyd George nor Hamar Greenwood, Secretary for Ireland who was staying at Chequers, believed their story. Over

David Lloyd George
with his daughter
Megan.

the years political terrorism has increased, and the security of public figures has become a greater problem; today the presence of armed police officers in flak jackets is all part of 'normal' life for the occupants of Chequers.

Although, as 'the man who won the war', Lloyd George had routed his opponents at the general election of 1918, he continued to lead a predominantly Conservative Coalition. The euphoria of victory, however, followed by the signing of the Treaty of Versailles six months later, soon gave way to unemployment and the realization that the promised land – 'a fit country for heroes to live in' – had not materialized. Before long there were signs of strain within the Coalition; a rift was forming between those Conservatives still under the spell of Lloyd George and those who were not.

The Irish treaty had not received wholehearted support and the Unionists were hostile to any concessions to the Irish rebels. In India, as Mahatma Gandhi's campaign for independence gathered pace, Lloyd George took the first steps towards Indian self-rule, while the Tories insisted the Raj must be preserved. But it was the Chanak emergency of September 1922 that proved the last straw, for although his resolute stand averted a war with Turkey, Lloyd George had few allies in the Cabinet. Those he did have were summoned to Chequers in mid-September to discuss the crisis and the future of the Coalition. Among them was Worthington Evans, Secretary of State for War, Lord Birkenhead, Lord Chancellor, Sir Robert Horne, Chancellor of the Exchequer, Austen Chamberlain, Foreign Secretary, and Winston Churchill, the Colonial Secretary who was also chairman of the Cabinet Committee for Defence Spending. Although Lord Lee, as First Lord of the Admiralty, had responded promptly to the emergency, he had declined the invitation to Chequers, still immensely depressed at the thought of returning there. Churchill, however, although supportive of Lloyd George's stance over Chanak, thought the Prime Minister's days were numbered, while Chamberlain's advice was to play their hand and dissolve Parliament once the crisis was over.

This was the last meeting of any significance held by Lloyd George at Chequers, for in the end the initiative did not rest with him. The following month, in his famous intervention at the Carlton Club in London, the President of the Board of Trade Stanley Baldwin made it clear that the Coalition had run its course. King George V reluctantly accepted the resignation of Lloyd George, who left Downing Street in October 1922, never to return. 'Damn,' said Megan, 'there goes Chequers.' For her, it had definitely been one of the sweets of office.

ANDREW BONAR LAW

Andrew Bonar Law was the shortest serving Prime Minister of the twentieth century, holding office for only 209 days between October 1922 and May 1923. He was also the only Prime Minister never to occupy Chequers. It has frequently been stated that Bonar Law's refusal to occupy Chequers was based on a loathing of the countryside, for which, together with his lack of interest in the arts, the Lees could make no allowances. Yet Law, visiting Chequers in November 1912, ten years before his premiership, had enjoyed a round of golf with his son, while Faith and Ruth had shown his daughter around the house. Over lunch Law confided to Lady Northcliffe, wife of the newspaper proprietor, how much he liked the house; after tea he had settled down comfortably in the Great Parlour, listening keenly as Arthur Lee outlined his plan for Chequers.

Although Law had kept his seat in Parliament, ill-health had forced his departure from the Coalition Government in March 1920, and Austen Chamberlain had taken over as leader of the Conservative and Unionist Party. Nevertheless, with the collapse of the Coalition and Lloyd George's resignation, the King sent for Bonar Law. For a man of robust health the Prime Minister's job is an arduous one; for a sick man it is an insupportable burden. Ten years earlier he would have taken it up with relish, but now he accepted it with reluctance. Furthermore, the Conservative Party was divided and he was only prepared to accept office with its total support. He appointed his Cabinet, dissolved Parliament and announced a general election, all in the space of a few days.

Andrew Bonar Law

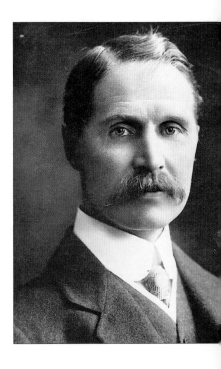

Meanwhile, the Trustees were pressing Bonar Law for a decision on whether or not he was going to take up residence at Chequers. With an election campaign under way, it was hardly surprising that Chequers was not the focus of his attention. Once the electorate had endorsed his Government, however, Law suggested that he and the Chancellor of the Exchequer, Stanley Baldwin, might share the occupancy of Chequers, with Baldwin taking the first shift. This arrangement was considered perfectly in accord with the spirit of the Trust and although disappointed at this breach of the principle they had endeavoured to establish, Arthur Lee was more relieved than anything else, since he held the Prime Minister in such low esteem.

Bonar Law was by then an increasingly sick man: he was found to have cancer of the throat. He cut short a Mediterranean cruise in the Easter recess and returned to London, too ill to tender his resignation to the King and too weak to involve himself in the complexities of recommending a successor. There were two potential candidates: Lord Curzon, Foreign Secretary, and Stanley Baldwin. But events had moved beyond the time when a Prime Minister could lead successfully from the House of Lords. In spite of Curzon's greater experience, it was Baldwin, whose stock had risen dramatically within the Party since the Carlton Club attack on Lloyd George, who took up the reins of office two days later.

So Bonar Law was denied his commemorative window and his memorial tree at Chequers. When he died in 1923, five months after leaving office, among the tributes in the House of Commons was this statement from his successor: 'There is no doubt that Mr Bonar Law gave his life for his country just as much as if he had fallen in the Great War.'

STANLEY BALDWIN

A countryman through and through, Baldwin appreciated the arrangement he had come to with Bonar Law. At the weekend, it allowed him to swap what were then the rather cramped living quarters of No. 11 Downing Street for the spaciousness of Chequers, and the wing-collar and bowler hat for plus-fours and a walking stick. Even if Baldwin felt that there was no place in England quite like his native Worcestershire, he found Chequers a congenial substitute for the family home at Astley Hall. In a letter to one of his daughters, he explained how he came to be at Chequers: 'You haven't heard probably that this house is mine. Bonar will only take it for a portion of the summer and I stand next on the list of people to whom Chequers is to be offered.' The peaceful and restful atmosphere, which the Lees had worked so hard to engender, made a deep impression on the Baldwins. After their first visit in December 1922, Lucy Baldwin wrote to Lady Lee of the loving care so obviously spent in bringing the house to its wonderful perfection. 'Words fail me,' she wrote, 'in which to tell you what I feel about it all ... even if our possession as tenants should be only months, we will be able to look back with happy memories upon the honour that has been ours.' These were memories to be shared generously with family, friends and closest colleagues on and off for the next fourteen years, as Baldwin alternated the premiership with Ramsay MacDonald.

With the help of Arthur Lee's little guidebook, Baldwin familiarized himself with the history of the house and took great pride in showing his guests the paintings, the furniture and, above all, the books. Since Rudyard Kipling and Stanley Baldwin were first cousins and childhood friends, the names of members of the Kipling family appear frequently in the Visitors' Book. The cousins shared a sense of history, and in a tribute to Baldwin's eloquence and love of literature Kipling once said that 'Stan was the real pen in our family.'

In the study overlooking the rose garden Baldwin put the finishing touches to his only Budget Speech; but it was fiscal policy rather than the 'calm tenacity of Chequers' that influenced his decision to cut 6d off income tax and reduce the duty on wines and spirits. The speech greatly enhanced his reputation in the House of Commons but, in spite of the part he had played in the Carlton Club dénouement, the name of Baldwin was not a household word. Neither was he an ambitious man and he told his Parliamentary Private Secretary, J.C.C. Davidson, that he would rather take a one-way ticket to Siberia than become Prime Minister. On the day after Bonar Law's resignation in May 1923, Baldwin left the political manoeuvrings of the succession behind him and took a train to Wendover. At Chequers he and his wife, driven out of the house by the incessant ringing of the telephone, took to the woods that they had grown to love during his five months' residence as Chancellor. Baldwin was thus in the unique position of being at Chequers – playing patience in the Long Gallery – when he received the message that the King wished to see him in London early the next morning.

The net was closing around Baldwin. In a two-horse race for the premiership, he was the favourite. The other runner, the Foreign Secretary Lord Curzon, was handicapped, as we have seen, by his position in the Upper House. Curzon also lacked support in the parliamentary party and in the constituencies, whereas Baldwin was perceived to have the tacit endorsement of Bonar Law and the qualities to unite a divided party. As Baldwin arrived in London quietly from Chequers, Curzon, hailed by press as 'the King's choice', received a triumphal

Stanley Baldwin's window at Chequers

welcome at Paddington Station. The King's choice, however, was
Stanley Baldwin and, as he returned to Downing Street later that
afternoon, to move from No. 11 to No. 10, he told the waiting
journalists, 'I don't need your congratulations but your prayers.'
Baldwin's official occupancy of Chequers thus continued
uninterrupted, much to the Lees' satisfaction. His mother's
signature is the first on a page in the Visitors' Book headed, 'The
Prime Minister's Tenancy'; it was Empire Day, 1923.

By the weekend Baldwin was back at Chequers, restructuring
the Cabinet that he had inherited. Lord Curzon, pledging loyalty,
continued as Foreign Secretary and Baldwin remained as
Chancellor for the time being, although Neville Chamberlain
took over at the Treasury three months later. Baldwin had a
difficult meeting at Chequers with Neville's brother Austen, for
Baldwin knew that the price he would have to pay for Austen, the
one coalitionist he really wanted in the Cabinet, would be the
resignation of colleagues he could not afford to lose. Austen
Chamberlain, a former leader of the Party who had held office as
Chancellor of the Exchequer in two previous administrations, was
devastated to be summoned to Chequers only to be offered the
post of Ambassador to the United States instead of the Cabinet
post he had hoped for. He refused Washington but eighteen
months later Baldwin made amends by appointing him Foreign
Secretary in his second administration.

Under the terms of the Chequers Trust, the Board of
Administrative Trustees – of whom the Prime Minister was
automatically Chairman – met annually and every third year the
meeting took place at Chequers. It was for the meeting at the end
of July 1923, three years after they had left Chequers, that the
Lees returned for the first time.

Ruth Lee did not find it as uncomfortable as she had feared,
taking her place as a guest at the familiar dining table. Mrs
Baldwin was evidently very much at home and had not been
tempted to move anything. Arthur Lee entertained his hosts at
lunch with cartoons drawn by Sir Mark Sykes, a former
Parliamentary colleague, which were captioned 'Rules of
Deportment for Chequers'. These do's and don'ts for an incoming
Prime Minister and his family – 'No object of plate to be
pledged', 'Do not strike matches on the Old Masters', 'Do not
cool your curling tongs on the tapestry, damask or Venetian velvet'
– reduced Mrs Baldwin to tears of laughter. The Prime Minister,
however, was tired and strained, having just returned from a visit
to the North and the atmosphere of Chequers had not had time
to do its work. Over lunch Baldwin discussed his problems over

Stanley and Lucy
Baldwin
*with their son Oliver in
the garden at Chequers,
May 1923.*

the future of the Fleet Air Arm and the immense strain on Anglo-
French relations caused by the continuing French occupation of
the Ruhr. The Admirals had wanted to continue their discussions
at Chequers but Baldwin had put them off until he was back in
London because he felt it would be contrary to the spirit of the
Trust. But nothing could have given more satisfaction to the Lees
than to hear that Chequers was providing a backdrop to the
deliberations and decisions that shaped the nation's destiny.

Reassured on this point, Baldwin initiated occasional small
conferences there, including one of considerable significance in
November 1923 when the Irish Boundary Commission met in the
Hawtrey Room at Chequers to carry forward the Irish Agreement
of 1921. The Treaty which established the Irish Free State had also
provided for an independent Commission to settle the boundaries
between Ulster and the South. William Cosgrave, the President of
the Irish Free State, had persuaded Baldwin to see the Sinn Fein
negotiator, Kevin O'Higgins. They were joined at Chequers by
Mr Justice Feetham, the Chairman of the Commission, who
spread out his maps in the Hawtrey Room as the options were
examined. The next day the discussions were broadened to

include the Ulster Prime Minister Sir James Craig and, sandwiched uncomfortably between Craig and O'Higgins at lunch, Mrs Baldwin reminded them both that she was 'much too plump' to be the 'bone of contention'. The Irish leaders trusted Baldwin but were anxious not to be compromised. When the time came to leave Chequers, one of them said to Baldwin, 'We had better travel separately, Prime Minister. To be seen arriving in London together would not be good for either of us.'

Baldwin's biggest domestic problem was unemployment, for which the best remedy, in his view, was a return to Protectionism. Unfortunately, on this issue his hands were tied, for Bonar Law, a Free Trader, had pledged that there would be no change in fiscal policy without reference to the electorate. The obligation to honour that pledge and the prospect of going to the country were on Baldwin's mind as he worked at Chequers on his speech to the Party Conference at Plymouth in October 1923. Eighteen days later, Parliament was dissolved and at the general election in December the Conservative Government lost its majority on the question of Protection. The Unionists were still the largest single party in Parliament, but they were in a minority in the new House of Commons, outnumbered by the combined Labour and Liberal Parties. Great Britain had its first Labour Government and Baldwin relinquished Chequers to Ramsay MacDonald. But MacDonald's first premiership did not last long either and within nine months Baldwin was back again at Chequers in an electorally strong position, which secured him a full term of office.

Thanks to Lord Lee, Chequers provided Baldwin with the ideal sanctuary. It was as he described it, a place where Prime Ministers 'will not be snap-shotted, where they can be private, and where they can perch on a fence and look at the landscape without being shooed off'. Baldwin claimed not to be able to think at Downing Street, and he refused to allow Chequers to become an extension of No. 10, where the hectic work of government went on as usual.

His critics, however, asserted that he used the burden of office as an excuse to disappear to the country, leaving the defence of his policy to others, and this earned him a reputation for indolence. The truth was that Baldwin tired easily and often found himself overwhelmed with exhaustion. When he collapsed after a dinner at the Royal College of Surgeons he was smuggled out of the back door and away to Chequers, and it was to its haven that he returned weary in mind and body after the General Strike of 1926 to recover his strength before returning refreshed to the political fray.

Meet of the Old
Berkeley at Chequers
1 January 1925.

Baldwin disliked parties, his own and those of others, and, apart
from family and close friends, he entertained rarely. The Baldwins
did, however, take part in local activities and welcomed at
Chequers the meet of the Old Berkeley West Hunt, as they
gathered in the sunshine around the statue of Hygeia for the
traditional stirrup cup. Afterwards Mrs Baldwin wrote to Lady Lee
assuring her that only the Hawtrey Room was made available and
that, 'everyone respected the grounds and behaved beautifully'.
The Baldwins also shared an interest in cricket – Lucy Baldwin
herself played a useful bat – and they gave the Chequers Estate

Stanley Baldwin
*with the Chequers
Estate Cricket Team.*

cricket eleven enthusiastic support in their matches in the south park against neighbouring village teams.

Although Baldwin had handled the General Strike with great finesse, once the crisis had passed he failed to maintain the political momentum. The coal strike dragged on into the winter. Unemployment rose inexorably and with it the ever-increasing burden of the dole bill. Baldwin lost the 1929 general election, a result at odds with the enthusiastic reception he had received during the campaign but, as they made way once more for Ramsay MacDonald at Chequers, they were philosophical about defeat. 'So we are beaten,' wrote Lucy Baldwin, 'but God willing we will flourish again.'

In the meantime MacDonald's minority Labour Government was heading for the rocks of the Great Depression, an economic catastrophe which ushered in the National Government, in which Baldwin became Lord President of the Council. In 1935, with a general election imminent, Baldwin, at the age of sixty-eight, reversed roles with MacDonald for the last time. Before the year was out he had won a victory for the Conservatives.

Baldwin's last two years as Prime Minister were overshadowed by Hitler's march into the Rhineland and repeated calls for greater rearmament. In the summer of 1936, weighed down with domestic and international problems, Baldwin sought sanctuary at Chequers. Since Parliament was sitting, his absence from the Commons could not be concealed and rumours of his resignation were rife. Even the loyal J.C.C. Davidson felt it necessary to tell Baldwin that: 'Every mongrel is yapping, believing that a very tired fox has gone to ground at Chequers with no fight left in him.'

The brief respite at Chequers got the Prime Minister through to the end of the session and he brushed aside rumours of resignation. Not well enough to travel to his habitual holiday destination at Aix-les-Bains in France, however, he began the recess at Chequers, where Lord Dawson, the King's physician, kept a close eye on him. In August, Dawson came to Chequers with a new-fangled contraption for testing the condition of the Prime Minister's heart. Baldwin described the procedure to Davidson:

> *I sat as if I was going to be electrocuted in a chair with wires attached to both arms and one leg. Anyway, my heart is sound and doesn't show any sign of one of the sixty-five ailments which may be revealed by the instrument. But I am to go very easy and lose all sense of time.*

This he contrived to do in both Norfolk and Wales. He returned in much better shape for the autumn session, only to be plunged

Stanley and Lucy
Baldwin
*in the Rose Garden
at Chequers.*

immediately into the events which culminated in the abdication of
King Edward VIII.

The constitutional implications of the King's determination to
marry a twice-divorced American went beyond the shores of
Britain. At Chequers, Baldwin had a meeting with the Canadian
Prime Minister Mackenzie King who made it plain that if a
collision was to take place between the King and the Government,
the handling of the matter required the utmost delicacy. In fact, it
was Baldwin's masterly handling of the crisis that restored him to
public favour. When he retired at the end of May 1937, after the
coronation of George VI, he did so on a wave of popularity.

It was over fourteen years since he had taken office as Prime
Minister for the first time and his last visit to Chequers, where he
had been the official occupant for seven years, was full of
nostalgia. It was as Earl Baldwin of Bewdley that he signed the
Visitors' Book for the last time and he took his seat in the House
of Lords, resolving 'never to make another speech, never to spit
on the deck, and never to speak to the helmsman.'

JAMES RAMSAY MACDONALD

When the Chequers Estate Bill came before Parliament in 1917, Lord Curzon, Lord President of the Council, was in complete sympathy with the philosophy behind Arthur Lee's generous gift. 'We like to think,' he said, 'of our statesmen at the end of a hard week of work in Downing Street going down to enjoy the repose and to bear their share in the interests of the countryside.' This was not, however, the view of the Liberal peer, Lord Haldane: he thought the time was past when a Prime Minister could afford to be away from town at the weekend out of reach of his colleagues, and feared that Chequers would prove a dangerous distraction to Prime Ministers unaccustomed to the charms of a country-house.

It was, of course, for a Prime Minister without wealth or famous descent that Arthur Lee had conceived his scheme and, by 1924, Chequers had already proved its worth both as a place of relaxation and for the quiet determination of policy. Carrying the awesome dual load of the premiership and the Foreign Office – a double role which would be unthinkable today – Ramsay MacDonald was greatly in need of such a sanctuary and he came to love Chequers with a passion.

In the early days of his marriage, MacDonald had bought a cottage at Chesham Bois and was no stranger to Buckinghamshire. A keen walker, he was familiar with the network of footpaths across the Chilterns. In the summer of 1914 he had asked Arthur Lee if he and his sons might walk through the Chequers Park and they had been entertained to lunch. The Chequers scheme was still only a germ of an idea and no-one could have predicted then that Ramsay MacDonald would have a part to play in its future. In the 1920s the Prime Minister's salary of £5,000 a year had to cover all the household expenses of Downing Street, including the provision of linen and china. There were two gas meters, one

James Ramsay MacDonald's window at Chequers

James Ramsay
MacDonald
*at work in his Study
at Chequers,
February 1924.*

for the private quarters and another for public entertainment paid
for by the Treasury. In contrast, at Chequers everything was
provided for a Prime Minister's comfort, including an allowance of
£15 for every weekend he was in residence. It was no wonder
that MacDonald took to his new official residence with such
enthusiasm.

While MacDonald's attachment to Chequers was applauded by
the Cabinet Secretary, Maurice Hankey, who thought it was
having 'a marvellous effect on these Labour people', others
believed that Haldane's fears had come to pass. Instead of seeing
his colleagues on Saturday and Sunday evenings, the Prime
Minister was now cloistered at Chequers, neglecting his duties and
taking evident delight in playing the country gentleman. Harold
Nicolson related in his *Diaries* how he was greeted on the
doorstep at Chequers by the Prime Minister in Lovat plus-fours,
carrying a log in one hand and wielding an axe in the other.
Charlie Chaplin, an overnight guest in 1931, also described his
surprise on meeting the leader of the Labour Party dressed like an
English country squire. The irrepressible comedian had walked
with MacDonald up Beacon Hill, where he had performed his
antics for the 'amusement of the crows'.

MacDonald had been a widower since 1911 and relied on his
eldest daughter Ishbel to take on the role of hostess. This included

Ishbel MacDonald,
the eldest daughter of
James Ramsay
MacDonald.

the formidable task of running No. 10 and it is no wonder that
Chequers became as much of a refuge to her as to her father. In
spite of Ramsay MacDonald's reputation for loving the trappings
of his position, neither of them cared much for the social side of
official life and he was proud of the way his daughter rose to it.
When Ishbel celebrated her twenty-first birthday at Chequers,
little more than a month after MacDonald took office, he wrote in
his diary: 'How happy I am with her. Daily she grows more like
her mother.'

   An invitation to Chequers was much sought after, but few
enjoyed the privilege. MacDonald defended his reluctance to
entertain ministerial colleagues on the grounds that the Trust Deed
did not encourage it. Neither, according to Beatrice Webb, was he
interested in the idea of ministerial tea-parties, when,
accompanied by their wives, ministers 'could make the desirable
acquaintance of Chequers without depriving the Prime Minister
of his weekly rest...' The Webbs neither liked nor trusted

MacDonald, but it rankled with them not to be invited to Chequers, especially since those he did entertain were friends he cultivated outside the Labour party.

MacDonald was a lonely man and he welcomed female companionship at Chequers. Especially welcome were Princess Martha Bibesco, Cecily Gordon-Cumming and Lady Londonderry. Martha Bibesco, the wife of a Romanian Diplomat, loved Chequers, which she described as 'this ancient house of muted ostentation'. She was a frequent overnight guest and corresponded with MacDonald almost weekly until his death. Cecily Gordon-Cumming, the daughter of the Laird of Gordonstoun and only a few years older than Ishbel, used to walk for miles with MacDonald at Chequers and after one of her visits he wrote to urge her to come again but warned her 'not to fall in love with old men'. She married in 1931 and her visits ceased, though they continued to correspond. The Prime Minister's closeness to Lady Londonderry, the famous political hostess, scandalized many of his friends and supporters. They had their political differences and she had strong views about his pacifism during the war, but they were both Highlanders and shared an interest in Gaelic myth and folklore.

Oswald Mosley, who had recently abandoned the Conservatives for the Labour Party, was another frequent guest at Chequers. But it was MacDonald's friendship with Sir Alexander Grant, chairman of McVitie Price, that caused a great furore and contributed to the fall of the first Labour Government. The two men had grown up together and maintained their friendship in spite of the divergence of their careers and politics. Appalled to discover that his friend, despite the pressures of office, still had to travel in the 'tube', Grant lent MacDonald a Daimler motor-car and gave him a parcel of biscuit shares to pay for the running costs. This generous and practical gift might not have presented a problem had it not been closely followed by the appearance of Grant's name in the Honours List. The honours scandal which had tarnished Lloyd George was still fresh in the public memory and MacDonald's detractors used this occasion to cast him in the worst possible light.

Out of this débâcle evolved a strict code with regard to gifts, not only to the Prime Minister but also to every member of the Government. Today, no gift can be accepted if it exceeds £125 in value, unless the difference between that amount and the value of the gift is paid to the Treasury by the recipient. While Lord Lee was alive, he continued to make donations to Chequers, but was circumspect about accepting on its behalf anything from third parties. Since then the Trustees have taken over the role of

Ramsay MacDonald
*with Ishbel and Malcolm
MacDonald, his son.*

protecting both the house and the Prime Minister from the presentation of embarrassing or compromising gifts. During Baldwin's premiership they accepted a car from Ford for use at Chequers, and in Harold Wilson's time the household benefited from a freezer from Bird's Eye. The General Electrical Company's offer to Edward Heath of a British television set to replace a Japanese model was, however, politely refused. Some gifts, though incapable of misinterpretation, can present the Trust with problems. One such example was the Chequers bell offered to Harold Wilson in 1965. When HMS *Chequers*, a destroyer built just before the end of the Second World War, came to the end of her useful life and was destined for the scrapyard, the Ministry of Defence decided to present the ship's bell to the house after which she had been named. Although the gesture was appreciated, the Trustees had no money to pay for its mounting. Three years passed before the presentation could be made and the bell now hangs on an oak frame with dolphin shoulders made by the Dartmouth cadets. As a gong it would raise the dead, so it hangs silently in the east porch.

When the Lees, accompanied by Faith Moore (now a Trustee), were guests for Sunday lunch in July 1924, Lady Lee, characteristically apprehensive, was reassured to find things exactly as they were even down to the scent of the white rose still struggling to climb in the window of her bedroom, which Ishbel now used. She was also pleased to note that, although beset with problems both at home and abroad, the Prime Minister seemed to be responding to the restorative effect of Chequers. In May of the same year the Belgian Premier and Foreign Minister had come to Chequers to negotiate a British commitment to blockade Germany if the Germans defaulted on war reparations. MacDonald was not prepared to give such a commitment but, in June, the French Prime Minister Eduoard Herriot joined MacDonald for a country-house weekend, and their talks paved the way for an inter-allied conference in London. The two Prime Ministers got on well together, and Herriot, whose English was not good enough to conduct negotiations without an interpreter, practised with Ishbel, whom he called 'my little English teacher'.

Ramsay MacDonald's first premiership was a short one. His liaison with the Liberals, upon whom he relied for his majority, had been unhappy from the start and on a Conservative motion of no confidence in October 1924 he lost their shaky support. He spent his last day at Chequers with his daughters and Miss Byvoets, the Dutch housekeeper who had looked after the children since his wife died. In his hour of defeat, the Lees were greatly touched to receive a letter from him of gratitude and appreciation:

*I praise you and congratulate myself that I have shared your
beautiful gift. Every room has become my own and I bid them
farewell in deep sadness of heart – truly the only wrench that the
change has brought.*

He asked if he could leave behind a memoir of his wife Margaret
'which would not be disturbing to the peace of the house'. The
gift was accepted, but for No. 10 and not Chequers, and when his
second book was published in 1925, he gave a copy to the
Chequers library. It was a collection of articles about his walking
tours in Britain and elsewhere, entitled *Wanderings and Excursions*,
which he inscribed 'A ghost for Chequers, May 1925'. On 2
November 1924 he wrote in the Visitors' Book, 'Farewell to this
house of comforting and regenerating rest'. He then escaped on a
walking tour of the West Country, leaving Chequers to Baldwin.

It was five years before Ramsay MacDonald was back, but once
again as Prime Minister of a Government without an overall
majority. To have Chequers to return to was an immense joy and
no weekend was complete without a walk up Beacon Hill where
he became such a familiar sight in fair weather and foul that it
became known as the Prime Minister's Quarter Deck. But his
favourite walks now seemed 'a little dishevelled', he wrote in his
diary, 'like a woman one has not seen for some time and upon
whose person carelessness had been stamped.' Great care had been
taken with the garden but the park was disfigured by dead and
fallen trees, thistles flourished unchecked and rabbits played havoc
on Beacon Hill. In a letter to the secretary of the Trustees, he
drew attention to the neglect, for which he blamed 'the feeble
hand of Toryism'. 'You will not mind my making these
observations,' he wrote, 'because I love the place.'

He also suggested that the old main drive from the south would
be improved by the planting of an avenue of trees. The restoration
of this ancient access was begun by the Lees during the First
World War, using German prisoners-of-war as labourers. It was
called Victory Drive and, later, new entrance gates were added
and two gatehouse lodges built. Lord Lee, however, had already
considered and rejected the idea, and he wrote to MacDonald:

*We know there had not been an avenue in Elizabethan times,
indeed the approach then must have been only a bridle track, and
we felt that for a manor-house of modest proportions an avenue
would be hardly appropriate ... Moreover it would take the best
part of 100 years before it would become sufficiently mature for it
not to be an eyesore.*

Ramsay MacDonald
*with his middle daughter
Joan at Chequers,
February 1924.*

Ramsay MacDonald
*with his daughter
Joan in the Great Hall
and in the Rose Garden
at Chequers.*

It was, however, not only the park which was in need of attention. Lee had worked hard to reclaim and improve the derelict agricultural land around Chequers. When he left, the farms on the estate were given over to the Ministry of Agriculture but the arrangement had proved unsatisfactory to him and to the Trustees. The farm buildings and fences were now in a deplorable condition, with damp, run-down estate cottages and a contaminated water supply which had all the makings of a public scandal. When the survey was extended to the house, a whole Pandora's box of problems was revealed. Extensive decay to both timbers and stonework was discovered inside and out; fungus was much in evidence and dry rot and death-watch beetle had done their worst. The Trust Fund, which had seemed generous in 1921, was inadequate to cover the vast amount of work necessary and in 1927 Parliament voted a grant-in-aid for a major programme of restoration which lasted on and off from 1927 to 1932.

Although Baldwin had his share of the upheaval, it was Ramsay MacDonald who bore the brunt of it, even though the Trustees did all they could to ensure that the Prime Minister's weekends were not disrupted. As the work dragged on, the foreman built himself a house in Princes Risborough, as though he had settled there for life, and MacDonald complained that, since he had resumed occupation, not a single weekend had been free from scaffolding, closed wings, dust and disorder. Eventually, in the interests of speed and efficiency, it was decided to evacuate the house altogether, with Lord Lee supervising the removal of its contents. Ramsay MacDonald went to his native Lossiemouth in Scotland for the summer and the house was up and running again in time for 'a great gusto' of guests to celebrate the wedding of his middle daughter Joan in September 1932.

Walking and reading were Ramsay MacDonald's main activities at Chequers. He also played golf, but so rarely that his game showed little improvement and he was not a regular at the Ellesborough Golf Club, of which the Prime Minister was automatically an honorary member. Having grown up in a household where books were a much coveted luxury, he took a special interest in the Chequers library, which he was also distressed to find so neglected.

Many of the leather-bound books in the Long Gallery were exposed to the north-facing windows and they had become faded and dry. Some were infected with worm and, with no system of cataloguing, many were upside-down and out of sequence. The 'lethal chamber' at the British Museum took care of those with the worm and Ramsay MacDonald offered to apply preserving cream to the rest himself. His application to Baldwin, as chairman of the Pilgrim Trust, for a grant to repair and reorganize the Library had to be refused since Chequers, not a charity, fell outside the remit of the Trust.

Perhaps MacDonald's preoccupation with the state of the house was a distraction from bigger affairs of state. Although the prospects for his second term had at first seemed bright, the optimism did not last. Within a year of his return to office, the Wall Street Crash sent the recovery into reverse. When the Cabinet could not agree on the necessary remedies, the Government resigned and in the following realignment Ramsay MacDonald found himself, with all-party agreement, as the leader of a National Government whose brief was to save the pound and restore confidence at home and abroad.

There was to be no quick fix, however, and when Geoffrey Dawson, editor of *The Times*, visited Chequers in September 1931, the two men came to the conclusion that an election could not be far off. A week later MacDonald was called back from Chequers for a meeting with officials from the Bank of England and the Treasury which resulted in Britain abandoning the gold standard. At the general election in October, the Conservatives unexpectedly won a massive majority, but with a pre-election agreement to retain a National Government, Baldwin, instead of pressing his claim to the premiership, remained Lord President of the Council. MacDonald therefore became Prime Minister of a predominantly Conservative Government – a betrayal in the eyes of the Labour Party, for which he was never forgiven. By the time he reversed roles with Stanley Baldwin in June 1935 he was a broken man, his health deteriorating, his eyesight failing. He remained as Lord President until 1937, when illness finally forced him to retire.

Ramsay MacDonald shared Arthur Lee's belief in the English countryside as a source of healing and refreshment. Earlier, in March 1930, he had broadcast from Chequers – the first Prime Minister to do so – and had paid a graceful tribute to the Lees. Speaking over the Columbia Broadcasting System to North America, he described the gift of Chequers (made possible by Ruth Lee's American wealth) as 'one of the blessings of good relations between our two peoples'. The house which had found its way so deeply into his heart was, he said:

an abode mellow with age and sanctified by the ghosts of vanished generations, given to the nation so that Prime Ministers might know that birds sing, flowers bloom and body and mind may rest.

Ramsay MacDonald
with his daughter
Ishbel in 1937.

NEVILLE CHAMBERLAIN

When Neville Chamberlain became Prime Minister two weeks after the Coronation of King George VI in May 1937, he was sixty-seven – an age at which most men contemplate retirement. But as he told the Party meeting which elected him as leader, he had 'led a sober and temperate life ... and was consequently sound in mind and limb'. Apart from occasional attacks of gout, he was robust and energetic and thought nothing of taking his dog and striding for miles around Chequers, while younger policemen panted at his side.

Chamberlain was an austere man of intellectual arrogance. He was not easy to get to know and did not take any trouble to make himself agreeable to his supporters, still less to his opponents. His Parliamentary Private Secretary, Lord Dunglass (later Sir Alec

Neville Chamberlain's window at Chequers

Douglas-Home) had the devil's own job in persuading him into the smoking room of the House of Commons. He shunned social life and was full of admiration and gratitude to his wife for taking the burden of entertaining from his shoulders. But there was a side of Chamberlain's personality that the public rarely saw: a love of the English countryside that he shared with Douglas-Home. With an almost encyclopaedic knowledge of wildlife, Chamberlain was overwhelmed by the profusion of moths, butterflies and wildflowers to be found on the Chequers estate. He and Annie discovered an infinite variety of walks amongst the boxwoods, and Cymbeline's Mount, Velvet Lawn and Silver Spring – where he was to venture by moonlight to try his luck with a fishing line – soon became favourite haunts. Although they anticipated spending less time at Chequers than the Baldwins, weekends there quickly took precedence over those in Birmingham, the city of his birth where, since 1929, he had represented the constituency of Edgbaston.

The Chamberlains felt that, despite their evident enjoyment of Chequers, the Baldwins had not taken a very intelligent interest in it. Neville's comment to his sister that he and Annie would 'very much enjoy what we can give to Chequers', indicated that he had no intention of being a passive occupant. In particular, he was able to indulge his passion for trees, planting many in the park, even though he could not expect to see the results of his efforts.

Like Ramsay MacDonald, Chamberlain discussed with the Trustees his concerns about the preservation of the woodlands and the feasibility of the Forestry Commission taking over their management. Lee and the Trustees had grave misgivings about the wisdom of such a move, but a lease was signed at the beginning of 1940, by which time the Forestry Commission was being pressed to supply quantities of sound timber for the war effort. 'It will ease our negotiations for timber from private estates,' explained the Commissioners, 'if we can point to definite action on Chequers Estate'. The Prime Minister of the time, Winston Churchill, had no choice but to comply and Chequers, already a recognized source of wood for clarinets and tennis rackets, thus became a supplier of rifle butts to the Ministry of Munitions. In the process, however, the boxwoods of Little Kimble Warren and Happy Valley, some of the finest in the British Isles, were decimated and Velvet Lawn, a Buckinghamshire beauty spot, was inappropriately planted with young conifers. Surveying the devastation, and convinced that the Forestry Commission was acting in breach of the Chequers Estate Act, Lee pleaded for a suspension of the 'massacre'. The Forestry Commission was turned out and the responsibility for the woodlands reverted to the Trustees.

Chamberlain was also taken with the idea of planting the main drive with an avenue of trees and after Lord Lee's predictable refusal, he sent a diagram to his sister revealing an alternative plan. 'This weekend I am having my revenge on Arthur Lee ... I am planting two groups of elms at the corner of the railings and a thicket of thorn and gorse at the end of the straight.' Neither the elms nor the thicket survived, but when the Churchills left Chequers in 1955, their wish to plant an avenue of trees as a gift to the Trust was accepted with alacrity. Lord Lee had died in 1947 and Lady Lee did not protest at the gift. Seeing the mature beech trees flanking Victory Drive in all their autumn glory, it is hard to imagine why there had been so much resistance in the past.

Although the 'pouches' always followed him to Chequers at the weekend, Chamberlain hated to be disturbed there. He never took a private secretary with him and the only telephone was in the pantry. Through the changing seasons he was enchanted by Chequers. If the weather or an attack of gout prevented him from

Neville Chamberlain
at his desk at Chequers.

getting out to examine his nesting boxes or root out undergrowth in Crow Close, he was plunged into gloom. He enjoyed showing his sisters his plans for the garden and liked to walk with his daughter to the top of Coombe Hill and sit in the sun by the Boer War Memorial, with the great Vale of Aylesbury spread out before them. It was with immense effort that he tore himself away from Chequers to return to the problems forced upon him by Franco, Mussolini and Hitler.

For his wife Annie, often exhausted by entertaining at Downing Street, Chequers was a veritable haven. She believed that a place such as Chequers, 'which one loves – where one can be oneself and do things upside down if one likes all day long', was a necessity. They shared it sparingly for, seeing the immense pleasure that other people derived from their brief visits to Chequers, she felt that the sacrifice of privacy was worth making now and again.

In October 1937 the Chamberlains succeeded, where Lloyd George and the Baldwins failed, in persuading the Lees to stay for the weekend. Conscious of the sensitivity of the occasion, the Chamberlains had gone to great pains to ensure that their guests' return to the house would be free from any awkwardness.

The Lees were met at Chequers by their own butler, who had stayed on. Mrs Chamberlain greeted them with the news that the Prime Minister was unfortunately laid up in bed with gout, but the other guests in the party – the Lord Chancellor and Lady Hailsham and the Cabinet Secretary Maurice Hankey and his wife – were old friends. Torrential rain prevented them from going out and after tea in the Long Gallery, Lee was shown to Neville's bedside, where the Prime Minister lobbied him about the avenue of trees for the south drive. Nonetheless it was gratifying for the Lees to see how much the Chamberlains appreciated Chequers and they left with a deep sense of pride that the scheme appeared to be working exactly as planned.

Shortly after the visit, Lee presented the Prime Minister with a silver inkwell which he had designed and inscribed in Latin. The inscription (see right) could be said to characterize Chamberlain's philosophy in a term of office dominated by the growing threat from Nazi Germany. But his tireless attempts to divert the gathering storm by diplomatic means were not to be rewarded. As the crisis mounted, it was clear that Chequers provided Chamberlain with a sanctuary where he was able to renew his strength and refresh his spirit. Returning from Munich, however, to the cheers of the multitudes clinging in hope to Disraeli's immortal phrase, 'Peace for our time', he came back to Chequers in a state of deep depression.

At this difficult time Chamberlain was greatly moved by the presentation from Lord Lee of an eighteenth-century silver-gilt dessert service for Chequers, inscribed with the words, 'In grateful homage to Neville Chamberlain'. In a letter to Lord Lee, he thanked him for the 'great and lasting honour, which I value all the more because I am so devoted to Chequers and get such infinite pleasure out of the use of it that I do want my memory to be somehow associated with it after I have gone'.

Within the year, Hitler had occupied Prague. Everything Chamberlain had worked for and believed in had crashed in ruins, and hope had turned to despair. Once England was at war with Germany, the solace of Chequers became still more important to him as a buffer against the overwhelming affairs of state. But Chamberlain, who only survived in office for eight months after

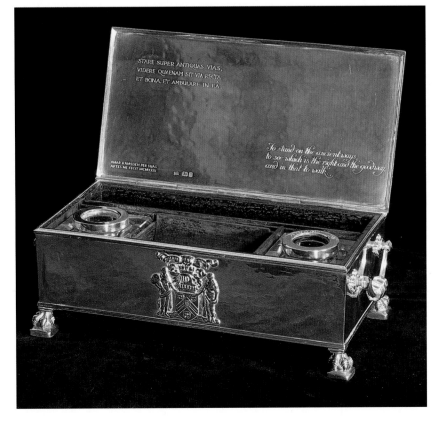

A silver and gold casket inkstand *Made by Omar Ramsden in 1931, designed by Lord Lee. His arms, carved from a single piece of gold, embellish the front. The Latin inscription inside the lid reads: 'To stand on the ancient ways, to see which is the right and the good way, and in that to walk.' In 1937, Lord Lee presented the inkstand to Neville Chamberlain. It stands on the desk in the Prime Minister's Study.*

Neville Chamberlain
at Chequers,
March 1939.

the outbreak of war, found the burden of decisions which would send men to their deaths insupportable. 'I groan in spirit over every life lost and home blasted,' he wrote to the Archbishop of Canterbury at Christmas 1939. Many Conservatives who had acclaimed the Munich Agreement now raised their voices in dissent and lack of co-operation from the Opposition was making Chamberlain's position untenable. In May 1940, in a censure motion in the House of Commons, his majority plummeted from around 200 to 81 and, since a National Government under his leadership was impossible, Chamberlain resigned.

With his official occupancy of Chequers over, Chamberlain wrote to his sister of the happy times they had enjoyed at Chequers, but that it was 'difficult to see how there can be much more happiness for any of us.' The wrench of having to part with the place to which he had grown so attached compounded the pain and distress caused by the circumstances of his departure from office. He and his wife returned one evening to say goodbye and collect his saw. Jones, the gardener, was in tears and needed no encouragement to take special care of the trees that Chamberlain had planted – the magnolias on the north lawn, the liquidamber, the tulip trees, the red oaks and the flowering cherries. Chamberlain gave him a copy of William Robinson's *English Flower Gardens,* in which he had written: 'In grateful appreciation of his unfailing help and interest in my endeavours to improve the gardens and trees at Chequers during three happy years there.'

Chamberlain's last months of life were poignant. Fiercely loyal to the new leader, he continued to serve in the National Government as Lord President of the Council, but he was already suffering from an inoperable cancer and he retired completely from public life a few months later. His illness denied him all the pleasures of the countryside that had been so much a part of his life and he did not live long enough to see Hitler, that 'most detestable and bigoted' man, destroyed and a liberated Europe re-established. Chamberlain had often said that he wanted his ashes to be scattered in Crow Close at Chequers, but when he died in November 1940 they were buried in Westminster Abbey, next to the tomb of Bonar Law. Having refused both a peerage and the Order of the Garter, he is commemorated with a simple coat of arms in a window in the Long Gallery. A tulip tree which he planted was designated as his memorial tree and it thrives gracefully for all to see as they approach the east forecourt. Still at Chequers as a reminder of his interest is an album of striking photographs taken by Chamberlain of some of the magnificent trees in the park.

WINSTON CHURCHILL

Winston Churchill's first visit to Chequers was in February 1921, just a month after Lloyd George had taken up residence. 'Here I am,' Churchill wrote to his wife. 'You wld [sic] like to see this place. Perhaps you will some day! It is just the kind of house you admire – a panelled museum full of history, full of treasures – but insufficiently warmed. Anyhow, a wonderful possession.' It was, not, however, until June 1940, when the evacuation from Dunkirk was at its height, that he was able to introduce his family to Chequers. Over the next five years almost everyone of any consequence connected with the allied war effort visited him there, and a weekend without house-guests was rare.

As it became increasingly difficult to obtain civilian domestic staff during the war, the house was run by volunteers from the ATS (Army Training School) and the WAAF (Women's Auxiliary Air Force), an arrangement which proved so successful that it was continued after the war. Under the capable management of the curator Miss Grace Lamont, the staff often had to cope with as many as three shifts of guests in a single weekend, as an endless stream of special advisers, politicians, diplomats, chiefs of staff and foreign guests flowed in and out.

Members of the Churchill family were almost always there. In November 1940 Pamela, the wife of his only son Randolph, gave birth to 'little' Winston – the first child born at Chequers since a kitchen maid unexpectedly increased the household overnight in 1910. Winston was baptised in Ellesborough Church, an occasion celebrated by an almost full turn-out of Churchills to lunch at Chequers after the service. The two elder married daughters, Sarah Oliver and Diana Sandys, often stayed for the weekend with their husbands. Mary, the youngest daughter, who was evacuated to Chequers during the Blitz and worked for the WRVS (Women's Royal Voluntary Service) in Aylesbury until she joined the ATS, looked forward to the weekends when the

Winston Churchill's window at Chequers

Winston Churchill
with his cigar.

'great gloomy' house came alive again. For Clementine Churchill,
however, who was always unstinting in her efforts to create an
atmosphere of comfort and calm, the weekends offered little
respite from the busy week in Downing Street.

Nobody came to Chequers expecting a long night's sleep.
Dinner was followed by discussion over the brandy and cigars and
a late-night film show in the Long Gallery. Sometimes the film
show was merely an intermission. On one occasion Churchill
watched the whole of *Gone with the Wind* with Anthony Eden,
then discussed the North Africa campaign until 3am. Finding it
impossible to cope with Churchill's nocturnal habits, Eden would
not go to Chequers if it could be avoided. For Field-Marshal Sir
Alan Brooke (later Viscount Alanbrooke), two years as Chief of
the Imperial General Staff had felt like ten. His diary describes
one evening at Chequers when, after a late dinner and even later
film show, the party adjourned to the Great Hall to discuss the
impending operations in North Africa and the Mediterranean. At

2:30am Churchill called for sandwiches and then, to a tune on the gramophone, capered around the Great Hall, pausing occasionally in front of the fireplace to deliver one of his epigrams. The Field-Marshal often wondered what Hitler would have made of Churchill in his siren suit demonstrating bayonet drill in the Great Hall.

In addition to attendant secretaries, detectives, switchboard operators and Churchill's chauffeur and valet, Chequers absorbed the staff of the Prime Minister's private office, without whom he can travel nowhere and who became part of the extended family. As a working environment, it was a welcome change from London. 'If only there wasn't such a rush,' wrote John Martin, Churchill's private secretary, in his diary, 'this work in a house, instead of an ordinary office, would be very pleasant. I'm afraid it will be very spoiling.' There was time, however, for the occasional walk in the park and even for games of croquet on the north lawn when Churchill wasn't using it for rifle practise or demonstrating some new explosive device.

John ('Jock') Colville, Churchill's junior private secretary, found it curious to stay in a country house not as a guest but on fairly close terms with the family. He never knew with whom he might be sitting down at dinner. Professor Lindemann, Churchill's old friend and scientific adviser, General Ismay, Deputy Secretary (Military) War Cabinet, Air Vice-Marshal Portal, Chief of the Air Staff Lord Mountbatten, General Eisenhower and Field Marshal Smuts were among those who came at various times to discuss the strategy of war. The first time John Martin visited Chequers he

The Long Gallery
facing east
*In wartime the Long
Gallery was turned into
a cinema.*

Anti-aircraft guns
on nearby Beacon Hill.

found there Lord Gort, Chief of the Imperial General Staff, and
Lord Dowding, Commander-in-Chief Fighter Command, and
among 'the lesser fry', he noted in his diary, was General de
Gaulle, who had taken refuge in Britain as leader of the Free
French. There was also Nelson, Churchill's fine black cat, who
liked to sit on a chair beside the Prime Minister and who, like
Mary Churchill, was an evacuee from London. Churchill had
found him at the Admiralty and taken him to Downing Street,
where he had held his own against the resident No. 10 cat,
Treasury Bill. 'Try to remember,' Churchill used to tell Nelson,
who was afraid of gunfire, 'what those boys in the RAF are
doing.' At Chequers Nelson slept on the bed, curled up on
Churchill's feet and Churchill was fond of telling people that, in
saving fuel as a hot-water bottle, the cat was more use to the war
effort than they were.

Although the Lees had installed central heating at a time when
it was by no means standard practice in British homes, it was
never really warm at Chequers. Great care was taken to conserve
fuel and it was a struggle to heat the house. Churchill virtually
lived in his siren suit and only the very hardy arrived at Chequers
without warm pyjamas and extra underwear. Commander C.R.
('Tommy') Thompson, Churchill's ADC, used to stuff sheets
around the window frames to keep the snow and the draughts
out, but it was President Roosevelt's special envoy Harry Hopkins
who really suffered from the cold. After the United States had
been drawn into the war, Hopkins made frequent visits to

A firewatcher's observation hut *on the roof above Winston Churchill's bedroom.*

A sentry box at Chequers

Chequers on the President's behalf and, although he described Chequers as 'this lovely old place', his fragile health caused him misery there in the winter months. His method of keeping warm when reading his papers was to wrap up in his overcoat and huddle in a ground-floor cloakroom, the only room small enough to benefit from any body-heat he might generate. He promised Mrs Churchill that he would try and raise enough money after the war to have proper central heating installed.

Once France had fallen, in the summer of 1940, the threat of invasion was taken very seriously and every effort was made to make Chequers as safe from attack as possible. A company of Coldstream Guards was billeted in Nissen huts along Lime Walk, anti-aircraft guns appeared on Beacon Hill and the park bristled with barbed wire. The usual air-raid precautions – along with sandbags, black-out curtains, gas masks and tin hats – were in force and, in case of an emergency dash to London, there was always an armoured car on stand-by.

In a hut on the roof close to the Prime Minister's bedroom was a 'spotter' in direct communication with the Observer Corps. To avoid drawing attention to the fact that Chequers was a target worth bombing, however, instructions were given not to open fire unless air attack was inevitable. In fact, Chequers was a clearly identifiable target from the air, easily located between Beacon Hill and Coombe Hill, the latter plain to see with the Boer War Memorial on its summit. On moonlit nights, when the landscape was virtually illuminated – with Victory Drive pointing to the

Winston Churchill and
Mackenzie King
in the garden at
Chequers in 1941.

house like an arrow – Chequers was particularly vulnerable to
night bombers. The memorial was relatively easy to camouflage
but Victory Drive proved more of a problem. At first, tennis court
stain was applied to the gravel, but this was soon worn away by
army vehicles. Then it was turfed over, but no sooner had this
been completed than Mr Randag, the tenant farmer – zealously
digging for victory – ploughed up the semi-circle of grass at the
end of the drive, thereby defeating the object of the exercise.

When the moon was full, it was Mr and Mrs Ronald Tree who
provided an alternative retreat, welcoming the whole Churchill
retinue into their home at Ditchley Park, Oxfordshire. (Ronald
Tree, M.P. for Harborough in Leicester, had been a staunch

GLASS
FROM
HOUSES OF
PARLIAMENT.
GERMAN AIR RAID
10 MAY, 1941.

Fragments of
stained glass
*These were salvaged
from the Houses of
Parliament after a
German air-raid in
May 1941.*

supporter of Churchill's campaign for rearmament.) But, although
Great Missenden received its share of bombs, Chequers
experienced a few near-misses but no direct hits. When Arthur
Lee attributed this immunity to the fact that Hitler did not want
to be bombed at Berchtesgaden, Churchill's response was
predictably robust: 'There has been no reciprocity with Hitler on
that or any other matter, and so far as I'm concerned I would
bomb the bastard wherever I could find him.'

One of Churchill's favourite ports of call was the operations
room at the Uxbridge headquarters in Middlesex of No. 11
Fighter Group, which controlled the air approaches over the
home counties. In July 1940, as London and the south-east came
under heavy bombardment, he followed the course of one battle
as it raged in the sky overhead. In the car travelling back to
Chequers with General Ismay, Churchill spoke the immortal
words: 'Never in the field of human conflict was so much owed
by so many to so few.' The words burned themselves into the
General's mind as they did into the mind of the nation when
Churchill used them again a week later, in the House of
Commons.

When the Battle of Britain was at its peak, Churchill was once again at Uxbridge following the progress of Fighter Command. 'The odds were great; the margins small; the stakes infinite,' he wrote afterwards. In this decisive engagement the Royal Air Force had the edge, and once the all-clear sounded Churchill returned exhausted to Chequers, where he put on a black eye mask and went to bed.

Chequers was the conduit for news both good and bad from the front, for Churchill was never out of touch. He was there in May 1941 when the devastating report came in that HMS *Hood* had been sunk by the *Bismarck* with the loss of 1,500 seamen. In December, on the wireless after dinner, he heard of the Japanese attack on Pearl Harbour. 'We shall declare war on Japan,' Churchill announced to his companions. The American Ambassador Gilbert Winant doubted the wisdom of declaring war on the strength of a wireless announcement and put a call through to the White House. 'We're all in the same boat now,' confirmed Roosevelt. When Churchill went to bed that night, the scale of the attack was not known, but he slept easier in the knowledge that within hours the United States would be at war with Japan on the side of the Allies. Two months later the Japanese took Singapore, and Churchill broadcast the grim news to the nation from the Hawtrey Room.

Although since 1940 the Parliamentary Labour Party had refused to allow Churchill's speeches in the House of Commons to be broadcast, he made full use of the wireless and many of his most stirring wartime speeches were made from Chequers.

Churchill's bedroom in wartime

Amongst them was the speech to Britain and the Empire in February 1941 which concluded, 'Give us the tools and we will finish the job' and two months later he was able to announce that the Americans had at last committed themselves to helping Britain with the production of munitions.

On 20 June 1941 Churchill arrived at Chequers, preoccupied with intelligence reports that Hitler was on the verge of attacking Russia. The Soviet Government had shrugged off the warnings, but at 4am on Sunday Jock Colville received the confirmation that the expected invasion had taken place and that German forces were making a rapid advance on a broad front. With orders only to disturb the Prime Minister in the event of an invasion of Britain, Colville did not wake him until 7:30am, when the news was received with trepidation, for if Russia was defeated, the Germans would turn on Britain. Along the corridor Anthony Eden received the news from Churchill's valet, together with the Prime Minister's compliments and a cigar on a silver salver. Churchill spent the whole day preparing his evening broadcast to the nation. He worked in bed, as was his custom, until lunchtime and in the afternoon he worked in his study or on a bench in the shelter of a yew hedge, from where he strode out across the garden, testing the powerful phrases. His secretaries transcribed the pages of his manuscript and then listened to the wireless in the Curator's sitting room checking his delivery against the script.

In his evening broadcast from the Hawtrey Room, Churchill promised the nation:

The Hawtrey Room
in wartime

We will never parley, we will never negotiate with Hitler or any of his gang. We shall fight him by land, we shall fight him by sea, we shall fight him in the air, until with God's help we have rid the earth of his shadow and liberated its peoples from his yoke.

In May 1942, a year after the German invasion of Russia, the Soviet Foreign Minister, Vyacheslav Molotov came to Britain with a Soviet-American draft communiqué concerning the creation of a second front in Europe. The talks were planned to be held in London but, at Molotov's request, arrangements were made for him and the Soviet Ambassador Ivan Maisky to stay at Chequers. Russian visits always presented Chequers with a challenge, but nobody was prepared for the size of the delegation which alighted from the train at Wendover.

The story of their arrival at Chequers has become part of Chequers history. Molotov was greeted by a Guard of Honour in the east forecourt where, to Ambassador Maisky's horror and the delight of the Coldstream Guards, Molotov attempted to give his host's famous 'V' sign but only managed a two-fingered salute of a different kind. He then harangued the troops for not being at the front. After some argument, the Ambassador was prevailed upon to persuade some of the delegation to return to London. Amongst the strange house-guests who remained was a typist who could not operate a typewriter, a bodyguard who turned out to be a Russian General travelling incognito and a secretary who refused to let his briefcase out of his sight, even when being introduced to the mysteries of croquet on the north lawn. Extraordinary precautions were taken for Molotov's personal safety, but when the housekeeper knocked on his door to ask him to observe the black-out, she was terrified to be confronted by Molotov waving a revolver. A collective sigh of relief went up when the Russians left for Washington with an Anglo-Soviet treaty of friendship, but with no guarantees of a second front much before 1943.

The need to offer endless hospitality made enormous demands on resources and the limitations of the ration books caused great concern both at Chequers and No. 10. In 1941 alone there were 432 lunches and dinners for the Army, Navy and Air Force top brass, political figures and diplomats. There were requests for extra diplomatic coupons for butter, margarine, cooking fat, cheese and tea and a shortage of soap meant that Miss Lamont was having trouble keeping the house clean for the guests, and the guests clean in the house. If the rations were stretched a bit, so was the ingenuity, although early arrangements for supplying Chequers with fresh eggs were not strictly in accordance with Ministry of Food regulations.

The pantry at
Chequers in wartime

The kitchen at
Chequers in wartime

Among the guests at Chequers who were able to bring a little light relief were Noel Coward and the Russian pianist Benno Moiseiwitsch. Moiseiwitsch, who was involved with Mrs Churchill's Aid to Russia Fund, played Chopin brilliantly and was not in the least put out by Churchill's comment that what mattered in music were 'the silences between the notes'. His virtuoso party-piece, however, involved rolling a couple of oranges up and down the keyboard, playing a selection of popular tunes without his fingers touching the keys. Noel Coward came to Chequers twice and loved indulging Churchill's request for his song 'Don't let's be beastly to the Germans', which had been censored by the Ministry of Information.

By December 1944 the Germans had withdrawn from Greece, and Churchill and Anthony Eden, anxious to prevent the Communists from taking power, left for Athens on Christmas Eve. A huge party of Churchill family and friends were left at Chequers to celebrate their last wartime Christmas there. But when peace came to Europe in May 1945, they were all gathered together at Chequers and the euphoria of victory was palpable. The principal topic of discussion, however, was the general election. Should the Government go to the country straight away and capitalize on Germany's defeat or should it wait for the defeat of Japan as well? While Anthony Eden favoured a June election, Rab Butler preferred to wait. But it was the Labour Party which refused to continue the National Government and Churchill resigned on 23 May 1945 and the election was called for 5 July.

The Lion and the Mouse
Rubens and F Snyders
This enormous canvas, depicting one of Aesop's fables, is one of the most important paintings in the house; it is on the Chequers inventory of 1837/8. Until recently it was hung high up on the east wall of the Great Hall, where the mouse was barely visible. As the story goes, late one night, Churchill called for his paints and brushes and, with the aid of a step-ladder, proceeded to highlight the mouse. Arthur Lee would surely have been horrified that anyone should dare to touch up a Rubens, even if the then Prime Minister was an accomplished artist in his own right.

In 1973, the Trustees loaned the picture to the Churchill Centenary Trust's exhibition. When it was returned to Chequers several months later, the painting had been cleaned and was minus Churchill's brushwork. It now hangs in the Great Parlour, at a height where the mouse is clearly visible.

In the meantime, the King asked Churchill to form a caretaker administration which, for the first time in five years, was a predominantly Conservative one. While the work of Government went on, Chequers was still a hub of activity and Churchill was reported to be in ebullient spirits by those who visited him there during the election campaign. Duncan Sandys, his son-in-law, and Sir Alexander Cadogan, Permanent Secretary at the Foreign Office, found him cheerfully sunning himself on the lawn, wearing his siren suit and a ten-gallon hat. Dinner that night, Cadogan revealed, was cold roast beef and mince pies, washed down with plenty of port and brandy, which were much better than the 'damned bad film' which followed it.

Churchill broadcast the first party political speech of the campaign from Chequers and drafted it with the same laborious care that went into all his speeches. But the words 'some form of Gestapo' (which he used to describe a necessary socialist 'political police') provoked widespread criticism. It was three weeks after polling day before counting could begin, to allow for all the service votes flown home from across the world. Churchill was devastated by the result: nobody had expected him to lose and his family and friends were stunned by the scale of the defeat.

A few days after the declaration Churchill was at Chequers, coming to terms with the dramatic change in his circumstances. With him were his wife, his brother Jack, his son and three daughters, together with Professor Lindemann (now Lord Cherwell), Brendan Bracken M.P., Jock Colville and the American Ambassador. There were games of cards and croquet, one last film to watch in the Long Gallery, but there were no dispatch riders speeding their way to Chequers with red boxes and there was no strategy to discuss. Playing Gilbert and Sullivan on the wind-up gramophone did little to dispel the gloom and it was late, as ever, when the family escorted Churchill to bed. Over champagne at lunch the next day, reflecting on the problems facing the new Government, Churchill became philosophical. 'They are perfectly entitled to vote as they please,' he said. 'This is democracy, this is what we have been fighting for.' Under his signature that day in the Visitors' Book, Winston Churchill wrote 'FINIS'.

In fact it was far from finished, for Churchill was one of only four Prime Ministers who returned for another innings. The second time, however, he spent many more weekends at his home Chartwell, although he continued to entertain officially at Chequers. In many ways the routine there had not changed and neither had the house. There were still weekends in the company of Field-Marshal Montgomery, Brendan Bracken and Lord Cherwell; a late dinner was still followed by a film, and with British troops in Korea, belligerent noises emanating from the Soviet Union and trouble in the Middle East, there was much to discuss into the early hours of the morning. Peter Thorneycroft (later Chancellor of the Exchequer) could remember how content young men were to sit at the great man's feet, listening to his vision of the future. A few weeks later, this late-night philosophy would reappear, fully fledged, on the floor of the House of Commons.

At this time Churchill was both preparing *The History of the English-Speaking Peoples* for publication and revising the second edition of *The Second World War*. He dictated anywhere and everywhere – even while sitting for the painter Graham Sutherland, who completed his controversial portrait of Churchill at Chequers. The portrait had been commissioned by the House of Commons to celebrate his eightieth birthday in November 1954. Sutherland allowed no-one so much as a glimpse of the canvas, but he carried out a number of sketches of the work in progress, and Lord Beaverbrook subsequently presented one of these Chequers sketches to the Beaverbrook Library in Nova

Winston Churchill *giving his famous V-for-Victory sign.*

Winston Churchill
*with Mrs Churchill,
Anthony Eden, then
Foreign Secretary, and
his bride Clarissa
Spencer Churchill, the
Prime Minister's niece,
in 1952.*

Scotia. When the portrait was finally unveiled, Churchill loathed it on sight and it never saw the light of day again.

The sculptor Oscar Nemon found Churchill an unpredictable subject, except at Chequers where he was much more relaxed. A Nemon bust of Churchill was commissioned by the Queen for the Queen's Guard Chamber at Windsor, by which Churchill was greatly honoured. This time, instead of dictating, he worked on his own clay model of Nemon and the sculptor was so impressed with the result that he later had it cast.

At the beginning of 1955, as the Government went into its fourth year, it was clear that Churchill would not be able to contest another election as Prime Minister. In early March, Churchill made his last important speech in the House of Commons; and on 5 April he resigned. The following day, after a final visit to Chequers in low spirits, he arrived back at Chartwell. Reporters mingled with the crowd of well-wishers. 'How does it feel not to be Prime Minister?' one of them shouted. 'It's always nice to come home,' he replied.

CLEMENT ATTLEE

Not even in his most optimistic dreams did Clement Attlee imagine that he could win the post-war general election. Churchill's wartime prestige would have seemed to make a Conservative victory a foregone conclusion. But with a compelling programme of employment, housing, welfare and promises to bring the 'boys' home quickly, the Labour Party won a landslide victory, and Attlee became Prime Minister of the first Labour administration to hold office with an overall majority.

Since the formation of the Wartime Coalition, when Chamberlain made way for Churchill, Attlee had been officially regarded as Deputy Prime Minister. He chaired the War Cabinet and Defence Committee when Churchill was away on war business, and excelled in his responsibility for the day-to-day running of the Government's affairs in the House of Commons. His wartime visits to Chequers, some with his wife Violet, encouraged him to look forward to their new home.

Clement Attlee's window at Chequers

Clement Richard Attlee, P.C., C.H., M.P.
Prime Minister July 1945-Feb 1950-Oct 1951

Jock Colville, who continued for a while as Attlee's Private Secretary, accompanied him to Chequers for his first official visit. It was apparent that things would be different now. Mrs Churchill's excellent cook was replaced by a new arrival from the ATS and, although Colville admitted that she did her best, her cooking was not in the same class. There was also an air of formality with the new Prime Minister favouring a stiff shirt and wing collar, in contrast to Churchill's habitual siren-suit over which, for dinner, he would sometimes wear a brightly patterned silk dressing gown, described by Lord Alanbrooke as his 'coat of many colours'. Colville found Mrs Attlee welcoming and friendly, but missed Mrs Churchill's caustic comments. He also welcomed the earlier nights and the more homely atmosphere that prevailed after the frenetic days of the war.

The entire Attlee family signed the Visitors' Book in August 1945. Unless the Prime Minister had engagements out of town, they stayed at Chequers every weekend and quickly came to appreciate the friendly hospitality of the house. Chequers was now run by Mrs Kathleen Hill, Churchill's private secretary for many years who had taken over when Grace Lamont retired at the end of 1945.

Games of tennis and croquet were popular on the north lawn and Churchill's cinema looked as if it would be a permanent feature. The complement of weekend staff always included two cinema operators, No. 10 kept a record of recently released films and occasionally there was a preview of a new film.

In 1948, H. Clifford Smith, Keeper of the Victoria & Albert Museum who acted as adviser to the Trustees, visited Chequers with Lady Lee. He was greatly embarrassed to find the Long Gallery still disfigured by projection equipment and rows of tubular steel chairs. An earlier small fire in the projection box had served as a warning of the fire risk, and the Attlees were now restricted to a limited range of fire-resistant 16mm films. But Lady Lee had no wish to deprive the Prime Minister of his film show. Numerous alternative plans were drawn up which would not infringe the Trust Deed, but none of them came to fruition. On high days and holidays films continued to be shown in the Hawtrey Room, where the screen and projector were set up as needed and the operator was on stand-by. In due course, the cinema gave way to the video film and satellite television.

Like their predecessors, the Attlees never tired of the park and surrounding countryside. In fact, they became so attached to Buckinghamshire that they bought Cherry Tree Cottage in Prestwood, just six miles from Chequers, so as to have somewhere to settle when the time came to leave.

At Chequers, Attlee also entertained his Parliamentary colleagues, amongst them Hugh Dalton, Chancellor of the Exchequer, Ernest Bevin, Foreign Secretary, Sir Stafford Cripps, President of the Board of Trade, and Aneurin Bevan, at the Ministry of Health and Housing; in contrast to Churchill's day, their wives were welcome too. Hugh Dalton found the house a little overpowering, 'like living in a museum, but very peaceful if you are prepared to let it be, and not try to find out all about everything'; but he and his wife enjoyed the obligatory walk in the beechwoods. Another guest, the Member of Parliament for Ormskirk who succeeded Stafford Cripps to become the youngest Cabinet minister at the age of thirty-one, was Harold Wilson. Attlee regarded Chequers as a great asset for entertaining foreign visitors, amongst whom, attending the Heads of Government meeting in January 1951, was Jawaharlal Nehru, the first Prime Minister of independent India.

Clement Attlee
with General Smuts.

In his autobiography Attlee recalls the many pleasant memories of Chequers shared by his family. They spent every Christmas there and on Boxing Day, the Prime Minister gave a party for the children of the estate workers and his private office. As they left, Attlee would stand on the doorstep to give each child a bag of sweets.

For many years the Chequers Trust Fund had been finding it increasingly difficult to meet all the expenses of Chequers, and during the war Churchill had even offered to waive his weekly allowance. In the end it was a Labour Government – with Labour Trustees – which decided that the Ministry of Public Buildings and Works should take on the full responsibility for maintenance of the house, leaving the Trustees simply to manage the domestic side. This arrangement seemed appropriate to the Lees, since Chequers had so emphatically proved its worth to the Government. 'The Labour Government,' Ruth Lee wrote in her diary, 'has certainly adopted Chequers almost as a pet child as no Conservative Government would ever dare to have done.'

In a period of post-war austerity, however, it was still no easier to get things done. For three years Mrs Attlee had complained about the garage roof leaking on to the family car, until eventually she offered to pay for the repairs herself. But the Attlees, who were far from extravagant, practised the same economies as the rest of the nation and they were mortified to be accused of burning fires in every room during the coal shortage of the freezing winter of 1947. Mrs Hill believed the rumours, which were quite untrue, to have come from a sacked coal-merchant. The plan to install wash-basins in some of the bedrooms was also postponed because wash-basins were in short supply and it was not considered good politics to install at Chequers what was not available for new houses elsewhere. Even before the days of political correctness, when the Old Berkeley West Hunt met at Chequers again after the war, it met in the south park rather than the east forecourt and the Attlees were advised to keep their distance.

There was much clearing up to be done at Chequers after the war, removing the camouflage and barbed-wired defences and taking down the barracks that had sprung up along Lime Walk. By 1947 the Nissen huts had gone, though the foundations remained, but the eastern entrance was in a sorry state. The lodge was dilapidated and the walls had been knocked down so often by army vehicles that all attempts at repair had been abandoned. Now even the public was complaining that visitors were receiving entirely the wrong impression of the Prime Minister's country residence, and the War office was asked to give the matter priority.

When the Labour Party lost the 1951 general election, Churchill had no wish to hustle the Attlees out of Chequers or No. 10. 'My wife and I,' he wrote, 'will not be coming to C for at least a month, so pray use it in any way convenient.' The previous year's election had left the Labour Government with a majority of five, and Attlee felt he needed a larger one to face the increasingly difficult economic situation. Had he won he would have been the first Prime Minister to win three consecutive election victories, but it was to be thirteen years before another Labour Prime Minister became the official occupant of Chequers. This was Harold Wilson, who described Attlee as 'the most reluctant of Prime Ministers'. Attlee was often underrated by his opponents and colleagues, but his achievements in government were considerable. He was perhaps one of the few Prime Ministers who left office satisfied with what he had accomplished. His epigram sums it up:

> *Few thought he was even a starter.*
> *There were many who thought themselves smarter.*
> *But he ended PM, CH and OM,*
> *An Earl and a Knight*
> *Of the Garter.*

Clement Attlee
*with Mrs Attlee at the
Durham Miners' Gala.*

POSTSCRIPT

In the early summer of 1994 I invited Attlee's youngest daughter, Lady Felicity Harwood, to come and see her father's stained glass window in the Long Gallery – this was a simple shield with his name and dates, for he had made no attempt to update it when the Queen conferred an earldom on him in 1955. After lunch we sat in the sunshine on the terrace before walking round to inspect Attlee's memorial tree in the east park; he had planted this fine hornbeam the day after his sixty-fourth birthday in 1947.

To mark the fiftieth anniversary of Attlee's premiership in August 1995, a surprise party was arranged by the family. After a picnic under an ancient tree in the park, they came back for a drink in the Long Gallery, where Attlee's great-grandsons investigated the secret door and were fascinated by the sight of Cromwell's 'head', stowed away in a drawer.

ANTHONY EDEN

When Anthony Eden succeeded Winston Churchill in April 1955, he was no stranger to Chequers. He saw the house for the first time in 1926, during Baldwin's first premiership, on 'a day of glorious sunshine and beautiful autumn colouring'. As the Foreign Secretary's PPS, he was helping to entertain the South African and Canadian Prime Ministers during the Imperial Conference. Among the fellow guests on that occasion were the Attorney General Sir Douglas Hogg, and the Colonial Secretary Leo Amery. Eden had been very hospitably received, although he was somewhat overwhelmed by what he described as the 'plethora of Prime Ministers'. With a collector's interest in the pictures, his attention had been particularly caught by Joshua Reynolds' self-portrait, Rembrandt's *Mathematician* and the Philips pastoral

Anthony Eden's window at Chequers

Sir Robert Anthony Eden. K.G., P.C., M.C., M.P. Prime Minister, April 1955 – January 1957

conversation pieces. The house he thought was 'much spoiled' on one side but 'very beautiful' on the other. In 1935, under Baldwin, Eden had become the youngest ever Foreign Secretary. But his relationship with Baldwin's successor was soured during the critical period of appeasement by a fundamental disagreement with Chamberlain's strategy for dealing with Mussolini. In his memoirs, however, Eden recalls a visit to Chequers in 1938, where he found Neville Chamberlain in excellent spirits, in spite of the gloom of the house and the widening rift between them. Eden resigned later in the year but was back in Government after the outbreak of war for two short periods as Secretary of State for the Dominions and Secretary of State for War, before being summoned to Chequers by Churchill to learn of his reappointment as Foreign Secretary, a post he held in both of Churchill's administrations, for ten years in all.

Notwithstanding Eden's dread of the late-night sessions at Chequers during the war, he was a frequent if reluctant visitor, especially when dragged away from his own garden in Wiltshire. On one occasion, after retiring exhausted at 1:15am, he accompanied Churchill on a morning walk to Happy Valley, where the Prime Minister, who had carried out some imaginative water schemes at Chartwell, explained how he planned to create an electrically driven waterfall.

Eden's second wife Clarissa, whom he married in 1952, was Churchill's only niece and therefore knew Chequers well. The Edens had not much cared for the Foreign Secretary's official country residence of Dorneywood (given to the nation in 1943 by Lord Courtauld-Thomson, following Lord Lee's example) and they had been loathe to leave their Wiltshire cottage at weekends. But once Eden became Prime Minister, they used Chequers often, soon recognizing its magical effect on his health and disposition.

The Edens took a close interest in everything to do with Chequers, including the management of the woodlands. They were particularly saddened by the removal of shrubbery, lilac bushes and the fine amphitheatre of yew on the north side where Churchill liked to sit during the war, and where seclusion was now no longer possible. An enthusiastic and creative gardener, Lady Eden reorganized the cultivation of the gardens to eliminate bedding-out, arranged for more fruit to be grown in the walled kitchen garden and improved the efficiency of the greenhouses. A replanting scheme for the south garden was abandoned in favour of her plan to incorporate many of her favourite, fragrant old-fashioned Damask and Hybrid Musk roses, as well as the Bourbon roses so popular with the Victorians.

A request to paint the depressing black panelling in the Prime Minister's Study proved more problematic. Since the panelling was not original to the house and therefore of no historical significance, Eden did not imagine that there would be any objection. But, although the Trustees were all in general agreement about the desirability of the change and Lady Lee felt she could not object, it was pointed out that to paint the panelling would be in direct contravention of the Chequers Estate Act. The only solution was to secure court approval for a deed of variation to the Trust. When the judge refused the order on the grounds that it was not a matter for the court but for the Attorney General, the Trustees considered going ahead regardless. 'No one will object, indeed I do not know who could,' wrote Lord Goddard, Lord Chief Justice who was also a Trustee, to the Prime Minister, 'and if they did, I think the only remedy would be impeachment and if you are impeached, I will offer my head to the block in your place!' Eden was grateful for Lord Goddard's commitment and anxious to get the painting done before the

Anthony Eden
in the Study.

Commonwealth Prime Ministers' visit to Chequers. But by now the course of the hearing was already public knowledge and they were alert to the political consequences of taking the matter into their own hands. Eden, by now thoroughly exasperated by the whole matter, abandoned the idea of painting the Study. 'I think that we can pickle the panelling without running the danger of being beheaded,' he wrote to Lord Goddard. So the panelling was stripped and bleached, and the room transformed for the better.

Although Eden had succeeded in increasing the Government's majority (from seventeen to sixty) in the 1955 election, he was allowed no political honeymoon. He had inherited a newspaper strike – a deprivation which, he said, the nation had endured with 'stoical calm' – and was immediately faced with strikes on the railways and in the docks. As the country was plunged into a state of emergency Eden spelled out the devastating effect of the disputes on the nation's economy in a broadcast from Chequers.

Eden was the first Prime Minister to make use of the relatively new medium of television. But his relationship with the BBC, as with the press, was uneasy and one incident at Chequers was seized upon with glee by the tabloid newspapers. Near the east drive lived a family who were sub-tenants of Mr Randag, the farmer. Mrs Butts had become accustomed to hanging out her washing, not on a line in her own garden but across Lime Walk,

Anthony Eden
with his son Nicholas.

where the Edens liked to walk and where it could be clearly seen by visitors to the house. When the Trustees approached her with suggestions for a more appropriate site for the washing line, Mrs Butts took her story to the press, who descended on Chequers in droves. The cartoonists had a field day, Mrs Butts had her fifteen minutes of fame, and Lady Eden, mortified by the furore, had to wrestle with some particularly unpleasant correspondence.

It was a supreme irony that Anthony Eden, who had been a brilliant Foreign Secretary, should meet his nemesis in foreign affairs. The Suez Crisis dominated the last six months of Eden's premiership, and not for nothing did his wife say that she often felt as if the Suez Canal was flowing through her drawing room.

In the spring of 1956, Eden was visited by Nikita Khruschev and Nikolai Alexandrovich Bulganin, newly appointed leaders of the Soviet Republic. On a recent tour of Asia the Russians had been echoing Egypt's anti-colonial propaganda and Eden, who set great store by personal contact, was glad of the opportunity to show his Soviet guests the reality of the British way of life. Chequers, where the Edens tried to introduce a family atmosphere, provided a useful contrast to Downing Street where the formal meetings took place. Eden's son Nicholas drove down from London with Kruschev's son, each speaking a little of the other's language, and the ensuing discussions were less inhibited and not overwhelmed

Anthony Eden

by political aides. Against a background of rising tension in the Middle East, Eden made it plain to his Russian guests that Britain was so dependent upon oil from the Middle East that if the supply was threatened, the Government was prepared to use force.

Three months later, Gamal Abdel Nasser, the Egyptian President, nationalized the Suez Canal. At Chequers, away from the publicity invariably attached to the comings and goings in Downing Street, Eden was visited by the Acting French Foreign Minister, Albert Gazier, and the Deputy Chief of Staff of the French Air Force General Maurice Challe. The purpose of this meeting was for Gazier to relay to Eden the French plan for overthrowing Nasser and taking back the Canal. The plan hinged on the belief that Israel, denied the use of the Suez Canal, would take the opportunity to settle its long-standing dispute against Egypt and attack her across the Sinai Peninsula. Once Sinai had been captured, the Israelis and Egyptians would be ordered to withdraw from the Canal Zone by the British and French, who would follow up with an invasion of the Canal to separate the combatants and thus safeguard their rights of navigation.

This Chequers meeting took place so secretly that neither the French nor the British ambassadors were present and no-one signed the Visitors' Book. Churchill, too, paid a secret visit to the Prime Minister and, in customary fashion, in the car on the way to Chequers had dictated a note to Eden in case the Prime Minister was too busy for a personal talk, stopping in a lay-by so that it could be typed up before his arrival. (Harold Wilson believed that there was another secret Suez meeting at Chequers, supposedly with a high-ranking Israeli officer, and that the name had been erased from the Visitors' Book. If so, there is no evidence of this to be seen today. Ten years later, however, when Guy Mollet, French Prime Minister at the time of Suez, came to Chequers for an International Socialist Conference in December 1966, he was reluctant to discuss it.)

Eden viewed Nasser as another Hitler, fearing the emergence of an Arab alliance under Nasser's leadership, supported by Communist money and arms. There were those, however, who were horrified by the Anglo-French plan, which was codenamed 'Musketeer', because they believed it would end in disaster. The Americans gave it no support either. When the proposed invasion took place, the United Nations called for sanctions against Britain and France, causing a run on the pound. Sterling collapsed and, in a humiliating defeat for the Government, British and French forces were obliged to pull out of the area they had occupied around Port Said.

Eden at that time was in Jamaica, convalescing from another bout of the illness which had plagued him following an unsuccessful gall-bladder operation four years earlier. He returned to London in the middle of December 1956 and went straight to Chequers to prepare for a difficult reappearance in the House of Commons. The Suez débacle had greatly diminished his authority within the party, but friends urged him to fight for his survival and Eden was determined to continue his leadership for as long as his health allowed.

He spent Christmas quietly at Chequers with his family and Lindemann, now Lord Cherwell. On Christmas Eve, Nehru dropped in on his way home from the United States with his sister Mrs Pandit, the Indian High Commissioner. Although the Indian Prime Minister had publicly condemned Britain's actions over Suez, the two had a mutual respect for each other that transcended differences of policy. On Boxing Day the party expanded with the arrival of Rab Butler, Lord Kilmuir, Lord Chancellor, Alan Lennox-Boyd, Colonial Secretary, Lord Salisbury, Leader of the House of Lords, and Gwilym Lloyd George (Lloyd George's son), Home Secretary.

In the White Parlour, Eden sought Kilmuir's advice about whether to remain in office. His old friend urged him to stay, but the fevers had returned and his doctor was called to Chequers. When further medical opinion confirmed that to continue in office would endanger his life, Eden's resignation became inevitable. He was only fifty-nine, with many happy years still ahead of him.

On 9 January 1957 Lady Eden accompanied her husband to Sandringham to see the Queen. The next day he broke the news to his unsuspecting Cabinet. Lord Salisbury, who had difficulty with his 'r's, canvassed the Cabinet for their views on Eden's successor. 'Well, which is it,' he asked each in turn, 'Wab or Hawold?'. That same afternoon, Harold Macmillan was summoned to Buckingham Palace and succeeded to the premiership.

The Edens returned for a few days to Chequers, where one of his last visitors was Paul-Henri Spaak, the Belgian Foreign Minister who had joined the exiled Belgian Government in Britain during the war. He and Eden had been through much together since Hitler's remilitarization of the Rhineland and they regarded each other as old friends. Having signed the Visitors' Book for the last time on 17 January 1957, the Edens set sail the following day on the *Rangitoto,* bound for New Zealand, where they were invited to be the guests of the New Zealand Prime Minister. Anthony Eden subsequently became Earl of Avon in 1961 and he died in 1977.

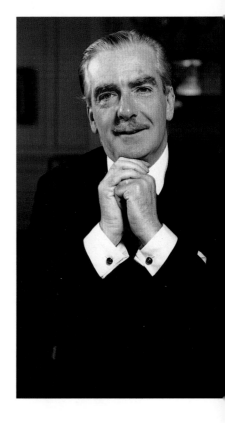

Anthony Eden

HAROLD MACMILLAN

Accompanied by his wife, daughters and grandchildren, Harold Macmillan made his first official visit to Chequers just a month after he succeeded Anthony Eden as Prime Minister in January 1957. He had been to Chequers often enough in the past to know what it was like. 'A fine house,' he had written in his diary, 'but it has been rather spoilt.' In fact, although Macmillan regarded Chequers as a noble gift, on a personal level he was indifferent to its charms. Lady Dorothy Macmillan never went there unless duty called, and, when not in London, she and her husband preferred to stay at Birch Grove House, the family mansion in Sussex. Perhaps, had Disraeli ever occupied Chequers (as at one time it seemed that he might), Macmillan might have used the house

Harold Macmillan's window at Chequers

THE
RIGHT HONOURABLE
HAROLD
MACMILLAN
M.P.
PRIME MINISTER
JANUARY 1957
TO
OCTOBER 1963

more, for he had a profound sense of history and from the earliest dawning of political awareness Disraeli had been his hero. On Macmillan's rare visits to Chequers he would visit Disraeli's Hughenden Manor, near High Wycombe, for inspiration and refreshment.

Nevertheless, Macmillan appreciated Chequers as a useful asset for conferences and entertaining foreign guests, for which Birch Grove was not really equipped. His installation in the Great Parlour of the large dining table made a valuable contribution to Chequers. This first-floor sitting room was surplus to domestic requirements and the addition of a table transformed it into a magnificent conference room, much used by subsequent Prime Ministers.

When drafting the Chequers Trust, Arthur Lee had considered almost every set of circumstances, including the possibility that a Prime Minister might not wish to exercise his right to use Chequers. To ensure that the house remained lived in, the Trust provided for a hierarchy of alternative occupants: the Chancellor of the Exchequer, the

Harold Macmillan

Foreign Secretary, the American Ambassador, the Speaker, the Minister of Agriculture, the First Lord of the Admiralty and the Ministers for the Navy and the Army. It also made provision for the Prime Minister to nominate a senior minister to make official use of Chequers and Macmillan generously made it available to his Cabinet colleagues. The minister who came to use Chequers most frequently was Selwyn Lloyd, Foreign Secretary and subsequently Chancellor of the Exchequer. He was recently divorced with his young daughter, Joanna, to look after and Macmillan took pity on his domestic plight, dismissing his own generosity with the excuse that Lady Dorothy had no enthusiasm for weeding other people's gardens. For this kindness and consideration Selwyn Lloyd was extremely grateful and he cherished the time he spent there.

For almost five years Selwyn Lloyd kept overnight things in Bedroom 3. At weekends he played croquet with Joanna, walked in the park with his black labrador, Sambo, and enjoyed nursery tea in the White Parlour. He also welcomed to Chequers his friends and his private office, and took pleasure in showing off his knowledge of the house and its treasures. Officially, every visit had to be sanctioned by the Prime Minister, and once or twice Macmillan magnanimously chose to make other arrangements rather than inconvenience Selwyn Lloyd at Chequers. Twice the Treasury team joined Lloyd at Chequers to prepare Budget Statements and on Budget Day itself, Joanna and Sambo were paraded in the park for the ritual photograph.

In July 1962 Selwyn Lloyd fell victim to the ministerial purge famously remembered as the 'Night of Long Knives', when Macmillan sacked seven members of his Cabinet. For Selwyn Lloyd, who had taken on the Exchequer on the understanding that he would remain there until the election, it was a devastating blow, for he lost not only his job but his beloved Chequers. Unlike Megan Lloyd George's reaction to her father's loss of office, the ten-year-old Joanna's response was 'Thank goodness, no more photographs.'

There was a poignant postscript to Selwyn Lloyd's departure. Several weeks later the new Cabinet met at Chequers for a strategy meeting, and as Macmillan gathered them together on the terrace for a Cabinet photograph the faithful Sambo, left behind in the Lloyds' move to London, made an appearance and sniffed around looking for his absent master. For several years Sambo was looked after by the Chequers staff and when he died he was buried in the grounds.

Another minister who benefited from Macmillan's generosity was Edward Heath, but his request, in December 1959, as Minister of Labour, to use Chequers for a working party on industrial relations caused something of a dilemma. Hitherto, with the exception of the Chancellor of the Exchequer, only Foreign Office ministers had been allowed to make use of Chequers and only for the official entertainment of overseas visitors. David Stephens, the Prime Minister's Appointments Secretary, feared that by going outside the official list of persons allowed to use Chequers, an awkward precedent would be created which could be seen as an unacceptable departure from the original purpose of the Trust.

The Prime Minister, however, who enjoyed a good relationship with Heath, the former Chief Whip who had presided over the transition of the premiership from Eden, gave the working party his blessing. 'I expect Mr Heath's guests will be more or less house-trained,' he scribbled in the margin of Stephens' memorandum,

Harold Macmillan

'Please arrange accordingly.' Later, as Lord Privy Seal with Foreign Office responsibilities, Heath entertained delegations from the six countries of the Common Market when Paul-Henri Spaak felt that being at Chequers had greatly enhanced an interesting and useful exchange of views. The Cabinet Secretary, Sir Norman Brook, also held a working party of Commonwealth officials at Chequers. In May 1960, just a few months after Macmillan's 'Winds of Change' speech to the South African Parliament, the African leaders came to London for the Commonwealth Conference and were entertained at Buckingham Palace, Windsor and Chequers. At the end of the year, when some of them met again for the Conference of the Central Africa Federation, they were once again welcomed at Chequers. Duncan Sandys and Ian Macleod, Colonial and Commonwealth Secretaries respectively, hosted the occasion, with Macmillan joining them for dinner in the evening. Dr Hastings Banda, leader of the Malawi Congress Party, and Sir Roy Welensky, Prime Minister of the Federation of Rhodesia and Nyasaland, had not met socially before. Macmillan held out few hopes that a weekend at Chequers would solve their differences, but he felt that at least they would get to know each other better.

The Secretary to the Trustees, pleased to see Chequers being used, was quite happy about these arrangements as long as the expense of the hospitality did not fall upon the Trust. The £15 allowance was only available for the Prime Minister and his immediate family. Selwyn Lloyd, as unofficial occupant, had had to pay his own way; Mr Heath's department had picked up the bill for his working party; the Government Hospitality Fund was responsible for foreign visitors and the Prime Minister pays for his private entertaining.

By 1958 it was clear that an Act of Parliament was required to put the running of the Chequers estate and house on a different footing. For forty years the Trust had worked exceptionally well – a tribute, in Lady Lee's view, to the care and thoroughness with which the scheme had been drafted forty years ago. But the 1917 Act had become impractical and, in some respects, a hindrance to the efficient management of the estate. Changes were necessary and, confident that the object of the Trust would be preserved, Lady Lee closely followed the passage of the new bill through Parliament. Among the amendments was the power to sell outlying land and buildings, to cut and sell timber and to use the proceeds from either of these for the improvement and maintenance of the estate. The composition of the board of Trustees was also changed and its numbers reduced.

Harold Macmillan
with his grandchildren at
Chequers in 1963.

The Chequers Estate Acts

T he Chequers Estate Act of 1917 provided for a board of *ex-officio* Trustees, whose functions or offices were likely to be permanent and of a kind to make them feel some interest in the objects of the scheme. The Prime Minister was Chairman of the board, which also included the Speaker of the House of Commons, the Chancellor of the Exchequer, the Foreign Secretary, the Minister of Agriculture, the Lord Chief Justice, the First Commissioner of Works, the Chairman of the National Trust and the Director of the National Portrait Gallery. With the 'power to add to their number', by 1958 the number of Trustees had risen to fourteen and, given the exigencies of office of five Ministers of the Crown and the Lord Chief Justice, it was becoming increasingly difficult to convene the full board.

The 1958 Act reduced the board of Trustees to six, including Lady Lee. Since her death in 1967 the board has remained at five: the Prime Minister's nominee, the Department of the Environment's nominee, the Chairman of the National Trust, the Public Trustee and, as Chairman the Lord Privy Seal, currently Viscount Cranborne.

Harold Macmillan *with Ted Dexter (left), England's cricket captain, and Frank Worrel, captain of the West Indies, in the Great Hall in September 1963.*

One of the most significant achievements of Harold Macmillan's premiership was the part he played in bringing about a test ban treaty. In August 1959, President Eisenhower came to Chequers on his way for talks with Chancellor Adenauer of Germany and President de Gaulle of France. Since the American President was shortly due to meet Khruschev at the White House, Macmillan wanted Eisenhower to persuade the Soviet leader to stop the testing of atomic and hydrogen bombs. Macmillan had done much to repair Britain's relationship with the United States after the Suez crisis and he and the President were old friends. When the President arrived, fresh from a visit to the Queen at Balmoral and bearing several brace of grouse for supper, there was much to talk about. The next day, while practising golf strokes, they lost a number of balls in the long grass of Victory Drive and in the evening, as they settled down to watch *Ice Cold in Alex*, the

Harold Macmillan *with the Reverend Cyril Norman White, after attending a service at Ellesborough Parish Church.*

President must have been reminded of similar evenings with Churchill during the war.

Eisenhower had been welcomed to Britain with a great show of public enthusiasm. The leafy lanes of Buckinghamshire looked their best as he was cheered through the villages in an open car between RAF Benson, in Oxfordshire, and Chequers. The largest congregation since Janet Attlee's wedding filled Ellesborough Church on Sunday morning, and the service was relayed to the overspill on the hill outside. The Prime Minister read the lesson, and the sermon was delivered by the Reverend Cyril White, who had preached to every Prime Minister since Baldwin. Later, in the north park, near to Roosevelt's cedar, Eisenhower planted a rare dawn redwood tree.

Having succeeded in reuniting the Conservative Party in the aftermath of Suez, Harold Macmillan enjoyed a good innings as

Prime Minister, presiding over a period of rising prosperity. Within a week of Eisenhower's departure, and with a personal poll rating of 67 percent, Macmillan called a general election, proclaiming the slogan, 'You've never had it so good'. The Conservatives were returned to power for the third time in succession with a majority of 107, which guaranteed a full Parliament. By the summer of 1962, however, although production was rising and unemployment falling, Macmillan was assailed by problems: de Gaulle's veto of Britain's membership of the Common Market, the Cuba crisis, by-election defeats and the scandal which embroiled the Minister of Defence, John Profumo. Inevitably, the press began to speculate about the leadership.

In the autumn, Macmillan spent a month at Chequers, preoccupied with the Denning Report on the wider aspects of the Profumo case. Between occasional visits from the family and the comings and goings of ministers, he brooded about the future. One of his visitors at this time was Rab Butler, Deputy Prime Minister, who took away from Chequers the clear impression that Macmillan intended to remain as leader. Having been passed over in the change of leadership between Eden and Macmillan in 1957, Butler had an interest in the succession and Macmillan knew that he would accept the leadership if there was a consensus for him. The Prime Minister, however, favoured either Hailsham or Macleod, who to him were the true inheritors of the Disraeli tradition of Tory radicalism, which was so dear to his heart.

When Lord Home came to Chequers, he was greatly distressed to find that Macmillan was considering retirement, especially since, in his view, there was no question of a revolt or a plot within the party. There were doubts, however, about whether or not 'super-Mac' could recover his image sufficiently to win an election. If retirement was an option, then the party had a right to know: he believed that the party conference due to be held in Blackpool would provide the opportunity for the Prime Minister to strengthen his position with a clear announcement of his intentions one way or another.

A week before the conference, and aware of the difficulties that lay ahead, the Cabinet endorsed Macmillan's decision to lead the party into the election. But ill-health overtook him and Lord Home, as President of the National Union, found himself in Blackpool telling the conference that Macmillan would not, after all, 'be able to carry the physical burden of leading the party at the next general election.' In the event, to the astonishment of all, it was neither Hailsham nor Macleod nor Butler who succeeded Macmillan as Prime Minister, but Alec Douglas-Home.

Harold Macmillan

ALEC DOUGLAS-HOME

Alec Douglas-Home, 14th Earl of Home, had not sought the premiership. He was content as Foreign Secretary in the House of Lords and viewed the prospect of relinquishing his title, finding a new constituency and contesting a by-election in order to take his seat in the Commons – to say nothing of the overwhelming responsibility of the highest office in the land – with some dismay.

He took office in October 1963 but it was not until January 1964 that Sir Alec Douglas-Home first stayed at Chequers officially. As Secretary of State for Commonwealth Relations in Eden's Cabinet and subsequently as Macmillan's Foreign Secretary, he had been the official occupant of nearby Dorneywood. The Douglas-Homes had made their home there since 'The Hirsel', the family home in Scotland, was virtually inaccessible while Parliament was

Alec Douglas-Home's window at Chequers

SIR ALEC DOUGLAS-HOME K.T., M.P.
PRIME MINISTER OCT. 1963-OCT. 1964

sitting and they were in no hurry to exchange Dorneywood for Chequers. In the meantime, Mrs Hill kept the WAAF girls busy cleaning the house and was uneasy when the Prime Minister allowed Duncan Sandys, the Commonwealth Secretary, to use Chequers privately. During Macmillan's premiership, Selwyn Lloyd was in almost permanent residence and so many ministers had used it for official entertaining that the 'booking' arrangements had become extremely complicated and Macmillan had complained that he was never able to go to Chequers himself when he wanted to. But if the Douglas-Homes were slow to take up residence, they soon became very attached to Chequers, and the acres of countryside at the Prime Minister's disposal compensated for the Scottish Borders, to which he was only able to go in the parliamentary recess.

Chequers was less generously endowed than Dorneywood, where Sir Alec had been continually pressed by the Trustees into making improvements. At Chequers the only deficiency, as far as he and his family were concerned,

Alec Douglas-Home
in the Study.

was the lack of a suitable reception room in which to receive and entertain guests. (It was not until Edward Heath's time that the ground-floor Hawtrey Room was turned into a drawing room.) When they were on their own, they used the White Parlour, since it was much lighter and more intimate than many of the other rooms. They found the Long Gallery more 'interesting' than 'comfortable', for in the jewel case is a ring worn by Elizabeth I, which has a historic link with the Douglas-Home family.

The ring, made of mother-of-pearl, has shoulders set with rubies. The bezel, bearing a monogram ER in rose diamonds and blue enamel, opens to reveal exquisitely miniaturized enamelled portraits of the Queen and her mother, Anne Boleyn. Beneath the bezel is the badge of the Boleyns, an oval medallion of a phoenix rising from a flaming crown. After Elizabeth's death, the ring was taken from her finger and delivered to her acknowledged heir, James I, the son of the executed Mary Queen of Scots, at Stirling Castle, as proof that she was dead. The new King in due course presented it to the first Earl of Home, who accompanied him south, as a special mark of his esteem and as a reward for his services. It was Arthur Lee who acquired the ring and gave it to Chequers.

During the Commonwealth Conference held in London in July 1964, a number of African leaders and their wives were invited to 'dine and sleep' at Chequers. Amongst them were President Obote of Uganda and President Nyerere of Tanzania. All appeared to go well until bedtime, when one guest pleaded urgent business in London and asked for arrangements to be made for his

Alec Douglas-Home
by Karsh of Ottawa.

immediate return. As his driver was prised away from his pint in the rest room, several other Prime Ministers also discovered important business that required them to leave. It fell to Dr Hastings Banda, a familiar visitor to Chequers, to explain to his bewildered host that they were all afraid of sleeping in the curtained and canopied four-poster beds. (Perhaps they were aware that the original purpose of the canopy was to catch droppings from the bats roosting in the open rafters. (This is not much of a problem today, although on several evenings in August 1995 the Prime Minister's secretary was driven out of the office by bats and the Great Hall filled up with them. The next morning a search revealed several peacefully sleeping behind the curtains; we put them out but they showed their gratitude by coming back the next evening.)

Of all the Prime Ministers who have used Chequers, Alec Douglas-Home had the shortest residence. He was in office for only a year from October 1963. In the general election of October 1964 the Labour Party had an overall majority of four seats, a long way short of the predicted landslide. Even before the votes were counted, Harold Wilson was being asked if he would make Chequers available to the outgoing Prime Minister, who is obliged to beat a hasty retreat through the back door of No. 10 by lunchtime the next day. It is, of course, understandable that the civil service has to make contingency plans for a change of government, but this treatment of a defeated Prime Minister does the British no credit. Alec Douglas-Home, conceding defeat in the early hours of the morning, and realizing that eviction from No. 10 meant that he and his wife had nowhere to go, was grateful for the sanctuary of Chequers. The house was full for that 'extra' weekend and among those staying were Lady Douglas-Home's young secretary, Lorne Roper-Caldbeck. Nearly thirty years later, Lorne came back to Downing Street to work with me, and she has become an indispensable personal assistant and friend.

When the time came to leave, Elizabeth Douglas-Home expressed her regrets in a letter to Lady Lee. 'Now that our time at Chequers has come to an end, I feel I must tell you that I am sure no Prime Minister's family can have appreciated it more. We have had all too short a time to enjoy it, but so many people have been here with us. Perhaps we have had our own children (plus seven-month-old grandchild) too much, but they will never forget it and I hope we haven't misused it .... We feel desperately sad in lots of ways at the result of the election,' she continued, 'but losing Chequers is one of the saddest aspects.'

Not until 1968, when he joined Harold and Mary Wilson for lunch, did Alec Douglas-Home plant his memorial walnut tree.

HAROLD WILSON

From the beginning of his premiership in October 1964, Harold Wilson recognized the value of Chequers as a place not only for entertaining, but also for 'contemplative discussion'. At Chequers, away from the interruptions inevitable in Downing Street, he found that there was the time and space to tackle complex issues – not always possible at the weekly Cabinet meeting.

It took rather longer, however, for Chequers to grow on Mary Wilson. According to Marcia Williams (later Lady Falkender), the Prime Minister's political secretary, she had been at a disadvantage following Lady Douglas-Home and the titled wives of the three previous Prime Ministers and everything had to be discovered by accident. Moreover, the Wilsons were under a misapprehension about the terms of the Chequers Trust and thought the Prime Minister's wife was not allowed to be at Chequers unless the Prime Minister was there as well. If he was called away on urgent business, Mary Wilson felt there was no encouragement for her to stay. In the interests of protecting the furniture and pictures, the minute the Prime Minister left the house the blinds were drawn, the rugs rolled up and the furniture covered in dust-sheets. (The present curator, Jane Uff, is more discreet about the dust-sheet and carpet-rolling routine.)

If Mary Wilson was never as much at ease at Chequers as she was at their favourite retreat on the Isles of Scilly, the house was nevertheless infinitely preferable to No. 10, where she felt the upstairs flat was simply an extension of the office and total privacy was difficult to come by. She became immensely fond of the White Parlour and it was here, free from distractions, that she wrote much of the poetry that has given such pleasure to so many people. When John became Prime Minister in 1990, Mary Wilson wrote to tell me how much she had enjoyed Chequers and to urge me to make as much use of the house as possible.

Harold Wilson's window at Chequers

SIR HAROLD WILSON KG, OBE, FRS, MP.
PRIME MINISTER OCT. 1964–JUN 1970 & MAR 1974–APR 1976.

Harold Wilson *in the Study at Chequers.*

In the 1960s, Chequers was rather dingy and run-down. Nothing much had been done to the house since the war and many at this time commented on its gloom and isolation. Today its isolated position is an advantage, but for Richard Crossman, Wilson's Minister for Housing and Local Government, it was a frustration. 'No-one knows how to find Chequers,' he grumbled in his *Diaries*. 'Today I had to be at Chequers by 9.45 for an all day Cabinet ... Thomas Balogh [Wilson's economic adviser] gave me exact details of how I could get in by the back entrance behind Kimble Church. When we got to Great Kimble we found two churches and finally got to the front entrance at 9.58 .... There must be hundreds of great country houses nicer than this. It is heavily restored and stuffy in atmosphere. After a day there one appreciates why everybody says they detest Chequers.' This was not, however, the view taken by Harold Wilson, who loved it enough to return every weekend, even after spending Friday evening in his Merseyside constituency of Huyton. After a year in office, he wrote appreciatively to Lady Lee: 'My wife and I ... owe a great deal to the generosity of you and your husband in making over Chequers for the use of the Prime Minister. I am sure you will have heard from my predecessors in office how much Chequers has been appreciated. I can assure you it is being used to great advantage.'

Wilson's first important meeting took place in November 1964, a little over a month after he had taken office. He gathered together leading ministers and chiefs of staff, plus their permanent secretaries and advisers, in order to look at the Government's overall defence strategy. Wilson described it as 'the most thorough ever undertaken by a British government'. Among the participants were Lord Mountbatten, Chief of Defence Staff, Patrick Gordon Walker, Foreign Secretary, Jim Callaghan, Chancellor of the Exchequer, Dennis Healey, Defence Secretary, Roy Jenkins, Minister of Aviation, Fred Mulley, Minister of Defence for the Army, and Solly Zuckerman, who, as the Government's chief scientific adviser, was to Wilson what Lindemann had been to Churchill. The conference began in the Hawtrey Room, where a screen had been set up for a visual presentation of Britain's defence commitments around the world. Discussions then continued round the conference table in the Great Parlour.

Such meetings became a feature of Harold Wilson's official occupancy of Chequers and the Cabinet met so often there that Barbara Castle, then Minister for Transport, took to referring to the Great Parlour as the 'Cabinet Room'. On one weekend alone, Wilson held an all-day conference of the National Economic Development Council, followed on Sunday by a meeting of the Economic Committee of the Trade Union Council. On other weekends there were meetings to discuss Britain's renewed application to join the European Community (EC) and a meeting of the National Executive Committee of the Labour Party which gave the trade union members an opportunity to 'blow their tops', as Wilson put it, while the Cabinet sat and listened.

In the late 1960s, when strikes and industrial disputes were endemic, industrialists and trade unionists were constant visitors. The reform of industrial relations enshrined in Barbara Castle's policy document, *In Place of Strife*, though popular with the public, was a contentious issue with both the Cabinet and the unions. Over roast duck and a decent bottle of claret at Chequers one Sunday evening in the summer of 1969, Wilson and Barbara Castle, now Minister of Employment and Productivity, discussed with the union leaders Hugh Scanlon, Jack Jones and Vic Feather how the document related to inter-union disputes and wild-cat strikes.

Nor were the conferences at Chequers restricted to domestic issues. Having represented the Labour Party at many International Socialist Conferences over the years, Wilson was on intimate terms with many of the European democratic socialist leaders, including Golda Meir of Israel and Willy Brandt of West Germany. Several times he welcomed the International Socialist Conference to

Chequers and at the first of these, in April 1965, the subject under discussion was the complex relationship between the six countries of the EC, of which Britain was still not a member, and the seven of the European Free Trade Association (EFTA), of which Britain was one. Out of this meeting came a proposal for a conference of EFTA Prime Ministers, and another international forum was brought into being. The next month, the summit was held in Vienna and in December 1966 they met again at Chequers.

The Commonwealth Prime Ministers' Conference was held in London three times during Harold Wilson's premiership, and on each occasion the Commonwealth leaders were entertained at Chequers. Since there were so many of them, however, the house-parties tended to spill over into several days, with several shifts of Prime Ministers and their wives, some of them dining and sleeping. Among the Prime Ministers were Dr Hastings Banda (Malawi), Sir Abubaka Tafewa Balewa (Nigeria), Keith Holyoake (New Zealand), Kenneth Kaunda (Zambia), Julius Nyerere (Tanzania), Lester Pearson (Canada), Robert Menzies (Australia) and Milton Obote (Uganda). When one of these splendid Conferences coincided with Mary Wilson's birthday, Keith Holyoake sang 'Happy Birthday to You' in a fine bass voice and eight Prime Ministers joined in. Many of them were by then old hands at these Chequers weekends, and Sir Abubaka had been a guest of three different Prime Ministers. But his visit in June 1965 was his last for, shortly after chairing the Commonwealth Conference in Lagos six months later, he was murdered in a tribal uprising.

The Commonwealth Prime Ministers had been heard to talk of the 'magic of Chequers' helping them to reach decisions more quickly, and Wilson made the most of these occasions for bi-lateral meetings. Away from the formality of the conference hall, problems could often be solved over a drink in the Long Gallery or during a stroll in the rose garden. It was on one such stroll, during the Commonwealth Conference of 1965, that Wilson conceived the idea of a Commonwealth peace mission on Vietnam. Although well received by the Commonwealth leaders, the mission subsequently floundered, and it was not until the visit to London in February 1967 of the Soviet leader, Alexei Kosygin, that Wilson attempted a new initiative.

It was significant that Kosygin's visit coincided with the traditional 'Tet' ceasefire of the Vietnamese New Year. Wilson, who had known the Soviet leader for many years and believed that he had contacts in Hanoi, hoped for Kosygin's endorsement of his plan to extend the truce and prepare the way for talks between the warring factions. One proposal had already been rejected by

Harold Wilson *meets some of Europe's top journalists at Chequers, during talks on the Common Market.*

President Johnson early in Kosygin's visit and Wilson had submitted another formula to the White House. When Kosygin and his advisers arrived at Chequers for dinner at the end of a week of discussions on a whole raft of other issues, Wilson had still not heard whether his revised formula was acceptable to the Americans. In fact, as Wilson and Kosygin sat down to dinner at Chequers, President Johnson was calling a meeting of the National Security Council in Washington to discuss it. A special telephone line linking Chequers to the White House had been installed in the Prison Room. Waiting there to take the call was the President's representative Chet Cooper, who was advising Wilson throughout the discussions. Fortified by a bottle of Bourbon and a tray of food, with a transistor radio for company, Cooper awaited the results of

Harold Wilson
with President Nixon
and Mrs Wilson (top)
and in discussion with
President Nixon in the
Long Gallery, 1969.

the deliberations with growing impatience, knowing there was a limit to how long Kosygin could reasonably be kept at Chequers.

Dinner was prolonged for as long as possible, and Wilson produced a number of points in the communiqué – the end-product of a week of talks – that required further clarification. After dinner, the two leaders retired to the Long Gallery, where the Prime Minister raised the subject of the Common Market and spun out a discussion on the future of the Soviet chemical engineering industry. It was early evening in Washington, but well past bedtime in Buckinghamshire. As both time and conversation ran out, the communiqué was ceremoniously signed in the Great Parlour. Wilson presented his Russian guests with copies of the Chequers guidebook, playing for time by slowly and laboriously writing a half-page inscription in each.

Meanwhile, in the Prison Room, Cooper was urging Washington to make haste. As the official cars gathered in the courtyard below he dangled the telephone receiver out of the window to carry the sounds of departure down the line to Washington. But the word from Washington came too late, and although the details of the formula, amended by the Security Council, eventually caught up with Kosygin, the timetable proved unacceptable in Hanoi. With the end of the truce, all hope of peace talks faded away.

Vietnam was also on the agenda for President Nixon's brief visit two years later. For Nixon, newly elected to the presidency, this was one of several European stop-overs and Wilson was keen to capitalize on his visit in the interests of the 'special relationship'. The value of the photo-opportunity was lost on neither party and television crews and press photographers crowded into the Great Hall to transmit the warmth of the welcoming speeches. (Arthur Lee would surely have turned in his grave.) In the Long Gallery the discussions touched on such major issues of the day as Vietnam, NATO, the Middle East, Europe, Rhodesia and Nigeria. Nixon, unlike Eisenhower, did not spend the night at Chequers and therefore did not qualify for the tree-planting ceremony.

All these meetings made for some very crowded weekends, but Wilson thrived on work and it was difficult to keep him from it either at No. 10 or at Chequers. A Prime Minister no longer has the luxury Disraeli often enjoyed at Hughenden of 'one week sauntering in his library' and 'another week sauntering in the park'. A so-called 'free weekend' is no such thing, with the inexorable pursuit of the red boxes. On one such 'free' weekend Sir Nicholas Henderson, then Ambassador to the Federal Republic of Germany, visited Harold Wilson to brief him on his forthcoming visit to Bonn. Paddy, the Prime Minister's golden labrador, greeted the Ambassador in the Stone Hall, closely followed by his master in his shirt-sleeves; Mary was sitting with some friends on the terrace. In his memoirs, Henderson described the scene: 'There was the usual P.G. Wodehouse atmosphere which hangs about Chequers: French windows leading on to large lawns and rose beds, many people hanging about apparently not doing very much; a feeling that someone is on the point of perpetrating some practical joke; and the shimmering presence, if not of Jeeves, at any rate of a servant or two ready to meet any need. One of these brought tea and scones with butter and jam. The P.M. and I helped ourselves.' (The hospitality had apparently improved considerably since 1964, when Tom Driberg M.P., one of Wilson's early guests, was scathing about the food at Chequers and suggested that if they wanted to extend their hospitality to anyone else, he could recommend some very good restaurants.)

Like his predecessors, Wilson took great pleasure in showing his guests around the house. He relished the historical associations, though Henderson recalled an uncomfortable occasion when Chancellor Schmidt was shown into the bedroom occupied by Churchill during the war and Wilson related the story of the great man touching up the mouse in the Rubens' painting. Wilson also had a romantic theory that the initials 'WH' were those of the mysterious 'WH' of Shakespeare's Sonnets. Having spent a night or two at the Ship Inn at nearby Grendon Underwood, Shakespeare has a tenuous connection with Buckinghamshire, but although the identity of the 'fair young man' of the Sonnets remains a mystery, there are others with a better claim than William Hawtrey who had been dead for several years when the Sonnets were published in 1609.

Harold Wilson played an occasional round of golf at Ellesborough, but otherwise his only recreation was walking with Mary and Paddy. Paddy was young and high-spirited, with a wanderlust that proved something of a problem at Chequers. He liked nothing better than to escape into the surrounding countryside, causing mayhem on the roads and trespassing on the golf course, where he used to run off with the balls. He soon learnt that if he turned himself in at the local police station when he had had enough, he would be sure of a lift home. But the lift was followed by a stiff letter from the Chief Constable to Mrs Hill – for it was her name and telephone number on Paddy's identity disc – urging her to keep him under better control. Mrs Hill had even subscribed to the Amersham, Chesham and District Rescue Society because of the frequency with which they had taken Paddy into care and when Paddy made a meal of some matting in the kitchen corridor, the Prime Minister received a bill.

Harold Wilson *planting his memorial tree with Paddy, his golden labrador.*

WITH ALL GOOD WISHES
FOR CHRISTMAS
AND THE NEW YEAR
FROM

Mary and Harold Wilson

Chequers
1969

The Wilsons'
Christmas card, 1969

In June 1970, Wilson unexpectedly lost the general election to Edward Heath. Like Alec Douglas-Home before him, he had nowhere to go and for a couple of weeks the Wilsons relied on the hospitality of friends. But they had taken to the charm and beauty of Buckinghamshire and in the autumn they bought Grange Farm in Kingshill, near Great Missenden, while leasing a house in Westminster's Lord North Street. When Wilson became Prime Minister for the second time in February 1974, he spent fewer weekends at Chequers. Grange Farm took over the role of refuge, especially for Mary Wilson who decided not to move back into Downing Street, and Chequers became primarily a place for meetings and entertaining, though on nothing like the same scale as before.

After three and a half years in opposition, the Wilsons returned to a very different Chequers from the rather shabby house they had left in 1970, for in their absence the house had been refurbished. Barbara Castle was horrified that 'someone with appalling taste had tarted up No. 10' but she approved of what had been done to lift the gloom at Chequers, which now looked less like a gentleman's club and more like a private home. 'We would never have dreamed of such extravagance,' Mrs Castle wrote in her diary, the implication being that Mr Heath had managed something the Labour Party would never have got away with – apparently spending a fortune on both No. 10 and Chequers, without so much as a whiff of criticism from the press.

By 1976 Harold Wilson had been leader of the Labour Party for thirteen years and Prime Minister for eight, having uniquely won four general elections. Although it meant that he failed by eleven months in his ambition to beat Asquith's record as the longest-serving Prime Minister of the century, he had determined to retire on his sixtieth birthday – 11 March – and Mary Wilson had pencilled the date in her diary well in advance. In the previous year they had become grandparents to twin girls, and it was in the Long Gallery that the babies were baptized by Bishop Colin Winter from a font that had been in the Wilson family for several generations. (Seventeen years later the twins came back to see the place where they had been christened.) The weekend before the announcement of his retirement coincided with the

twins' first birthday, which was celebrated at Chequers. Wilson had already warned Jim Callaghan of his intentions, and that same weekend, sitting in the rose garden where the previous year Lady Falkender had persuaded him not to make the announcement at the Blackpool Conference, he told her of his decision. Three days later he tendered his resignation to the Queen before breaking the news to a Cabinet whose surprise was almost total. In the election for his successor, after a third ballot on 5 April 1976, Jim Callaghan succeeded as leader of the Labour Party and Prime Minister.

After a formal farewell visit to Buckingham Palace, the Wilsons returned to Chequers – a visit which was by no means their last, for they were to return as guests of Jim Callaghan. The last photo-opportunity showed Harold Wilson nursing a pint in the Bernard Arms, the pub at the end of Kimble Drive, which for eight years had been his 'local'. The picture still has pride of place in the saloon bar, beside photographs of Macmillan with President Eisenhower and John Major with President Yeltsin.

Harold Wilson at the twins' first birthday party, in the White Parlour, March 1976.

EDWARD HEATH

When he took office in June 1970, Edward Heath already knew Chequers well. He had been a frequent visitor during Macmillan's premiership and, since he had been Chairman of the Board of Trustees during the four years in which he was Lord Privy Seal, he was familiar with the workings of the Chequers Trust. He grew to love Chequers as his country house and used it almost every weekend for official entertaining and for entertaining his friends and colleagues.

Since his earlier visits, however, the 'muted ostentation' described by Princess Bibesco in the 1930s had given way to a depressing gloom, and the house was shabby and run-down. The interior had remained very much under the influence of the Lees. After Lord Lee's death in 1947 Ruth, and her sister Faith, reserved the right to have the final say in any decision relating to the decoration and soft furnishings. Having lavished so much care, affection and money on its restoration, the Lees were naturally anxious to protect Chequers from the future onslaughts of interior designers, and their wish that nothing in the house should be altered or added to had been respected by the Trustees. The only challenge to the stipulations of the Trust had been Anthony Eden's attempt to have the panelling in the Study painted. This had proved such a legal headache that it did little to encourage anyone else to make changes. Apart from maintenance programmes and budget limitations, there are, quite rightly, all kinds of restraints upon a Prime Minister – or Prime Minister's wife – who might wish to move in and change everything.

Lady Lee had been dead for several years when Edward Heath became the official occupant of Chequers and thanks to the generous benefaction of Sir Harold (later Lord) Samuel, who thought the endowment needed topping up, Heath was able to bring about a transformation at Chequers which liberated it from the

Edward Heath's window at Chequers

THE RIGHT HONOURABLE
SIR EDWARD RICHARD GEORGE HEATH
K.G., M.B.E., M.P.
PRIME MINISTER
JUNE 1970–MARCH 1974

Edward Heath
*arriving at Chequers by
helicopter with President
Nixon, September 1970.*

gloom of the past. Sir Roy Strong, then Director of the National
Portrait Gallery, suggested that John Fowler, of Colefax & Fowler,
carry out the redecoration of the interior, but there was no
question of anyone telling the Prime Minister what to do and he
took a close personal interest in every aspect of the work.

Since stripping the panelling in the Study had made such a
difference to the brightness of the room, the same treatment was
given to the dark panelling in the Stone Hall, the Great Hall and
the Hawtrey Room. The latter, in particular, had become so
dismal that it had almost been relegated to the status of a storeroom. But with new curtains and covers, a comfortable drawing
room was created in which guests could be entertained. Upstairs,
the main bedrooms were redecorated and curtains and bed-
hangings replaced and the dark panelling in the Long Gallery was
'white-washed blue' as it had been in the eighteenth century.
Under-utilized furniture and pictures were rearranged to better
advantage and Mr Heath, a keen collector of antique china,
rescued pieces from the attic cupboards and displayed them around
the house.

Another dramatic addition to Chequers at this time was the
swimming pool, which was completed in 1973 and became Mr

Heath's pride and joy. The swimming pool was made possible by a generous donor, in this case the American Ambassador, Walter Annenberg, who wanted to commemorate the two occasions on which President Nixon had visited Chequers: in 1969, as Harold Wilson's guest, and again in October 1970, when the Queen broke her holiday at Balmoral to join the President and the Prime Minister for lunch.

The Queen in conversation with President Nixon *in the garden at Chequers, with Edward Heath and Mrs Nixon, October 1970.*

Royalty and Chequers

The Queen's visit in October 1970 was not the first visit of a reigning monarch to Chequers, for the Queen's father and grandfather had both been there. In April 1927 King George V and Queen Mary had been received by Baldwin, when it is believed they discussed the marriage of their youngest son, Prince George (later Duke of Kent). King George VI, when Duke of York, had been to lunch with both Baldwin and Ramsay MacDonald, and during the war he had visited Churchill, who was recovering from pneumonia and unable to keep his weekly audience at Buckingham Palace.

During the First World War, Queen Mary had come to Chequers accompanied by the Princess Royal, Prince Henry (later Duke of Gloucester) and Princess Alice (later Countess of Athlone), to visit wounded officers in the convalescent hospital at Chequers. They had all toured the house and had tea with Ruth Lee in the Great Parlour, before donning rubber boots from the cupboard under the stairs to take a walk in the garden. In her diary, Queen Mary described Chequers as 'a lovely old Tudor and Jacobean house ... a delightful place, very well restored and in perfect taste.'

As with the earlier plans for the cinema, numerous possible sites for a swimming pool were examined and the one most favoured was in the style of an orangery that was linked to the house on the west side of the rose garden. Opinions vary as to its aesthetic merit, but it has the advantage of creating an enclosed walled garden on its far side, thus providing the only completely private area in which to sit.

Heath liked to include members of his family whenever he could and they often joined him at Chequers. He had been specially proud to present his father to the Queen on her visit. His father, step-mother, brother and sister-in-law always made up the Christmas party at Chequers, together with his close friends the Aldingtons and the Seligmans. Lord Aldington, a former Member of Parliament and Deputy Chairman of the Conservative Party, was a dependable friend in good times and bad. Madron Seligman had been at Balliol College, Oxford, with Heath, who was godfather to two of his children.

Edward Heath was the first Prime Minister to bring music to both Downing Street and Chequers, and much of his entertaining had a musical dimension. He installed a state-of-the-art stereo system in the Great Hall and enjoyed demonstrating it to his guests, who did not always share his taste for Bruckner or Richard Strauss. His conducting of the annual Carol Concert at Broadstairs had become a national event and at Chequers he invited the church choir to sing carols in the Great Hall, restoring a tradition begun by Ramsay MacDonald – but with a difference. Whereas MacDonald used to bring the choir in up the back stairs and have them sing from the Gallery, Heath welcomed them at the front door and invited them to join his guests around the Christmas tree in the Great Hall, and to share in the mince pies and mulled wine. In subsequent years he also invited the choirmaster and members of Winchester Cathedral Choir.

The 1910 Steinway Boudoir grand piano, which Moiseiwitsch and Noel Coward had played during the war, was not really good enough for the recitals Mr Heath had in mind – nor, for that matter, for a pianist as accomplished as the Prime Minister, although Heath and his Private Secretary Robert Armstrong, a fine amateur musician, used to play duets together at Chequers. Mr Heath had a lifetime's experience of music to draw upon and there were many professional musicians among his friends who were happy to entertain the Prime Minister and his guests. Since Heath's own piano had been moved into No. 10, a Steinway was hired for the concerts at Chequers and the Great Hall – so thoughtfully roofed in by Sir Robert Frankland Russell – provided the perfect auditorium.

It was, however, in Macmillan's famous phrase, 'events, dear boy, events,' which conspired to keep the Prime Minister away from his first concert at Chequers, just a few months after taking office. It had been arranged for the Parliamentary recess, but Heath had counted without the Popular Front for the Liberation of Palestine hijacking four airliners and holding more than 300 passengers hostage. On one of them the hijackers had been overpowered and the plane had flown to Heathrow, where the

Christmas at Chequers *with family and friends.*

only surviving terrorist was taken to a London police station. The British Government was therefore one of several Governments involved in negotiations for the release of the terrorists in exchange for hostages and the Prime Minister remained in Downing Street while the Isaac Stern Trio entertained his guests at Chequers. The programme, which included the Cello Sonata No. 3 in A Major, the 'Spring Sonata' and the 'Archduke Trio', was recorded for Heath to listen to when the crisis was over.

On another happier occasion the eminent violinist Yehudi Menuhin brought children from the Menuhin School to Chequers. As a finale to the evening, Menuhin and Heath played Handel's Sonata in D Major for violin and piano in an apparently impromptu performance, but the Prime Minister had in fact compared notes with the maestro and practised conscientiously. Nevertheless, in spite of a rehearsal beforehand, the Handel did not go quite as planned. Although Menuhin had the score open in front of him, it soon became evident to Heath that Menuhin was actually playing from memory, and that his edition was different from the score Heath was using. 'In the second movement, he began to play faster and faster,' the Prime Minister recalled; ' ... in the third movement we settled down, but in the last movement we began a race to the finish for he had jumped four bars ahead of me.' With some frantic page-turning by Robert Armstrong, Heath caught up, and as they finished in triumph together, the audience seemed to have enjoyed the sense of competition.

Anniversaries of all kinds were important to Edward Heath, and for two successive years, his birthday was celebrated with music at Chequers. In 1972, on a warm July evening, Clifford Curzon played Beethoven's Variations on a Theme of 'Prometheus', his own particular favourite, and Schubert's 'Posthumous' Sonata in B flat.

When, in the following year, the Greek pianist Gina Bachauer played on his birthday, the great conductor Sir Georg Solti provided the encore with what he announced was 'a new and important' recording. Solti had just completed a recording of Mozart's *Cosi Fan Tutte* with a fine cast. Everyone listened in rapt attention as the voices issued from the Prime Minister's impressive stereo in the opera's famous sextet 'Alla bella Despinetta'. Then, to the accompaniment of the harpsichord, each member of the cast sang 'Happy Birthday, dear Ted' in their own language before a grand finale in English. The record was inscribed with the names of the artists and the accompanist – G. Solti – and Mr Heath treasures it to this day.

The last concert the Prime Minister gave at Chequers, in October 1973, was as fraught as the first. Isaac Stern and Pinchas

Zuckerman were due to play a programme of violin duos but in the meantime the Yom Kippur war had broken out. Zuckerman cancelled but, although aware that he would be criticized for doing so, Isaac Stern chose to play as a tribute to those who died. The Amadeus Quartet, invited as guests, opened the evening with a Haydn Quartet. Then, on a screen in the Great Hall, Heath's guests watched Pablo Casals' last performance in Tel Aviv before he died, when he played an intensely moving piece for unaccompanied cello called 'The Nightingale'. In memory of the great Spanish cellist, Stern ended the programme with Bach's Chaconne in D Minor, in the course of which the violinist's bow broke. Afterwards Robert Armstrong retrieved the hairs from the broken bow and had them mounted in perspex for the Prime Minister as a souvenir of one of his most memorable evenings at Chequers.

Mr Heath's other recreational passion was sailing, at which he excelled. He sailed whenever he could and hated his boat, *Morning Cloud*, going out without him. Field Marshall Sir Michael Carver, Chief of the Defence Staff in 1973, recalled one occasion at Chequers when Heath seemed unusually withdrawn and morose, until news came that *Morning Cloud* was safely at anchor and his spirits lifted. In 1969, he had captained the British team to victory in the testing Sydney-Hobart race and in 1971 he was looking forward to competing in the Admiral's Cup. But he needed a larger boat to qualify. Owen Stephens, the designer of the first *Morning Cloud*, brought his plans for *Morning Cloud II* to Chequers to talk them over with Heath. His crew were frequent guests and, as the race drew nearer, they gathered there to discuss tactics. As it happened, official business prevented the Prime Minister from taking part in the first leg of the race, but the three-boat British team won this prestigious event and Mr Heath was still euphoric with victory when the Irish Taoieseach, Jack Lynch, came to Chequers a few weeks later. In the search for a solution to the Irish problem that had defeated so many Prime Ministers, Heath had also received the Mayor of Belfast and civic leaders at Chequers, invited Brian Faulkner, the Prime Minister of Northern Ireland, for the weekend and succeeded in getting Faulkner and Lynch together at Chequers for an historic tripartite meeting – the first such meeting since partition in 1921.

If the solution to the Irish question remained beyond his reach, success in another area brought Heath great satisfaction. For ten years he had worked hard to fulfil his ambition of taking Britain into the European Common Market. De Gaulle, whose veto in 1963 had been such a crushing disappointment, had resigned in 1969 and his successor Georges Pompidou was much more

Edward Heath *with Brian Faulkner and Jack Lynch at Chequers, 1971.*

Edward Heath
and Pierre Trudeau
at Chequers.

sympathetic to Britain's application. Heath had wooed him assiduously, building a warm personal relationship which reached its apotheosis in January 1972, when Britain at last became the seventh member of the European Community.

In the spring of that year Heath reciprocated the hospitality he had received at the Elysée Palace by welcoming the French President to Chequers. Heath still chuckles when he relates how Pompidou arrived at Chequers in a check suit, every Frenchman's idea of the typical attire of an English country gentleman, to find all the British wearing sober dark suits. Pompidou was greeted and shown to his room where he hastily changed; the British, meanwhile, anxious that Pompidou should not be made to feel uncomfortable, changed into country casuals. Later, Pompidou planted a commemorative beech tree in the park and when he returned to Chequers the following year, he and Mr Heath signed the Channel Tunnel Treaty. It was a further demonstration of Heath's commitment to Europe, and he was bitterly disappointed when the Treaty was jettisoned by the Labour Party as soon as it was back in power in 1974.

During his time as Prime Minister, many other important figures on the world's political stage came to dine at Chequers. They included the German Chancellor Willy Brandt, the Indian Prime Minister Indira Gandhi and Marshall Tito of Yugoslavia. Unlike Wilson, Heath did not make a habit of holding fully-fledged Cabinet meetings at Chequers. But he held strategy seminars and entertained businessmen and industrialists there and although Heath seldom mixed friends with political colleagues, wives were often included.

Among the Prime Minister's other guests were Harold Macmillan and two women who had followed his career with affectionate interest – Thelma Cazalet-Keir and Lady Spencer-Churchill. Macmillan came to dinner and delivered one of the carefully prepared 'impromptu' speeches for which he was so famous, on the now topical 'one nation' concept. Lady Spencer-Churchill had presented Chequers with one of her husband's paintings, *The Lake of Geneva*. Thelma Cazalet-Keir, a close friend of Megan Lloyd George, had been among Chequers' earliest visitors in 1921. She and Heath had met when both were seeking adoption as the prospective Parliamentary candidate for the constituency of Sevenoaks in the 1950 election; neither was selected but they remained friends. It was she who introduced Heath to Augustus John, whose work he both admired and acquired.

Not all visits were so congenial, however. President Nyerere had come to Chequers in 1970 to denounce the British Government's stance on South Africa and had threatened to withdraw Tanzania from the Commonwealth. The visit in September 1971 of the newly elected Prime Minister of Malta, Dom Mintoff, also had an awkward twist. One of Mintoff's first actions as Prime Minister had been to raise the rent on the Maltese naval facilities used by Britain and NATO. When Mintoff came to England for negotiations, however, Heath found himself in the midst not only of a diplomatic imbroglio but a domestic one as well, for Mintoff's estranged wife had followed him to Chequers, where she was determined to discuss things with her husband *à trois* over a cup of tea. Heath, uneasy in the role of marriage counsellor, managed to extricate himself but found the situation hugely embarrassing.

Quite soon after taking office, industrial relations had begun to go sour for Edward Heath. Throughout his premiership he was plagued by strikes, and in 1972 the Industrial Relations Act – the cornerstone of the Conservative manifesto – collapsed. In July of that year, Jack Jones, leader of the powerful Transport and General Workers Union, came to Chequers to discuss a possible way out of a damaging dock strike. Then, in the wake of the Arab–Israeli war of 1973 came the quadrupling of oil prices. This, combined with another confrontation with the miners and the three-day week, of January 1974, delivered the *coup de grace* to the Heath Government. Having failed to secure a settlement with the TUC after weeks of talks but with a four-point lead in the opinion polls, Heath called an early general election in February on the issue of 'Who governs?' The voters, however, gave neither Party an overall majority. Heath's ability to stay in government depended upon any deal he could come to with the Liberals and the Ulster Unionists. Since he could not honourably come to an accommodation with either, he ceased to be Prime Minister at the end of the first weekend of March 1974.

It was a painful wrench for Mr Heath to leave Chequers, which he looked upon as home and which he had done much to improve. Like Harold Wilson in 1970, Heath had nowhere to go, for he had seen no point in renewing the lease on his flat in Albany, Piccadilly, when it expired a few weeks after he had moved into Downing Street. With his Bexley constituency so close to London, he had no alternative address, so friends took him in until he was able to make other arrangements. He signed the Visitors' Book for the last time on 5 March. A year later he returned to plant a Dawyck beech in the south lawn, but not until he became a Knight of the Garter nearly twenty years later could he be persuaded to install his window in the Long Gallery.

JAMES CALLAGHAN

James Callaghan did not expect the Labour Government to last long after he became Prime Minister in April 1976. In February 1974 Labour had been returned to power without an overall majority, and another election eight months later had only marginally improved the situation. By the time Harold Wilson had retired, the majority of four had been whittled away by defections and Callaghan therefore had no majority to tackle the difficult economic situation which he inherited. Nevertheless, against expectations, the Government lasted almost a full term and as Prime Minister, Callaghan was able to enjoy Chequers for three years and one month.

James Callaghan's window at Chequers

Since Harold Wilson's first administration in 1964, Callaghan had been a regular visitor to Chequers and thought that Arthur Lee's gift to the nation of 'this lovely old house' could not have been a more imaginative one. As Foreign Secretary, he had had the use of Dorneywood, but the official entertaining and constant travelling that the job entailed prevented him from appreciating it quite as much as Chequers. In any case, the staffing arrangements at Chequers were more conducive to entertaining and, although they had a farm in Sussex, the Callaghans often used Chequers privately. Nothing brought them more pleasure than having their family around them, and with nine grandchildren (a tenth was born in 1981) under the age of eleven, there were frequently three generations of Callaghans gathered together at Chequers. The house was a paradise for the children: the swimming pool was used whenever possible and the interconnecting rooms and the secret door in the Long Gallery were an endless source of fascination and of rediscovery.

THE RIGHT HONOURABLE
LORD CALLAGHAN
OF CARDIFF K.G.
PRIME MINISTER
APRIL 1976·MAY 1979

The Callaghans were regarded with great affection by the staff; and the family deeply appreciated the cheerfulness with which the staff gave up their Christmas to look after them. They went to great pains with the extra touches that mean so much; the children were delighted by the life-sized 'snow-covered' reindeer and sleigh, made by the staff, which greeted them on Christmas morning and the youngest had never before seen an indoor Christmas tree as tall as the one in the Great Hall, with its star almost touching the ceiling.

On Boxing Day 1977, in a simple family ceremony, Jim and Audrey Callaghan both planted trees in the park. The Prime Minister's tree was a South American beech, while Audrey planted a catalpa, an Indian bean tree. Mrs Callaghan was only the second Prime Minister's wife to perform this pleasant ritual (the first being Lady Spencer-Churchill). But while all the other memorial trees bear identifying plaques, these two trees remain anonymous.

Callaghan's experience of meetings at Chequers during Harold Wilson's premiership encouraged him to adopt the same practice. Cabinet and ministerial colleagues often gathered for discussions around the table in the Great Parlour, and many bilateral talks took place with visiting heads of state in front of the fire in the Long Gallery.

The German Chancellor Helmut Schmidt, who had succeeded Willy Brandt in 1974, had absorbed much of the history of Chequers on earlier visits, and was in accord with Arthur Lee's philosophy, 'The better the health of our rulers, the more sanely they will rule.' At a Downing Street dinner in his honour, after a weekend at Chequers in 1978, he paid tribute to the house: 'The ability to relax is a political virtue which comes easier after a stay at Chequers.' The German Social Democrats had much in common with the British Labour Party and Callaghan and Schmidt had long ago found common ground in their attitude to Europe. But when he visited Callaghan at Chequers for the first time in October 1976, the Government was in the midst of a currency crisis and Schmidt was anxious to do all that he could to help the Government weather the storm. The survival of the Government depended upon the outcome of negotiations between Denis Healey, the Chancellor of the Exchequer, and the International Monetary Fund (IMF), but the reductions in public spending agreed after a fierce debate in the Cabinet fell short of the draconian cuts demanded by the IMF. Callaghan was at Chequers in December when he received the news that Healey's package had been accepted and he began immediately to prepare for a week of difficult meetings with cabinet ministers whom he knew would fight tooth and claw to protect their departmental programmes.

When the German Chancellor returned to Chequers in January 1977, exchange rates had stabilized and interest rates had begun to

James Callaghan
*with his wife Audrey on
the terrace at Chequers.*

James Callaghan
*showing Malcolm Fraser
and his wife around the
grounds of Chequers,
June 1977.*

fall, yet two months later the Government faced an opposition motion of 'No Confidence'. With the IMF negotiations completed and with hopeful signs for the economy, Callaghan was not prepared to throw in the towel. At Chequers over the weekend of 19 March, he walked up Beacon Hill with Audrey but spent much of his time on the telephone rallying support for the crucial vote. The Government survived but only with the help of the Liberals which led to a formal agreement with the Liberal leader David Steel and the birth of the Lib-Lab pact.

Another of the Prime Minister's guests was President Giscard d'Estaing of France who came to Chequers in December 1977. The French did not share German sensitivities about the role Chequers played in the war and Giscard, always at home in a country-house atmosphere, found Chequers congenial. He also liked Callaghan's easy informality, and when the Prime Minister greeted the President in the Great Hall wearing a blue pullover, Giscard immediately shed his jacket and there was none of the sartorial confusion that had marked the start of Pompidou's visit five years before.

As had become customary, talks continued in the Long Gallery after dinner, although these were somewhat handicapped by the somnolence induced by good food, a fire piled high with logs and brandy liberally dispensed by the Prime Minister. Under similar circumstances in Edward Heath's time, the German Chancellor Willy Brandt had fallen asleep in his chair, leaving Karl Otto Pohl to look after Germany's interests. The fatherland was in safe hands though, for Herr Pohl, at that time Deputy Chief in the Federal Chancellery, was later to become Governor of the Bundesbank. Giscard, however, managed to keep his mind firmly focused on the issues and Anglo-French relations blossomed. As was often the case on such occasions, Chequers was not able to accommodate the whole of the visiting retinue, but local hostelries have become accustomed to providing for the overflow.

Before his departure, President Giscard planted a beech tree in the south park. Chancellor Schmidt, however, in spite of being a more frequent visitor, did not have the opportunity to plant his horse chestnut until the first year of Mrs Thatcher's premiership – the only tree planted by a visiting head of state during Mrs Thatcher's eleven years in office.

For Callaghan, the summer of 1977 was packed with official activity over and above the usual Parliamentary and constituency responsibilities. It was the year of the Queen's Silver Jubilee, and London was also host to a NATO conference, the G7 Economic Summit and the Commonwealth Heads of Government Meeting.

The Commonwealth Conference opened in London with Trooping the Colour, after which the Prime Minister took the Commonwealth leaders to Scotland. While, north of the border, James Callaghan negotiated the Gleneagles Agreement banning official sporting links with South Africa, Audrey entertained the wives of the Commonwealth heads of government at Chequers. Amongst the guests in colourful national costume arriving by coach from London were Mrs Ramphal, the wife of the Secretary General of the Commonwealth, Mrs Bunmi Anyaoku, whose husband Chief Anyaoku succeeded as Secretary General in 1990, and Mrs Kenneth Kaunda, whose husband was President of Zambia. With other ministers' wives, they toured the house after lunch and, in spite of poor weather, walked in the park.

In the midst of the Jubilee celebrations in the last weekend of June, the Prime Minister called an informal Cabinet meeting at Chequers sandwiched between visits to Cardiff, a speech to the Labour Party in London and a naval review in Portsmouth. The purpose of the meeting was to discuss the pros and cons of calling an election in the autumn. The economy was showing signs of revival: public expenditure seemed to be under control, the balance of trade was improving and the forecasts for employment and inflation – which was down to 17 per cent – were optimistic. With North Sea oil soon on tap, the revenue could be used to support the economic recovery. These were heartening signs. But the mood in the country did not reflect overwhelming support for the Government and there were problems ahead. The consensus was to renew the agreement with the Liberals and to soldier on until 1979, by which time the economic recovery was expected to be in full swing.

On New Year's Day 1978, in a broadcast from Chequers, Callaghan exhorted the nation to work together to overcome the economic difficulties. By February, with inflation now down to 10 per cent, re-election, which had earlier seemed improbable, now looked possible. But, as the Prime Minister called his ministers together at Chequers to discuss the priorities for the 1978 Budget, the optimism was overshadowed by calls for more public expenditure and for faster growth; there was also great concern that the unemployment figures stood obstinately at a million and a half.

In July 1978, the Callaghans celebrated their fortieth wedding anniversary at Chequers and, as Christmas approached, the family was aware that it might be the last it would spend there, because the present Parliament would have run its full course before Christmas 1979.

James Callaghan
*with Valéry Giscard
d'Estaing at Chequers,
December 1977.*

James and Audrey
Callaghan
*celebrating their Ruby
Wedding anniversary at
Chequers with their
three children – Julia,
Margaret and Michael –
and nine grandchildren,
29th July 1978.*

The ending of the Lib-Lab pact in November 1978 had not brought down the Government and the prospects of winning another term had increased. But the unions were straining at the leash after three years of Government-imposed pay restraint and, as the so-called 'winter of discontent' ushered in 1979, there were strikes right across the public sector, and the Conservatives were again in the ascendant. Losing the referendum in February 1979 on Scottish devolution – a central plank of Labour's election manifesto – was the final nail in the Government's coffin. On 28 March 1979 the Government was defeated by one vote and a general election followed. In May the Conservatives regained power with a healthy majority of forty-five and for the first time a woman was Prime Minister of the United Kingdom.

Unlike Harold Macmillan, who steadfastly resisted discussing his commemorative window while still in office, Callaghan was receptive to the idea when first approached by the Trustees in 1977. Macmillan was not interested in a coat of arms to which he was not entitled and even when an earldom was bestowed upon him in 1987 he resolutely refused to update the design of his window. He wanted it to represent his status when he was Prime Minister and, to this day, it is the plainest window in the Long Gallery, bearing simply his name and dates. By contrast, Callaghan's original window, installed in April 1981, was a highly symbolic one.

Seven of the Prime Ministers who have occupied Chequers have also been Chancellors of the Exchequer: Lloyd George, Stanley Baldwin, Neville Chamberlain, Winston Churchill, Harold Macmillan, James Callaghan and John Major. Many have been Foreign Secretary: Ramsay MacDonald, Anthony Eden, Harold Macmillan, Alec Douglas-Home, James Callaghan and John Major. Only Callaghan, who also served as Home Secretary, had consecutively held all four of the great offices of State and his window reflected the fact. A galleon in full sail signified his wartime naval service and his home city of Portsmouth; the Welsh dragon symbolized his connections with Wales, where he had represented Cardiff in Parliament since 1945. (He was Father of the House when he retired in 1983, having been a Member of Parliament for thirty-four years.) His terms of office as Home Secretary, Chancellor of the Exchequer and Foreign Secretary were symbolized respectively by the Tudor rose, the chequerboard and the globe. In 1987 when he became a Knight of the Garter and took his seat in the House of Lords as Baron Callaghan of Cardiff, his window was updated. He regards it with pride as a small footnote in the nation's history.

MARGARET THATCHER

No Prime Minister has taken up the official occupancy of Chequers without having previously been an often regular visitor to the house and Margaret Thatcher, who took office in May 1979, was no exception. She had been Prime Minister for ten days before she was able to spend her first official weekend at Chequers. In the meantime she had formed her Cabinet – which had already met twice – filled other numerous ministerial appointments in the Government and received an official visit from Helmut Schmidt, Chancellor of West Germany. Following her address to a triumphant Scottish Conservative Party conference, she was flown into RAF Northolt, which was conveniently close to Chequers.

Margaret Thatcher's window at Chequers

'I do not think anyone has stayed long at Chequers without falling in love with it,' wrote Margaret Thatcher in her memoirs, and it was no secret that she and her husband grew to love Chequers with a passion. After the 1983 election they sold their Chelsea house and the house they subsequently bought in Dulwich was never intended to be anything other than an investment and somewhere to retreat to in a hurry if necessary. Chequers therefore became a home of which she and Denis were both immensely proud. The playwright, Sir Ronald Millar, who added so much zest to her speeches, recalls coming across her sitting on a stool before the fire in the Great Parlour. 'Sitting there, like that,' he said, 'you look for all the world as though you belong to Chequers, and Chequers belongs to you.' 'But it doesn't,' she told him and she never lost sight of the fact that it was one of the ephemeral trappings of office. Nevertheless, she quickly became familiar with every detail of its history, contents and administration.

In the modest flat above the office in No. 10 there was neither a housekeeper nor a cook. Mrs Thatcher preferred it that way because she felt that no housekeeper could possibly cope with the long and irregular hours. There were often official lunches and dinners and she often ate at the House of Commons. At other times there was always something in the freezer to fall back on and her constituency secretary Joy Robilliard and the girls in the Political Office were co-opted into shopping or lending a hand in the kitchen.

At Chequers, however, although Mrs Thatcher paid close attention to the preparations for any entertaining she did there, everything was taken care of by a team of excellent chefs and stewards under Wing Commander Vera Thomas. Over the years the cuisine at Chequers had improved immeasurably and fresh fruit and vegetables from the well-stocked kitchen gardens are used as much as possible in the inspired menus of the head chef, Flight Sergeant Alan Lavender.

With national and international affairs of state, and a constituency occupying so much time, the Prime Minister is not expected to get involved with the local community, but Mrs Thatcher always took a close personal interest. When one Wendover shopkeeper, who had supplied groceries to nine Prime Ministers, said that Mrs Thatcher was the first to thank him personally, she told him: 'That was because the others were not ladies.'

At Christmas the Prime Minister used to invite to drinks and buffet lunches many of the people who contributed to making Chequers the refuge it was. Among her guests were the Chequers Trustees, the president of Ellesborough Golf Course and representatives of the parish church, together with personnel from nearby RAF Halton, which supplied many of the Chequers staff, and the Chief Constable and other personnel from the Thames Valley Constabulary who were responsible for the security of Chequers. She also took trouble to meet the Chequers Estate employees, some of whom had witnessed the comings and goings of several Prime Ministers.

Bob Goodwyn, Churchill's driver, had lived in one of the lodges since his retirement and even after his death his widow used to open the gates for the Prime Minister until she became too frail to do so. In the other lodge, until his death in 1996, lived Douglas Wilkins, the house carpenter, and his step-mother Jean. Douglas had worked at Chequers, man and boy, since before the war, when Jean used to clean the fireplaces for the Chamberlains. There was nothing he could not turn his hand to, and not a corner of the house with which he was not on intimate terms. The families of her Private Office were not forgotten either, with twenty-one children attending a party at Christmas. She also hated the idea of anyone being alone at Christmas and when Keith

Joseph, a Cabinet colleague, and Gordon Reece, her media guru, separated from their wives, they too were invited to join the family at Chequers. Ronald Millar was a regular Christmas guest and when his mother died, Mrs Thatcher had sent a message: 'If you're a bit down, drop everything and come to Chequers.' For Norman Tebbit, however, horribly injured in the bombing of the Grand Hotel at the Brighton Conference in 1984, the hospitality, although appreciated, was not without its difficulties. When he was well enough to leave hospital, the Prime Minister invited him to Chequers for Christmas so that he would be near Stoke Mandeville Hospital, both to visit his wife, Margaret, paralysed in the blast, and for his own treatment. Chequers looked beautiful beneath a carpet of snow that year and, as always, the staff were caring and kind. But Tebbit found the stairs awkward and in Churchill's old bedroom, alone for the first time since the bomb, he found it hard to undress himself without help. He also slept on the floor, painfully dragging the blankets off the bed, because the feather mattress in the great four-poster was too soft for his traumatized bones.

To anyone asking how Chequers was run, Margaret Thatcher was apt to snap 'on a shoe-string'; renowned for her thrifty nature, she was not the 'grocer's daughter' for nothing. Every one of the King of Morocco's annual consignment of fresh dates was used in some form or other and while guests not already sated with them relished the chef's date pudding, Denis could be heard to mutter 'not more bloody dates'. Even the Chequers Christmas tree was not always what it seemed, for Miss Thomas's instructions to the estate woodsman was to cut only the trees which were weak and failing. To achieve a symmetry worthy of the Great Hall, a little cosmetic surgery was performed which involved drilling holes in the trunk and rearranging some of the trimmed branches. The Prime Minister's first concern when a stray cat strolled in with the obvious intention of taking up residence was whether the housekeeping could stretch to feeding another mouth; it could, and after enquiries about ownership in the neighbourhood had drawn a blank, the tortoiseshell tabby was allowed to stay. Unlike Humphrey, her celebrated counterpart in Downing Street, Kitty knew she was well off at Chequers and never roamed far.

During Mrs Thatcher's time, the swimming pool was used only in summer – except by a few stoics – because she felt that the cost of heating it was an unjustifiable extravagance. There was, however, an occasion when she asked for the pool to be specially heated in order to show it to her American guests, including

Margaret Thatcher
with her family for
Christmas at Chequers.

Margaret Thatcher *applauding Helmut Schmidt as he plants a chestnut tree in the grounds of Chequers.*

Walter Annenberg, whose generosity had enabled the pool to be built. To demonstrate its success, the Prime Minister's daughter Carol, together with Rosalind Runcie, wife of the Archbishop of Canterbury, Lord Hailsham, the Lord Chancellor, and Katherine Day, the wife of the recently knighted television presenter, Sir Robin, engaged in a race. Among the guests who had come to admire the pool was Lord Whitelaw, who mischievously relates how Lord Olivier and Nancy Reagan, the principal guest, were splashed by their collective dive.

Any money thus saved on heating the pool could be used for improvements and repairs, always necessary in a house the age and size of Chequers. During Mrs Thatcher's time, the cupola in the Great Hall, which had been boarded up because it leaked, was repaired and unblocked to allow in more natural light, and the beautiful panelling in the Great Parlour was stripped of layers of polish and grime. Some of the bedrooms also needed attention, and the Prime Minister was also keen to take the neglected attic floor in hand and make the Astley Rooms usable again.

Mrs Thatcher liked the furnishing fabrics of Laura Ashley, which she had seen used to great effect in the Washington and

Bonn Embassies and had a high personal regard for Mrs Ashley herself. She thought the company's designs would be perfect for the two small Astley Rooms, with their lopsided ceilings and small windows, and she turned for advice to Mary Henderson (the wife of the diplomat Sir Nicholas Henderson), who was a design consultant. It was a daunting task, for the two musty rooms, illuminated by a single naked light bulb, were full of broken furniture and the walls were cracked and dirty and festooned with cobwebs. Once the rooms were cleared and the walls made good, the plan was to cover the walls and as much of the furniture as possible with fabric. To keep the costs down, all the work was done in the Laura Ashley workroom, from Mary Henderson's detailed drawings, using fabric based on sixteenth-century designs.

In the absence of a suitable wardrobe, Mary utilized a corner to create a tent cupboard; a mattress was found for an old discarded mahogany bedstead, and the walls around it and the sloping ceiling above it were ingeniously draped with fabric. The oak floorboards were covered with inexpensive cord matting; an old sofa was re-upholstered for the companion sitting room and tables and chairs and a couple of antique rugs were retrieved from a storeroom and cleaned up. A bathroom was created from a large adjacent cupboard and a pair of dingy attic rooms were thus transformed into a charming guest suite.

Mrs Thatcher used Chequers a great deal for entertaining and the guests attending her buffet lunches tended to be a mix of Cabinet colleagues, ministers, captains of industry and media moguls. As with all Prime Ministers, the circle of close friends with whom she could relax was relatively small, and tended to be those whose jobs brought them into close contact with her, but her guest list was often leavened by celebrities from other fields. It would gladden her heart if all the cars parked neatly around the statue of Hygeia in the forecourt were British. Sir Jimmy Savile's gold Rolls Royce was quite acceptable, whereas the sight of the white Mercedes belonging to Sir Larry Lamb, then Editor of the *Daily Express*, would make her eyes flash with patriotic fervour.

As the lunch parties expanded, so the format evolved. Since the dining table could seat only twenty at the most, several round tables, each seating eight or ten, were set up in the Great Hall, so that up to fifty guests could be accommodated. The first course was pre-set at the tables and thereafter guests helped themselves from a buffet – both hot and cold – set out in the Dining Room. By serving drinks before lunch in the Hawtrey Room, and coffee afterwards in the Long Gallery, the Thatchers gave their guests an opportunity to see more of the house. One guest recalled being

Margaret Thatcher *with Helmut Kohl at Chequers, May 1985.*

asked to examine the stained glass windows in the Long Gallery, where a singular omission was drawn to his attention. 'A tragedy,' the Prime Minister proclaimed. 'He thinks he'll be back, you see.' Mrs Thatcher was, of course, referring to Edward Heath, whose window, long after he had ceased to be Prime Minister, had still not been installed.

Even if entertaining was necessarily an intrusion upon the work, Margaret Thatcher was solicitous and hospitable towards her guests. Organized carol singing did not generally feature on the programme at Christmas, but there was usually a tour of the house and the grounds, weather permitting, followed by a film show. But while her guests were watching *Around the World in Eighty Days* or *Ring of Bright Water*, the Prime Minister was likely to slip quietly away to immerse herself in a hefty report in much the same way as the rest of us might curl up with the latest novel or thriller. She did not find it easy to relax and Harold Macmillan, visiting her privately at Chequers, was astounded by her compulsive appetite for work and afraid that she might burn herself out with so little relaxation. He urged her to unwind with a good book but stopped short of recommending his own habit of 'going to bed with a good Trollope'.

Among her many international guests, none was of greater political significance than Mikhail Gorbachev. His visit to London in December 1984, at the head of a large Communist delegation, was the first by a major Soviet figure since Harold Wilson had entertained Kosygin at Chequers in 1967. A seminar at Chequers with experts from the Soviet Union contributed to the meticulous briefing and once again Chequers was chosen for the meeting because the atmosphere was so conducive to easy conversation. There being no place in Mrs Thatcher's lexicon for small-talk, the dialogue with Gorbachev rapidly moved on to more substantive issues of arms control and human rights. Gorbachev's style was poles apart from that of the archetypal Soviet bureaucrat, and he and Mrs Thatcher spoke together with such ease that the interpreting was hardly perceptible. They clearly charmed each other and having overstayed his schedule by more than an hour, Mr Gorbachev left the Prime Minister on the steps of Chequers with an old Russion proverb: 'Mountain folk cannot live without guests any more than they can live without air. But if the guests stay longer than necessary, they choke.' As the Russians departed, Mrs Thatcher endorsed Gorbachev as 'a man with whom I can do business', and afterwards, Geoffrey Howe, the Foreign Secretary, recorded that their four hours of dialogue 'changed the shape of the world'.

When Konstantin Chernenko died three months later, Gorbachev succeeded him as leader of the Soviet Union. Between him and Mrs Thatcher there developed an extraordinary personal relationship, which demonstrably contributed to the eventual ending of the Cold War.

On 2 April 1982, Argentina invaded the Falkland Islands and for eleven weeks Chequers once again played an active part in the planning and strategy of a military operation. Within days a British task force set sail for the South Atlantic and in the weeks that followed the War Cabinet met regularly at Chequers, where Mrs Thatcher felt the atmosphere 'helped to get us all together'. En route to and from Chequers, Mrs Thatcher also became as familiar with the Operation HQ at Northwood as Churchill had been with the Uxbridge HQ of Fighter Command during the Second World War.

It was at Chequers a month later that the crucial decision was taken to sink the heavily armed Argentine cruiser, the *General Belgrano*, which, with its escort destroyers, was zigzagging in and out of the exclusion zone. The Chiefs of Staff had left the War Cabinet in no doubt about the threat she posed to the task force, now only hours away, and they were in total accord that the cruiser must be dealt with without delay. Before the order could be given, however, a change had to be sought in the Rules of Engagement. This was duly authorized by the Prime Minister. By lunchtime the order was given and by 8pm the deed was done – the *Belgrano* had been sunk by the nuclear submarine, HMS *Conqueror*. Mrs Thatcher never doubted the rightness of that decision. On a later occasion, guiding her guests around Chequers, when the possibility of making a film of the Falklands conflict was suggested, she is said to have pointed out the chair in which she had sat when she gave the order to sink the *Belgrano*.

The sinking of the *Belgrano* had effectively put paid to the peace initiative conducted by the American Secretary of State Alexander Haig. The task force meanwhile was nearing its destination; HMS *Sheffield* had already been hit by an Exocet missile and sunk, and several ships had been damaged. Time for further negotiations was running out and it would not be possible to keep the task force on hold, in worsening weather conditions, indefinitely. In one last attempt to find a peace formula, Mrs Thatcher summoned to Chequers Sir Nicholas Henderson and Sir Anthony Parsons, respectively British Ambassadors to Washington and the United Nations. They were joined by the Defence Secretary John Nott and Antony Acland, head of the Foreign Office, and in the Great Parlour, with sheep grazing peacefully in the park beyond the

Margaret Thatcher *with Robert Mugabe in the garden at Chequers, October 1988.*

Margaret Thatcher with Benazir Bhutto in the Rose Garden at Chequers, July 1989.

windows, the Prime Minister harangued the Foreign Office mandarins for not being supportive enough of British interests. In uncompromising mode, she repeatedly emphasized the virtues of democracy and the evils of aggression; she insisted that the principle of self-determination could not be stated often enough in this final diplomatic manoeuvre. She had not accepted the Ministry of Defence's initial position that the Falklands, once occupied, could not be retaken. It was Henderson's view that the Prime Minister preferred the idea of a fight to the accusation of a compromise.

On May 14th, as she and Parsons meticulously drafted the final ultimatum, they received news that the SAS and SBS had landed at Pebble Island, off North Falkland, destroying the air-strip and all the enemy aircraft on it. As Mrs Thatcher anticipated, the Argentine Junta rejected the ultimatum. The following week 5,000 troops were landed on East Falkland, establishing a bridgehead at San Carlos and fighting began in earnest as the hazardous traverse of the island got under way. The British destroyer, HMS *Coventry*, was sunk defending Falkland Sound, and as the casuaslties mounted the conflict became the Prime

Minister's total preoccupation. Cecil Parkinson, a member of the War Cabinet, remembers the Prime Minister and the Attorney General Michael Havers crawling around the floor of the Great Parlour examining maps of the south Atlantic in an effort to locate the whereabouts of the Argentine aircraft carrier, *25 de Mayo,* which posed such a threat to the British troops.

In interludes from the War Cabinet, the Prime Minister worked on her boxes, sometimes in the tranquillity of the walled garden at Chequers. But there was to be no peace of mind until the British flag flew over the Falkland capital, Port Stanley, which it did once again on 14 June 1982.

A year later, taking advantage of her enhanced political standing and the so-called 'Falklands Factor', Margaret Thatcher won a second election victory with an increased majority. She now had a powerful mandate which enabled her to take on the unions and press ahead with the reform of local government finance. It was at a Chequers seminar attended by ministers and officials that the community charge was born. Based on the premise that everyone should contribute something for services received, this new form of taxation, otherwise known as the poll tax, was to prove fatally controversial for Margaret Thatcher.

In May 1989, when Mrs Thatcher celebrated the tenth anniversary of her premiership with a lunch at Chequers, she had well exceeded Asquith's record as the longest serving Prime Minister of the twentieth century. A dinner for the Cabinet – 'the Long Marchers' as Denis Thatcher called them – had already been held at Downing Street, and the Cabinet had reciprocated with a dinner in her honour at the Conservative Carlton Club. The Chequers lunch was attended by friends, Conservative Party grandees and senior politicians, including John Major because he had been unable to go to the Downing Street dinner. For the first time I found myself on the Prime Minister's table and John hosted a table, as the only Cabinet Minister present. Ronnie Millar was not alone in thinking this *placement* deeply significant but I ignored the observation from a source, as they say, 'close to the Prime Minister', who saw John as Mrs Thatcher's 'logical successor' because he had no 'political baggage'. There were many, in retrospect, who thought that Mrs Thatcher should have used this anniversary to stand down from office. Her achievements had been considerable, but from this time or, more accurately, from the time of the European Council in Madrid the following month, things began to go badly wrong for the Prime Minister.

In July 1989, Geoffrey Howe was sacked as Foreign Secretary (becoming Deputy Prime Minister and Leader of the House) in one of the most dramatic Cabinet reshuffles since Macmillan's 'Night of the Long Knives'. Three months later Nigel Lawson resigned as Chancellor of the Exchequer and so strident was Mrs Thatcher's hostility to Europe that in November there was a 'stalking horse' challenge to her leadership. Though she won, she was seriously wounded by it and exactly one year later Geoffrey Howe's resignation from the Government triggered a much more serious challenge.

While the Prime Minister was working at Chequers on her speech for the debate on the Queen's Speech, which had now assumed even more importance than usual, Bernard Ingham, her Press Secretary, telephoned with some disturbing news. Michael Heseltine, who had been in the political wilderness since his resignation over the Westland affair in 1986, was deemed to have made a not so thinly veiled challenge to her leadership in a letter to his constituency chairman. The day after Howe delivered his devastating resignation statement in the House of Commons, Michael Heseltine, believing that he had a better chance than Mrs Thatcher of leading the Conservatives to a fourth election victory, announced that he would contest the leadership.

Once the process had been set in train, Mrs Thatcher gathered her family and her campaign team around her at Chequers, including the Party Chairman Kenneth Baker, Deputy Chairman Alastair McAlpine, Energy Secretary and former Chief Whip John Wakeham, the media guru Gordon Reece, her Political Secretary John Whittingdale and her PPS Peter Morrison. After some time spent working out the arithmetic of support within the party, they reached the conclusion that the Prime Minister would win.

According to Kenneth Baker, there was an air of complacency about the discussions – not, however, shared by Mrs Thatcher. Discussions also took place about the future unity of the party, including a suggestion, not immediately kicked into touch, that something would have to be done about the politically damaging community charge. Since Mrs Thatcher could not be dissuaded from attending the Conference of Security and Co-operation in Europe, she was at the British Embassy in Paris when the inconclusive result of the first ballot reached her. 'I fight on, I fight to win,' she declared from Downing Street the next day, but twenty-four hours later she had resigned and the second round of the ballot was wide open. Before the end of November, the Conservative Party had elected a new leader by the same voting mechanism that had enabled Margaret Thatcher to displace Edward Heath in 1975, and a new Prime Minister was installed in Downing Street.

Margaret Thatcher *and Denis Thatcher with Mr and Mrs de Klerk at Chequers, October 1990.*

The leadership election had not yet run its course when the Thatchers spent their last weekend at Chequers. At Ellesborough Church the hymns chosen for morning service – 'Guide me Oh thou Great Redeemer' and 'Through all the changing scenes of life' – were particularly apposite. Well-wishers gave her flowers and the photographer Srjda Dukanovic, who had taken pictures of Mr and Mrs Thatcher strolling in the grounds when they arrived at Chequers, was there to record their departure. Moving out was not a difficult operation, physically. There is no need, nor any encouragement, to accumulate personal effects at Chequers, so books, golf clubs and personal odds and ends were piled into a Range Rover. Emotionally, moving out was another matter. Mrs Thatcher was undoubtedly going to miss Chequers, but her greatest sadness was in saying goodbye to the staff who had served her so loyally and of whom she had become fond. As she had pre-lunch drinks with them in the Great Hall, many were in tears.

As Margaret and Denis Thatcher looked nostalgically, and for the last time, around the house that they had been privileged to call home for nearly twelve years, they reflected upon the fact that in nearly forty years of marriage they had lived nowhere longer than at Chequers.

John Major
*in the Study at
Chequers.*

To become Prime Minister just a few weeks before Christmas, as John did in 1990, was not ideal timing. For one thing, it threw the Christmas cards into chaos! John and I inherited the card that Mrs Thatcher had selected, featuring an artist's impression of a red carpet before the open door of No. 10, which some thought looked more like blood pouring over the step. I was sorry when some people were upset not to receive a Christmas card at all that year, while others received three. I was also haunted by the huge pile of letters awaiting my reply, and although many were letters of congratulation, it was apparent that I was already regarded as a Member of Parliament, a social worker and a counsellor, all rolled into one. Most of the other problems of Christmas were solved by spending it at Chequers. In spite of an incredibly crowded diary, which included a visit to the troops in the Gulf, a visit to Washington and a European Summit, ten days before Christmas we found an opportunity for lunch at Chequers so that we could meet the staff. We were joined on this occasion by the Prime Minister's Appointments Secretary, Robin Catford, and his wife Daphne. Robin (now Sir Robin) had his office at No. 10, and was an invaluable source of advice and support through a minefield of delicate problems.

It was coincidental that as we were preparing to take up residence at Chequers, Dorothy Haynes, who had been curator since 1987, was leaving to start a family and was in the process of handing over to Jane Uff, a retired Naval Commander. We were served drinks in the Great Hall, where a log fire burned in the enormous hearth, and lunch was served at the small table in the window recess of the Dining Room. Afterwards we were shown around parts of the house we had not seen before, including the Prime Minister's Study, the swimming pool and various backstage offices. Although unaware of it at the time, we chose the bedroom that Winston Churchill had used because I thought it was the prettiest of all the bedrooms. It was not until later that we discovered the fierce draught that blew in through the bathroom window. Our daughter Elizabeth, not in the least disturbed by the story of Mary Grey's imprisonment, adopted the Prison Room, like Carol Thatcher before her. Our son James, who had been unable to come with us, eventually made himself comfortable in the Astley Room which had been so successfully redecorated in 1985.

It was wonderful to spend Christmas at Chequers, with the traditional tree from the Park towering up to the ceiling of the Great Hall. There were Christmas cards on every conceivable surface, tactfully sorted so that those from relatives, friends and acquaintances were drawn to our notice; afterwards they would be channelled in the direction of various charities. That year, and in subsequent years, we maintained Mrs Thatcher's tradition of a Boxing Day lunch for ministerial colleagues and personal friends, but shifted it to New Year's Day so that it would not interfere with our family Christmas.

After that initial foray we made regular visits to Chequers and lunch parties soon became a feature of our weekends. During the G7 Economic Summit in July 1991, I entertained the wives of the heads of delegations and of ministers, including Barbara Bush, Milla Mulrony, Sachiyo Kaifu and Hannalore Kohl – the wives of the American President, the Prime Ministers of Canada and Japan, and the Chancellor of Germany respectively. There was the obligatory photo-opportunity in the rose garden and after lunch, while coffee was being served, a string quartet from the Royal College of Music played in the Long Gallery. The lunch had followed a visit to nearby Stoke Mandeville Hospital, where we had been shown around the Spinal Injuries Unit by its most celebrated and dedicated fundraiser, Sir James (Jimmy) Savile wearing an unforgettable gold lamé track suit. Since the 1960s the hospital, which has a worldwide reputation for the treatment and rehabilitation of people with spinal injuries, has enjoyed a special relationship with Chequers. Both Harold Wilson and Edward Heath had been regular Christmas visitors, and on Boxing Day 1968, an occasion Wilson recalled as one of the happiest of his premiership, those patients able to travel had come to Chequers for a party.

The journalists who persistently wrote that I did not like Chequers were entirely wrong. The curator and the staff could not do more to ensure the absolute comfort of the Prime Minister, his family and guests, and what woman would not relish the thought of being relieved of all household responsibility for two days out of every seven. It is true that at first several factors stopped us using it quite as often as we might have liked. Our home, Finings, is in John's Cambridgeshire constituency of Huntingdon, and that is where our children have their friends and their interests. In 1990 Elizabeth was still at home, just beginning her training as a veterinary nurse, while James, who was studying for his 'A' Levels, attended school on Saturday mornings and football matches in the afternoons.

Huntingdon is a large constituency with an active Conservative Association and a weekend without engagements was very rare. It was difficult to get away for a full weekend and, in any case, to use

John Major
*standing in the east
forecourt at Chequers.*

Chequers every weekend would have meant seeing little of the children, the constituency or our home. We quickly discovered that Finings was the only place where we were able to escape, to some extent, from the tyranny of the clock. As time has passed, however, Chequers has been used more and more for entertaining, for seminars and even for Cabinet meetings – even though productivity tends to fall away a little after one of the chef's excellent lunches.

From the beginning of our occupancy I was keen to bring opera to Chequers. I had seen Freddie Stockdale's touring company, Pavilion Opera, on several occasions and it seemed to me that the Great Hall would provide the perfect setting. With the help of a supremely efficient committee, we arranged four such occasions: two with Pavilion Opera and two with Philip Blake Jones' excellent company, Opera Interludes. Amongst our guests for the first opera, *Lucia di Lammermoor*, was the wife of the Japanese Prime Minister and their son, who were in London for the Japan Festival, and the Prince of Wales was our guest on another occasion for *The Barber of Seville*. Opera in such intimate surroundings is opera in the round and it is good to see an audience relax as they gather around the twelve-foot carpet, which is Freddie's 'stage', closer to the action than one is used to and becoming utterly involved in the performance.

Before the performance, drinks were served in the Long Gallery and the north lawn provided the perfect site for the magnificent marquee in which dinner was served afterwards. These were occasions when the talents of the Chequers chefs were brilliantly displayed. Ex-staff, husbands and wives were drafted in to help and, hard work though it certainly was, a good time was had by all. An added bonus was the £2.5 million that we raised for Mencap, the Arthritis and Rheumatism Council, the heart charity CORDA and the inspirational Chickenshed Theatre Company.

Chequers has witnessed several family celebrations and we gave lunch parties for our silver wedding and for my 50th birthday. At Elizabeth's twenty-first birthday party we danced in the Great Hall to the Kimbolton School band. James had his first driving lesson on Victory Drive and I taught myself to swim in the pool, where a plaque commemorates the Queen's presence at Chequers on 3 October 1970 – our wedding day.

Apart from its obvious appeal as a place for rest and relaxation, Chequers is also of tremendous value as a place for official entertaining, especially as No. 10 has neither the facilities nor the staff to accommodate overnight visitors. In 1921 the Lees had left Chequers with a full complement of staff, which included a butler, housekeeper, parlour maid, valet and lady's maid. Today their duties are undertaken by a curator and a staff of Service personnel, a tradition begun during the War when it was difficult to obtain civilian staff and security had to be taken into account. At that time, the house was run by representatives of both the Air Force and the Army, but after the war the Army, without the same tradition of stewardship, was replaced by the Navy. It is essentially a weekend job and Vera Thomas, the much respected curator, had no sympathy for any member of staff who didn't pull their weight at the weekend: if, as Denis Thatcher put it, the Prime Minister 'wants moose on toast at three in the morning, that's what you're here to do – white jacket as well.' Now, all the housework, including the cleaning of the silver, is done during the week. (Today's girls are amused by H. Clifford Smith's report on the silver in the 1940s: 'The WREN chief in charge of the pantry appears to take a genuine interest in the silver [but] the task is a difficult one for a woman and seems to call for a family butler to keep it in really good condition.') Some of the staff have their own homes in the vicinity of Chequers; others are provided with cottages in the grounds, but there is always a nucleus on duty in the house.

With a staff of RAF and Naval personnel and three chefs, an excellent security system and several principal bedrooms, Chequers is perfectly equipped for the task of entertaining foreign visitors, who are always charmed by the quintessential Englishness of it all. In a hard, unsentimental world, the warmth, hospitality and relaxed informality of Chequers make a great difference to our relationships with other heads of government.

1994 was a busy year for foreign visitors, when Chancellor Kohl, President Clinton and President Yeltsin all came to Chequers. Chancellor Kohl arrived by helicopter on a fine spring day and saw Chequers at its best. Lambs in the fields at the side of Victory Drive were indifferent to the clatter of the rotors as the helicopter set down in the south park, and in Lime Walk a thick carpet of daffodils nodded gently in the breeze.

The German Chancellor likes Chequers and he and John had a well-established routine. Their talks, minus officials, always began with a session of political gossip, Kohl's charming interpreter, Dorothea, never turning a hair as she translated his sometimes risqué jokes. As always on such occasions, the discussions between the Chancellor and the Prime Minister covered a range of issues, not least at this time Bosnia and European Security, the situation in Russia and the Ukraine, the forthcoming presidential election in France, the presidency of the European Commission and European enlargement. Inevitably, they touched upon the mischief

John Major

that had been made by the media with regard to the German participation in the D-Day commemorations.

The visits of Chancellor Kohl were relatively relaxed affairs in comparison to visits by other heads of state, though all are conducted with military precision, involving weeks of detailed planning. In the case of the President of the United States, it also involves a cast of hundreds, including administrative and security personnel who minutely reconnoitre every detail of the President's programme. The fact that a Presidential aide is prepared to shut himself in a toilet cubicle in order to check for himself that the President's personal attack alarm can be heard by the Secret Service agent outside the door, gives some indication of the detailed 'advance' that is carried out.

When President Nixon came to Chequers in 1970 during Edward Heath's premiership, the Secret Service were particularly concerned about sabotage of the water supply. In order to check it out, one of the Prime Minister's security staff accompanied the President's men to the top of the hill, where he identified the Chequers reservoir. Further down, he showed them where the supply divided for the village and the house, and a little further still, for the house and the police bothy. It was evident to them that the water supply was potentially so vulnerable that the only solution was to bring in a supply of the bottled variety. A few weeks after the President's visit a perplexed steward queried the vast quantity of bottled water in the pantry.

The American Presidential retreat of Camp David, deep in the forest of Maryland, has a chain-link perimeter fence, punctuated at intervals with control towers reminiscent of a German Stalag. There are no intersecting public footpaths, as at Chequers, and an American President out for a stroll will not encounter ramblers who pass by with a cheery 'Good morning' and regard the Prime Minister as part of the scenery.

In the 1970s, when political violence was on the increase (although not the serious concern it was later to become), a proposal was made to divert an ancient footpath which passed too close to the house for safety. At the inevitable public inquiry, one of the most colourful witnesses was Percy Brace, a retired octogenarian poacher, who explained how he had been nipping undetected in and out of the Chequers grounds since Lloyd George's time. He recalled people from the village peering through the windows to watch Ramsay MacDonald eating his breakfast and Baldwin taking tea. All Percy was interested in was snaring rabbits, not Prime Ministers, but in his view anyone bent on doing harm to the Prime Minister would not use the footpath to launch an attack. With all the legal procedures involved in moving an ancient right of way, it took four years of wrangling before the footpath was moved.

Perhaps fortunately for the staff at Chequers, President Clinton's visit in May 1994 for the D-Day commemorations did not involve an overnight stay. In fact, it was literally a flying visit – a brief interlude in a hectic schedule that was to take us all to the beaches of Normandy. John and I greeted the President and Mrs Clinton on their arrival in 'Air Force One', the Presidential plane, at Mildenhall, Cambridgeshire, and again, an hour later, at the American Cemetery at Madingly. We had leap-frogged ahead of the Presidential party at every stage, and arrived before them at Chequers in our battered Westland helicopter, its rough canvas seats in stark and embarrassing contrast to those of the President's sleek and gleaming 'Marine One' helicopter. In the south park already was the massive US Chinook transport helicopter carrying the two armoured limousines which would convey the President the hundred yards or so to the front door of Chequers.

I recorded the occasion:

John Major
*showing Helmut Kohl
around the gardens of
Chequers.*

As we greeted the President and Hillary Clinton on the doorstep, the house began to fill up with people, including representatives of the Foreign Office and US State Department, wearing colour-coded badges indicating where they could and could not go – particularly in relation to arrangements for lunch. Many of them were strangers to me. The Chequers staff were at full stretch. The log fire burning in the Great Hall was a great success with the Americans and, although time was short, John was anxious to show the Clintons something of the house before his short bilateral with the President in the Hawtrey Room. During the bilateral I show Hillary a little more of the house but we end up in the Study looking down Victory Drive and comparing the restraints of Camp David with the apparent openness of Chequers. We are determined to dine à quatre and the entourage is shaken off. Behind the scenes a posse of aides – green badges – are fed in the curator's sitting room, among them the President's doctor, nurse and kitchen steward. In the Great Parlour, lunch is served to the Ambassadors and members of the respective Private Offices – blue badges. We dine at the small round table in the window recess of the Dining Room in a surprisingly relaxed manner, given the constraints of the schedule. In the rose garden beyond the window the police are rather more in evidence than usual, boosted by American Secret Service agents. Over lunch, John briefs the President on the latest developments in Northern Ireland, and we talk in general terms about the international political scene and, more specifically, about

John Major
*with Bill Clinton at
Chequers, June 1994.*

*American health care reforms. After lunch President and Prime
Minister face the press coralled together in the east forecourt, the
closest they ever get to Chequers. A lectern and microphone have been
set up and it's pouring with rain. While John is speaking, a
Presidential aide asks Chris Meyer [the P.M.'s Press Secretary] if the
Prime Minister would move out of the picture while the President is
speaking! Chris's reply is unambiguous. We wave goodbye to the
President as his armoured limousine sweeps through the gates to join
the monstrous motorcade through the leafy lanes of Buckinghamshire
to a hotel outside Aylesbury, from where he is to broadcast live to
America. He apparently arrives with ninety seconds to spare. John
and I clamber into the battered Westland and tree-hop to Portsmouth
with rain coming in around our feet …*

Although not on quite the same scale as that of the American
President, when Boris Yeltsin came to Chequers a few months
later, he was accompanied by a sizeable retinue, including a doctor
with a suitcase full of electronics, a very curious medic. The
Russians also brought with them copious supplies of black bread,
water and Russian Coke. John had proposed the visit over dinner
in the Kremlin earlier in the year, for he and the President had
forged a close relationship when Russia was in the grip of an
attempted coup in August 1991.

The plan was to give Boris and Naina Yeltsin a taste of a typical
English country weekend and we hoped that the autumn colours
would compensate for the overcast September sky. The Russian
President was given Bedroom 3, Arthur Lee's old room, and since
eighteenth-century four-posters were not built for men of Boris's
height, the house carpenter had ingeniously extended the bed. A
walk was planned, John was keen to take Boris to the nearby
Bernard Arms for an unscheduled pint and our opera evenings had
proved so successful that we invited British Youth Opera to
entertain him.

I made some notes of the weekend:

*John and I are driven by Robbie, with a Thames Valley Police
escort from Chequers to RAF Brize Norton. The escort is
unnecessarily fast and we cause mayhem at road junctions. We are
not in danger of being late so we ask the caravan to slow down.
Waiting at Brize Norton are Brian and Delmar Fall [our
Ambassador in Moscow and his wife], who it is always a pleasure
to see, the Russian Ambassador and Mrs Adamishina (very new,
having only just presented their credentials), Douglas Hurd and,
reassuringly, Pamela Ridler [Foreign Office Escort Officer] and Tim*

Earle [the former Life Guards Officer, who is head of Government Hospitality] together with Tony Bishop, Ivan and Kate [interpreters]. There is time for coffee and, as the President's Ilyushin jet touches the runway, we begin to assemble for the receiving line with red carpet and ceremonial carpet-lining party of the Queen's Colour Squadron, Royal Air Force. We all greet each other warmly, pose for photographs and listen to speeches. At length the convoy forms up. John travels with the President in a specially stretched armoured Daimler which will allow Brian Fall and Tony Bishop to travel with them. A second limousine accommodates me and Naina, together with Pamela Ridler and Tatyana [Naina's interpreter]. This is Tatyana's first visit to the UK, though from past experience I know she speaks English like a native. We engage in mostly insubstantial conversation as we travel by the scenic route. Chequers is heaving with people I do not recognize, but eventually everyone is allocated a room. I make sure that Naina is comfortable while John has talks with Boris in the Hawtrey Room.

There were fourteen of us in the Dining Room for lunch and, with the exception of Douglas Hurd, John and myself, everyone seemed able to speak Russian. Although John urged me to tell the story of Mary Grey, which, with pauses for interpretation, seemed to take a long time, there was a lot of laughter and not much serious talk over lunch. Afterwards, with Boris and his bodyguard wearing identical blue and white tracksuits, we set off for a walk via the east forecourt, pointing out a few of the memorial trees along the way. Naina and I made good progress along Kimble Drive through Whorley Wood, the start of a circuit that could take us around Beacon Hill and back to the house along Church Way. We soon discovered, however, that we had left the men behind, since they had come to a standstill hardly a hundred yards from the house, deeply engaged in conversation. We waited for them to catch us up and made our way together around Beacon Hill toward the church. A woman walking her dog was completely unfazed when we introduced her to the Yeltsins and an elderly cleric wove his way up the hill utterly oblivious of our party. It was soon evident that the complete circuit, some of it uphill, would be too much for Boris, and incidentally for John's knee, so we called up the cars to meet us at the church.

Once again, my notes take up the story:

John is with the President and I am with Naina, but we are hardly out of second gear before the convoy is pulling up outside the Bernard Arms and we see John and Boris knocking on the door.

John Major
*with Boris Yeltsin in
the Bernard Arms.*

The pub is closed but we are within licensing hours. John tells me later that when someone announced the Russian President a voice jokingly called 'Oh yes, and I'm the Kaiser!' Pierre welcomes us in and our party fills the Saloon Bar. We hastily lock the doors against the pursuing paparazzi and John orders a pint for the President. A Russian rouble note is added to Pierre's collection of international currency pinned to a beam.

During our absence from the house the furniture had been removed from the Great Hall and the chairs set out for the evening's recital by British Youth Opera. Many of our hundred or so guests had a special interest in Russian affairs, amongst them Princess Alexandra and Sir Angus Ogilvy. In a varied programme the Yeltsins were very impressed with excerpts from *Eugene Onegin* sung in Russian, and before taking our seats in the marquee for dinner we introduced the Ogilvys and the Yeltsins to the singers.

I return to my notes:

Boris is anxious to get to the marquee and Rod Lyne [John's Private Secretary] tries to slow him down so that he doesn't arrive in the marquee before everyone is seated. I have already expressed concern about the placement, which has Boris opposite John, with his back to the room. I don't think he will be happy with this arrangement, but I am assured by those who 'know' that this is alright. Well, it isn't alright with Boris, who takes one look at the seating arrangement and sits down beside John. Tony Bishop interprets for them and, as the meal progresses, the three heads get closer and closer together – talking about NATO, John tells me later. After the toasts and the speeches, coffee is served in the Great Hall, where order has been restored, but it is late and people started to drift away. Boris is flagging. I didn't think to tell him that he was sleeping in the same bed as Molotov …

Joining the American Presidents and other Heads of State appeals to the Russian sense of history and Boris was the first Russian President to plant a tree at Chequers. The site chosen was in the east park, close to the beeches previously planted by Edward Heath and President Pompidou. A neat hole had been dug by Bill Johnson, the gardener, and a black poplar securely staked in the ground. In Siberia, however, they apparently plant trees three feet (90cm) deep and the President was not prepared to add the ceremonial shovel-full of earth until he was completely satisfied that the tree was correctly planted. A pool of press photographers recorded the event for posterity, and the tree thrives.

After a press conference at Brize Norton, at which the President stressed once again the excellent relationship that now existed between Britain and Russia, the Yeltsins departed for New York, where Boris was due to address the United Nations General Assembly. He took with him a Stilton cheese and some sage from the garden because he had enjoyed the Sage Derby so much at lunch. The Russians had cleaned Chequers out of vodka and gin.

In October 1995, the only thing that threatened to spoil the visit of President Chirac was a group of demonstrators protesting at the French nuclear testing in the Pacific. The chanting and the klaxons could not be heard inside Chequers, however, and therefore did not detract from British Youth Opera's recital in the Great Hall. In the morning, before bilateral talks with John in the Hawtrey Room, President Chirac planted a beech tree, bringing the number of Presidential trees in the south park to four. The two men then went on to High Wycombe for the inauguration of the Franco-British Euro Air Group, while I accompanied Madame Chirac on a visit to Stoke Mandeville Hospital.

The changes that have taken place at Chequers in our time have all been part of a programme of mostly invisible maintenance. Restoration work has been carried out on the windows of the south front, where rain used to pour in when the wind was blowing from the south, and a state-of-the-art central heating system has been installed. The chimneys in the White Parlour and the Hawtrey Room have been opened up and 'living' gas has given way to the real thing (Harry Hopkins would be retreating to the downstairs cloakroom to cool off). Any decorating required to 'make good' has simply restored the status quo, so that, for example, although the Long Gallery had to be emptied of books and completely dismantled, it has been rehung with the same classic Colefax & Fowler wallpaper chosen by Edward Heath.

It has been our privilege to use Chequers often during John's premiership, and the Cromwell connection has been of particular interest to us and to our guests from Huntingdon, where Oliver Cromwell was born in 1599. For nearly 200 years – from 1715, when Cromwell's youngest grandson John Russell married Joanna Rivett, the young owner of Chequers, to the death of Delaval Astley in 1912 – Chequers had remained in the hands of the Protector's descendants. How fascinating that these historic links should have been revived when Chequers became the official residence of the twentieth-century chief executive of State – the Prime Minister – when in 1990 that office was once again held by the Member of Parliament for Huntingdon, the seat which returned Oliver Cromwell to Parliament in 1628.

John Major
with Boris Yeltsin at the tree-planting ceremony.

Bibliography

Lysons Magna Britannia: A Concise Topographical Account of Buckinghamshire, 1806

The History and Antiquities of the County of Buckinghamshire, Lipscomb, 1847

The Victorian History of the County of Buckinghamshire, ed. William Page; University of London

Royal Commission on Historical Monuments in Buckinghamshire; HMSO, 1912

An Edwardian Architect, Reginald Blomfield; A Zwemmer Ltd.

The Life and Times of Sir Thomas Gresham Vol.II, John William Burgon; Robert Jenings, 1839

The Sisters of Lady Jane Grey, Richard Davey; Chapman & Hall, 1911

The Genealogical History of the Croke Family, Sir Alexander Croke; privately published, 1823

The King's Servants: The Civil Service of Charles I 1625-1642, GE Aylmer; Routledge & Kegan Paul, 1974

Genealogical and Historical Memoirs of the Families Allied to the Cromwells Vol. II, Mark Noble, 1784

Cromwelliana: A Chronological Detail of Events in which Oliver Cromwell was engaged from years 1642 to his death in 1658: with a continuation of other Transactions to the Restoration: 1810. Compiled from Mercurius Politicicus published during the Civil War (Political Messages/Papers)

Cromwell Our Chief of Men, Antonia Fraser; Weidenfeld & Nicolson, 1973

Chequers Court Manuscripts, Frankland Russell Astley; Historical Manuscripts Commission, 1900

The Search for a Style 1897-1935, John Cornforth; André Deutsch with *Country Life*, 1988

A Good Innings, Lord Lee of Fareham; ed. Alan Clark; John Murray, 1974

Chequers: A History of the Prime Minister's Buckinghamshire Home, J Gilbert Jenkins; Pergamon Press, 1967

Chequers, Plantagenet Somerset Fry; HMSO, 1977

Chequers and the Prime Ministers, DH Elletson; Robert Hale, 1970

Disraeli, Robert Blake; Eyre & Spottiswoode Ltd, 1967

The Life of Benjamin Disraeli, Vol.1, Moneypenny & Buckle; Murray, 1929

A Life of Sir Henry Campbell-Bannerman, John Wilson; Constable, 1973

The Decline and Fall of Lloyd George, Lord Beaverbrook; Collins, 1963

War Memoirs, David Lloyd George; Odhams, 1938

The Years That Are Past, Frances Stevenson; Hutchinson, 1967

A Radical Life, Mervyn Jones; Hutchinson, 1991

From the Wings, Thelma Cazalet-Keir; privately published, 1967

The Unknown Prime Minister: The Life and Times of Andrew Bonar Law, Robert Blake; Eyre & Spottiswoode, 1955

Baldwin, Roy Jenkins; Collins, 1987

Baldwin, Middlemas & Barnes; Weidenfeld & Nicolson, 1969

Stanley Baldwin, GM Young; Rupert Hart Davis, 1952

Memoirs of a Conservative: J.C.C. Davidson's Memoirs & Papers 1910–1937, ed. Robert Rhodes James; Weidenfeld & Nicolson, 1969

Ramsay MacDonald, Tiltman; Jarrolds, *c.*1925

Ramsay MacDonald, David Marquand; Jonathan Cape, 1977

The Nicolson Diaries 1930–1939, Harold Nicolson; Collins, 1966

Neville Chamberlain, Iain Macleod; Muller, 1961

Neville Chamberlain, Keith Feiling; Macmillan, 1946

Chamberlain papers; Birmingham University

Downing Street: The War Years, Sir John Martin; Bloomsbury, 1991

Fringes of Power, John Colville; Hodder & Stoughton, 1985

Churchill: A Life, Martin Gilbert; William Heinemann, 1991

Finest Hour: WSC 1939–41, Martin Gilbert; Heinemann, 1983

Clementine Churchill, Mary Soames; Cassell, 1979

High Tide and After: Memoirs of Hugh Dalton; Muller, 1962

Anthony Eden, Robert Rhodes James; Weidenfeld & Nicolson, 1986

Full Circle, Anthony Eden; Cassell, 1960

Facing the Dictators, Anthony Eden; Cassell, 1962

The Reckoning, Anthony Eden; Cassell, 1965

The Memoirs of Harold Macmillan, Harold Macmillan
  Winds of Change: 1914–1939; Macmillan, 1966
  Blast of War: 1939–1945; Macmillan, 1967
  Tides of Fortune: 1945–1955; Macmillan, 1969
  Riding the Storm: 1956–1959; Macmillan, 1971
  Pointing the Way: 1959–1961; Macmillan, 1972
  At the End of the Day: 1961–1963; Macmillan, 1973

Harold Macmillan Vols. I & II, Alistair Horne; Macmillan, 1988/89

The Last Edwardian at Number 10, George Hutchinson; Quartet Books, 1980

Selwyn Lloyd, DR Thorpe; Jonathan Cape, 1989

The Art of the Possible, Lord Butler; Hamish Hamilton, 1971

RAB: The Life of RA Butler, Anthony Howard; Jonathan Cape, 1987

The Way the Wind Blows, Lord Home; Collins, 1976

The Governance of Britain, Harold Wilson, Weidenfeld and Michael Joseph, 1976

Final Term: The Labour Government 1974–76, Harold Wilson; Weidenfeld & Nicolson and Michael Joseph, 1979

A Prime Minister on Prime Ministers, Harold Wilson; Michael Joseph, 1977

Harold Wilson, Ben Pimlott; HarperCollins, 1992

Harold Wilson, Philip Zeigler; Weidenfeld & Nicolson, 1993

The Crossman Diaries: The Diaries of a Cabinet Minister, Richard Crossman; Hamish Hamilton and Jonathan Cape, 1975

The Castle Diaries: 1964–1976, Barbara Castle; Weidenfeld & Nicolson, 1984

Inside Number 10, Marcia Williams; Coward, McCann & Geoghegan Inc., 1972

Sailing: A Course of my Life, Edward Heath; Sidgwick & Jackson, 1975

Music: A Joy for Life, Edward Heath; Sidgwick & Jackson, 1976

Travels: People and Places in my Life, Edward Heath; Sidgwick & Jackson, 1977

Edward Heath, John Campbell; Jonathan Cape, 1993

Heath and the Heathmen, Andrew Roth; Routledge & Kegan Paul, 1972

Ministers and Mandarins, Nicholas Henderson; Weidenfeld & Nicolson, 1994

Time and Chance, James Callaghan; Collins, 1987

The Downing Street Years, Margaret Thatcher; HarperCollins, 1993

A View from the Wings, Ronnie Millar; Weidenfeld & Nicolson, 1993

A Conflict of Loyalty, Geoffrey Howe; Macmillan, 1994

Catalogue of the Works of Art at Chequers; HMSO, 1923

Downing Street Records

The papers of Arthur Lee

Chequers papers (including Lady Lee's diaries)

Dictionary of National Biography:
  1901–1921; Oxford University Press, 1927
  1922–1930; Oxford University Press, 1937
  1931–1940; Oxford University Press, 1949

Photographic Credits

Index